Contemporary Capitalism
and Marxist Economics

Contemporary Capitalism and Marxist Economics

JACQUES GOUVERNEUR

Translated by
Richard LeFanu

BARNES & NOBLE BOOKS
Totowa, New Jersey

English edition © Jacques Gouverneur, 1983

Original French edition published in 1978
by Contradictions, Brussels, © Contradictions, 1978

Revised English edition first published in the USA 1983 by
Barnes & Noble Books,
81 Adams Drive,
Totowa, New Jersey, 07512

Library of Congress Cataloging in Publication Data

Gouverneur, Jacques.
   Contemporary capitalism and marxist economics.

   1. Marxian economics. I. Title.
HB97.5.G669 1983   335.4'12   83-9992
ISBN 0-389-20416-1

Printed in Great Britain

Contents

List of Tables and Figures

TABLES

FIGURES

Preface to the English Edition

I have taken the opportunity of this English edition to make substantial revisions and additions to the original text. The main changes are as follows.

The introductory chapter has been substantially rewritten to improve the presentation of the concepts, also omitting the specific data on the Belgian working population, which appeared in the original text. Some passages of chapter 2 (on value) have been rewritten in order to stress the concept of value as indirectly social labour (as against embodied labour); the passages referring to money have been simplified and/or developed in a new chapter (chapter 10).

Chapter 4 (on the basic ratios of Marxist economic theory) has been extended to provide a clear analysis of the factors affecting the rate of surplus value and the composition of capital. Chapter 6 (on the transfers of surplus revenue) has been divided into two separate chapters, corresponding to the broad division of the English edition into two parts (I: Theory; II: Applications) and the second half (now chapter 7) has been revised to show more clearly the relevance of the surplus revenue transfer schemes to the analysis of present-day situations.

Chapter 9 (on crises) and 10 (on inflation) did not appear in the French edition and are entirely new. Chapter 11 (estimating the rate of surplus value) has been completely rewritten, both to take account of more recent data and to make a comparative analysis of five European countries including the United Kingdom (instead of dealing only with Belgium, as in the French edition).

Finally, a theoretical appendix has been added which sets out an alternative to the concept of productive labour adopted throughout the book, considers the Marxist ratios when the period of turnover is not equal to unity and presents and discusses the famous 'transformation problem'.

I remain greatly indebted to Michel De Vroey, not only for the chapter on value, but also for many ideas developed in the two new chapters on crises and inflation as well as in the theoretical appendix. I am also indebted to Philippe Van Parijs, who read the whole manuscript of the new edition and made a great number of useful suggestions.

J.G. November 1982

Preface to the French Edition

This book has its origin in teaching activities, started at the Catholic University of Peru in 1970 and 1971 and continued since 1972 at the Catholic University of Louvain. In both universities, pressure from the student body had induced the faculty and academic authorities to agree to the setting-up of a course on Marxist political economy. Under different titles, both teaching activities consisted in a presentation of the Marxist economic theory of the capitalist system.

My previous education had hardly given me any serious initiation into Marxism: here and there some brief résumés, followed by sketchy and facile critiques, whose simplistic and fallacious character completely escaped me at the time. I must add that my previous education had not fired my enthusiasm either: the divorce between the abstract sophistications of theory and the concrete problems of reality had nourished a growing disenchantment with the prevailing teaching of economics. It was when I began the study of Capital, in 1970, that I realized to what extent my views on Marxism were mere clichés passed on by the prevailing ideology and also how the Marxist approach made it possible to combine the rigour of scientific method with attention to the most concrete and topical problems.

Yet subsequent reading of works by Marxist economists left me with a confused general impression: the concern for integrating theory and reality was certainly there, but a great deal of fuzziness seemed to hover over the most elementary theoretical notions. This is what motivated the writing of this book, in the hope of presenting, in a much clearer and more rigorous way, the basic concepts and elementary analyses specific to Marxist political economy.

While Marxism is at one and the same time a world-view, a science of history, a multidisciplinary approach to social problems and a social praxis, what is presented here is concerned almost exclusively with the *economic theory of capitalist society*. Lacking the necessary competence, I will not attempt to touch on the much vaster domains constituted by materialist dialectic, historical materialism, the study of the historical origins of capitalism and of societies in transition between capitalism and socialism. The study of capitalism will itself be approached from an essentially economic point of view and logically rather than historically: it will present, one might say, the *inner logic of the capitalist economy* rather than the concrete history of capitalism under its various facets. But the emphasis on the economy should not allow us to forget a basic originality of Marxism: Marxism approaches social realities in a comprehensive perspective, which does not allow the hiving-off of the discipline of economics from the other disciplines of the social sciences. From time to time, I shall myself point out in passing some important socio-political implications of the Marxist economic analysis developed here.

Although the direct outcome of university teaching, the book is nevertheless not intended for the exclusive use of students. Having had many opportunities of taking part in seminars, conferences, discussions or training courses for militants of organizations of the left, I have written it just as much for them: I have tried to take into account as far as possible their remarks and suggestions and to limit what might appear to be 'gratuitous theorizing' to a strict minimum. The book is also intended for every intelligent person, who is moved to react against the traditional anti-Marxist clichés and anxious to find a serious and non-partisan presentation of the socio-economic bases of Marxism.

With such a varied and relatively wide readership in view, the book is not altogether easy reading. This is due to the very complexity of the material discussed (which I have not wished to gloss over) as well as to the density of the argument. These difficulties should, however, be offset by the concern for clarity and rigour throughout the exposition.

The text which follows deliberately refrains from all citation and bibliographical reference: both in order to lighten the presentation as much as possible and also because it would have been impossible for me to indicate in detail the different works which have stimulated my thought (and against which I have often felt bound to react).

I should like to thank Michel De Vroey most cordially for his valuable collaboration in the preparation of this book. The frequent discussions I have had with him, as well as his critical observations on the manuscript, have made it possible to improve the content and the presentation of the text in numerous places. This is particularly true of the chapter on value, which owes much to him. Rightly or wrongly, however, I have not been able to agree with all his remarks and suggestions: a further reason for me to assume full responsibility for the text.

J.G. June 1978

1

The Essential Features of Capitalist Production and of Marxist Analysis

The Marxist analysis presented in this book focuses on capitalist production and capitalist profit. The introductory chapter begins by *placing capitalist production* in the context of other existing types of production and so bringing out its two distinctive and essential characteristics (on the one hand, production intended for the market; on the other, production carried out by wage-earners working for capitalists who own the means of production). It then puts forward the *central thesis of the Marxist economic analysis* (that is, that capitalist profit is created by the labour of the wage-earners) and indicates the three main paths (theoretical, empirical and statistical) which will be followed in order to prove this thesis in the course of subsequent chapters. It finally sets out the *logical structure of the book* as a whole.

CAPITALIST PRODUCTION AND NON-CAPITALIST PRODUCTION

Social and Domestic Labour

Individuals and societies live and reproduce themselves, *consuming* an extremely varied range of goods and services, from the air and basic food to sophisticated means of military defence. Apart from some exceptions (the 'gifts of nature', like the air we breathe), these goods and services have to be *produced* by the individuals of which society is composed.

We can, therefore, distinguish two main types of activities in the life of every individual: on the one hand, activities through which he participates in the aggregate *production* of goods and services in society; on the other, activities through which he participates in the *consumption* of the goods and services produced. The breakdown between the activities of production and consumption obviously varies according to age: the individual is a 'consumer' throughout his life, but is rarely a 'producer' until he reaches 'working age' and he gradually ceases to be one as his strength diminishes in his declining years.

A part of an individual's 'budget time' is therefore devoted to *consumption* activities. These can be set out under a certain number of important headings. Thus we can distinguish in our societies the time devoted to *studies* (during which the individual prepares for his integration into social and professional life), the time devoted to *journeys* between home and place of work, the time devoted to *shopping*, the time devoted to *leisure* and *rest*, the time devoted to meals and to health care etc.

The other part of an individual's 'budget time' is devoted to *production* activities, to which we apply the term '*labour*'. *Labour* can therefore be defined as the set of *activities through which individuals participate in the aggregate production of goods or services.*

In every country, the aggregate production of goods or services is carried out in two distinct areas: on the one hand, the area of professional life (in which we 'earn our living'), on the other, the area of non-professional life (or of 'private life').

Certain people remain confined exclusively in one of these two areas. Such is the case, in our societies, of 'housewives': they produce a variety of goods and services, which are useful·and necessary to the family and to society (cooking, care of children, education etc.) but their participation in aggregate production remains confined to the non-professional area. Such is also the case of men who, in their private life, refuse to 'lend a hand' and behave purely and simply as 'consumers': their participation in aggregate production is confined to the professional area.

Other people, by contrast, participate simultaneously in both areas of production: such is typically the case of women who go out to work, and also of men who, in addition to their occupation, take part in unpaid activities (in the family or elsewhere).

In *labour* (the general concept), we will therefore distinguish two specific categories, which we will call respectively *social labour* and *domestic labour*. *Social labour* can be defined as the set of *production activities carried out in the professional area*, and *domestic labour* as the set of *production activities carried out in the non-professional area*.[1]

Social labour can be classified according to three different and distinctive criteria.

(1)   The nature of the products made by the workers: this first criterion makes it possible to define the concepts of the *division of social labour* and of *socially useful labour*.

(2)   Whether the products are (or are not) intended to be sold: this second criterion makes it possible to contrast *indirectly social labour* and *directly social labour*.

(3)   Whether the workers offer (or do not offer) their services on the 'labour market': this third criterion makes it possible to contrast *waged labour* and *non-waged labour*.

The division of social labour and socially useful labour
The first distinctive criterion concerns the *nature of the goods or services* which the workers produce or help to produce.[2] Obviously, 'everyone does not make everything' but everyone works in some more or less specialized branch of activity: metallurgy, foodstuffs, textiles, health services, law, energy, banking, commerce, administration etc. In other words, there exists what is called a *division of social labour*, that is, a *distribution, as between different branches of activity* (of varying degrees of specialization) *of the total amount of social labour* available.

The different branches of activity are obviously not independent of each other. On the contrary, they produce in conditions of mutual *interdependence*: thus metallurgy produces sheet-metal which is used in the car industry, agriculture produces the primary materials of the foodstuffs sector, the energy and banking branches provide services for the whole of industry as well as for individuals, the foodstuffs and health services sectors ensure the maintenance or the improved efficiency of the workers and thus enable work to proceed in every branch of activity etc.

On consideration, it appears that every individual helps to produce goods or services which are normally used by others. If this is so, we can say that the labour of every individual in a specialized branch constitutes *socially useful labour*, this is, *labour useful to others than the producer himself* in a society founded on the division of social labour and on the interdependence of the producers.

Indirectly social labour and directly social labour
If 'everyone does not make everything', *how* is the division of social labour made between different branches of activity? and how is the labour of any individual recognized as socially useful labour?

In the hypothesis of a completely centralized economy, it is the central authority which plays this double role (whether democratically or not, is not important here). It is the central authority which allocates the individuals among the various activities to be carried out: in this way, it effects the division of social labour. And it is the central authority which determines which activities are useful and necessary for the satisfaction of social needs: an individual's labour is, therefore, recognized straightaway, *a priori*, as socially useful labour, by the simple fact that the central authority has decided that such and such an activity should be carried out.

What actually happens in a capitalist country?

1.   In a capitalist country, the distribution of social labour is generally based on the *free initiative* of entrepreneurs (whether capitalist or self-employed).[3] It is they who decide, each for himself, the nature of their production (what to produce), the volume of production (what quantity to produce), the technique of production (how to produce). Each of them, in taking these decisions, affects the distribution of social labour between the different branches of activity.

However, if the thousands of entrepreneurs take decisions in this way, independently of each other, nothing ensures *a priori* that these products will be mutually interdependent and that the labour employed will be socially useful labour. In fact, this 'social recognition' and this interdependence are only ensured subsequently, *a posteriori, by means of the market.*

It is the *market sale* which *determines the socially useful character of the different types of labour.* If goods or services find a purchaser, this is the proof that the labour put into producing them is useful to others than the producers. On the other hand, if goods or services are not sold, it would appear that the labour carried out by the producers is socially useless labour.

At the same time, it is *the market* which *directs (and redirects) the choices of individuals towards this or that particular branch of activity.* The market comes in here in two ways: for in fact every enterprise enters the market not only to sell its products (for which it seeks the highest possible revenue) but also to purchase its machines, materials etc. (the cost of which it seeks to minimize). As long as its revenue exceeds its costs by an amount which is judged sufficient, it continues production in the same branch; but if its profit becomes insufficient (for want of customers and/or because of excessive costs), it must redirect its activity so as to come up with a sufficiently 'profitable' line of production.

2. Even in a capitalist country, however, a market sale is not the sole criterion of the social usefulness of labour. A relatively large number of activities are recognized as socially useful without their productions having to find a purchaser on the market. This is so for a variety of *productions for collective use* (local and central administration, law and order, education etc.). Services produced in these areas of activity do not have to be sold on a market in order to be considered useful; they are useful *a priori*, by virtue of the public authorities' decision. Similarly, it is not market criteria (comparison of returns and costs) which direct labour towards this or that production, but political decisions which are in theory independent of such criteria.

We call '*indirectly social labour*' all social labour, the usefulness of which is recognized indirectly and *a posteriori*, by means of the market. The aggregate of indirectly social labour constitutes the *market production* sector.[4]

We call '*directly social labour*' all social labour, the usefulness of which is recognized directly and *a priori*, independently of a market sale. The aggregate of directly social labour constitutes the sector of *non-market social production* which we call, for brevity's sake, the *administration* sector.[5]

Waged labour and non-waged labour
The previous criterion divided the workers according to the market or non-market character of the *goods or services* which they help to produce by their labour: some help to produce goods and services intended for the market; others, goods and services which do not come onto the market. The next criterion classifies these same workers according to the market or non-market character of their *labour-power*: some hire out their labour-power on the 'labour market', while others do not enter this market to offer their services.

What difference is there between *labour* and *labour-power*? *Labour-power* is the sum of the physical and intellectual faculties which fit a man for work, it is his *capacity* to work. *Labour* itself consists in the *use* of these faculties, of this capacity to work. The difference between the two concepts is similar to that which exists, for example, between *nuclear capability* and a nuclear *strike* (a bombardment): the first is a potential, the second is the use of this potential. The distinction between *labour* and *labour-power* is not a simple question of semantics; we will see later that it is essential for an understanding of capitalist profit.[6]

What are the general conditions which must be fulfilled for a worker to hire out his labour-power? On the one hand, he must be *free* to hire it out, that is, he must be the owner of his labour-power and be able to dispose of it freely: this would not be so in the case of a slave (the property of his master) or of a serf (attached to the feudal domain by personal ties). On the other hand, he must normally be *obliged* to hire it out, which would normally imply that he has no other means of earning his livelihood. It is this second condition which gives us the next breakdown of the working population.

1.   The first category of workers comprises all those who, not owning any means of production, ensure their livelihood by the *sale of their labour-power*, in exchange for a wage. This category is that of the *wage-earners* and includes blue- and white-collar workers, executives and officials. These wage-earners can be divided into two groups, according to whether they work in the *administration* sector or the *market production* sector. The wage-earners in the market-production sector can in their turn be divided into two sub-groups, according to whether they work in capitalist *private* enterprises or in *public* enterprises (producing goods or services intended for sale).

2.   The second category comprises the owners of means of production (owners of enterprises), who ensure their livelihood by means of the *sale of goods or services* produced in the enterprise. In this category we distinguish *independent* (self-employed) owners and *capitalist* owners.

Capitalists are owners of means of production, who in order to produce goods or services for sale, use the labour-power of wage-earners. (This does not rule out the capitalists themselves taking part in production: but this participation is secondary in relation to the employment of waged labour-power).

The *self-employed* (artisans, shopkeepers, members of the liberal professions), also called *simple market producers*, are owners of means of production who personally produce goods or services for sale, and who do not use waged labour-power. (This does not rule out the self-employed having recourse to the services of 'helpers' or 'family helpers': these are members of his family who help, without payment, to produce goods and services within a family firm producing for the market; they thus belong to the area of market production but their labour-power, used by the head of the family and of the firm under whose authority they work, is not purchased on a 'labour market'.)

Domestic labour

Going back to the definitions made above in the analysis of the concept of social labour, we can briefly describe domestic labour in the following way.

(1) Domestic labour is characterized by a very *low level of division of labour*: the same person (usually the housewife) carries out a varied range of activities which, in the social labour framework, are carried out by specialists (catering, education, health care . . .). It constitutes, like all social labour, *socially useful labour* (useful to others than the producer himself, useful to the reproduction of individuals and of society).

(2) The products of domestic labour do not have to be sold on a market for this labour to be recognized as socially useful: in the same way as collective goods and services, domestic goods and services are a part of *non-market production*.

(3) The labour-power is not offered on a market (any more than the products of the labour): domestic labour therefore constitutes *non-waged labour*.

Synthesis

Figure 1.1 gives a breakdown of the whole of the labour carried out in a capitalist society (social labour and domestic labour) according to two of the three criteria put forward, namely: the *market* (or non-market) character of the goods and services produced and the *waged* (or non-waged) character of the labour provided.

The respective size of the different rectangles gives only an imperfect indication of the relative importance of the different types of labour. Lacking adequate statistics, it is impossible to give an exact picture of this distribution: the statistics available do not provide any indication of the time spent on domestic labour (which must be distinguished both from professional labour and from consumption activities); they give us very scanty information on the distinction between market production and administration; it is only the overall distribution between the waged and non-waged labour in the whole professional area that can be estimated with any precision.

Figure 1.1 tells us nothing about the first criterion mentioned above, namely, the nature of productions which are carried out. In fact, the same production, defined by the nature of the product, can appear in two or more of the different rectangles, even in all of them:

	Market Production = INDIRECTLY SOCIAL labour		Non-market production
WAGED labour	1. Labour of waged producers		4. DIRECTLY SOCIAL labour (Labour of officials of the 'administration' sector)
	1a (Capitalist enterprises)	1b (Public enterprises)	
			5. DOMESTIC labour (Labour of domestic producers)
NON-WAGED labour	2. Labour of capitalists		
	3. Labour of the self-employed (+ helpers)		

Figure 1.1   Distribution of labour (social and domestic) according to the market character of production and of labour-power.

the production of steel can take place both within private (rectangles 1a and 2) and public (1b) enterprises; teaching and education are provided primarily in the area of non–market production (state education = rectangle 4, education at home = rectangle 5) but also in the area of market production (private crèches, private schools, driving schools etc. = rectangles 1a and 2 and/or 3); we could produce many more examples.

Figure 1.1 enables us to bring out two essential and distinctive characteristics of capitalist production (rectangles 1a and 2): whatever the nature of the goods or services produced, capitalist production is production *intended for the market* and *carried out by wage-earners*, working on behalf of and under the orders of capitalists (owners of the means of production and exercising the power of decision). We can indicate at this stage two other essential features of capitalist production: it aims at *profit* and it is based on *competition* between enterprises (or between groups). These different characteristics will be analysed in detail later on.

Independently of the respective size of the different rectangles, one thing has to be made clear: what makes capitalist society specific, what distinguishes it from every other society, is obviously the existence and the dominant character of *capitalist production* (rectangles 1a and 2). Domestic labour (rectangle 5) and independent (self-employed) labour (rectangle 3) can be found in different degrees in practically every society, from the feudal to the centrally planned. The prevalence of directly social labour (rectangle 4) would be typical of a centralized society, while the prevalence of public sector enterprises (rectangle 1b) would indicate some form of 'state capitalism'. It is the existence and the dominant character of capitalist production which alone enable us to distinguish specifically the so-called 'Western' societies.

This book, concerned exclusively with the study of these 'Western' societies, will therefore seek primarily to achieve a thorough understanding of what is specific to these societies, namely capitalist-type production. This will first be analysed *in itself*, disregarding the existence of other different types of production (which are also to be found in every capitalist society). These other types of production will not be brought in until later in the analysis (and at different stages) and we will then see how they relate to capitalist production as such.

THE CENTRAL THESIS AND THE STAGES IN ITS PROOF

The Thesis: The Wage-Earners' 'Surplus Labour' as the Source of Capitalist Profit

As we have just said, the primary object of the study is to achieve a thorough understanding of capitalist production. We know intuitively that this is directed by the search for *profit* and that profit constitutes the logic of capitalist production. But the question immediately arises: where does this profit come from? A central thesis in the Marxist approach consists in pointing out that *the whole profit accruing to the capitalist class is based on the exploitation of the wage-earners*: a part of the labour-time supplied by the wage-earners is exchanged for a wage, the other part of this labour-time (called '*surplus labour*') is supplied free of charge and accounts for capitalist profit.

A switch of perspective
The statement that profit arises from free 'surplus labour' by the wage-earners certainly goes against common sense. It runs up against two everyday 'facts'. First of all, a wage-earner, paid at the rate of £5 an hour, earns £40 for a working day of 8 hours: where then is the surplus labour, supposedly 'free', which he gives the capitalist?

Secondly, highly mechanized or automated enterprises normally make a larger profit than rival enterprises which make a greater call on manpower: is this not proof that profit is due to mechanization, to technical progress, rather than to alleged 'surplus labour' by the wage-earners?

These objections, based on straightforward common sense, are not decisive for anyone who wishes to look at the facts in a scientific way. For science involves going beyond 'appearances' to discover the 'essence' or the reality of phenomena. This can be illustrated in a simple way by an example taken from astronomy: to all appearances, the sun seems to move around the earth; in reality, the science of astronomy proves that it is the earth which moves around the sun and it also explains how the illusion of the contrary arises. In the same way, Marxist theory proves that, contrary to appearances, profit comes from the surplus labour of wage-earners; it also explains how it actually comes about that the most highly mechanized enterprises are normally the most profitable.

Let us pursue the comparison. The switch of perspective brought about by astronomy was indispensable in order to *understand the real movements* of the planets and to turn this knowledge to our advantage (consider space exploration, satellite launching etc.). In a similar way, the switch of perspective concerning the source of capitalist profit enables us to *understand the real movements of capitalist society*: having established the reality of free surplus labour, one can understand and interrelate various other aspects of capitalist development, such as the struggles over working hours, the increase in productivity, state intervention in the economic and social field, exports of capital to less developed countries etc.

But a switch of perspective rarely takes place smoothly. Galileo was condemned because his ideas ran counter to the opinions and interests of the thinkers and learned men of the time. If astronomy is generally accepted today, Marxist science is not. For Marxist analyses not only run counter to current opinions and to the generally accepted ideology but also to the interests of the dominant capitalist class; this class, rather than open up a discussion on basic questions (the reality of 'free' surplus labour), prefers to take refuge in the comforting reassurance of immediately 'visible' appearances (for example, the rise in real wages).

A state of affairs which is both old and new
Let us return to the main proposition we wish to demonstrate: that capitalist profit comes from exploitation, from the 'free' surplus

labour of the wage-earners. It is true that 'free' surplus labour is not a phenomenon that made its first appearance with capitalist society: it already existed in earlier times, but its forms and functions have changed along with the evolution of society. Let us consider, by way of example, surplus labour in feudal society and see how it provides a first intimation of the reality and the form of surplus labour in a capitalist society (see Figure 1.2).

A *feudal* society recognizes two basic classes: that of the feudal lords and that of the 'serfs'. The feudal lords are owners of the estates, which constitute the principal means of production at the time. Each feudal lord divides his estate into two groups: the *demesne* which he keeps for himself and the *holdings or plots of land*, the use of which he grants to the serfs dependent on him. The serfs can work these plots for their own needs, in return for which they are obliged to work without payment for a part of the time on the feudal lord's demesne. The labour-time of each serf (for example a week of 6 days) is thus divided into two parts. A first part (3 days on the plot leased to him) allows the serf to assure his and his family's subsistence. This labour is called *necessary labour* and the product resulting from it is called the *necessary product* (necessary to the subsistence of the serf and his family). The second part (3 days on the demesne) brings in nothing for the serf but ensures the subsistence and the enrichment of the feudal lord. This labour is called *surplus labour* and the product resulting from it is called the *surplus product*; the latter is taken without payment by the feudal lord.

Necessary labour and surplus labour in feudal society may be defined in the following way. Necessary labour is the labour-time during which the peasant-serf produces the means of consumption intended for himself and his family. Surplus labour is the difference between the total labour-time and this necessary labour.

A *capitalist* society in the same way recognizes two basic classes: capitalists and wage-earners. The former have control over the means of production and get the wage-earners, who lack the means of production, to work for them. The total labour-time of the wage-earners, like that of the serfs, can be divided into two parts; but at the same time we must make clear what differentiates the serfs labour from that of the wage-earners.[7]

A first difference, an essential one, arises from the fact that the wage-earner does not himself produce his means of consumption but has to purchase them out of the wages he receives. The necessary labour of the wage-earner cannot therefore be defined as the time he needs to produce his means of consumption; it must be defined as the *time corresponding to the labour devoted (by others than himself) to producing the means of subsistence he has to purchase.* Thus in the example in Figure 1.2, the means of consumption required by the wage-earner having cost 4 working hours, the wage-earner's 'necessary

A. In a feudal society

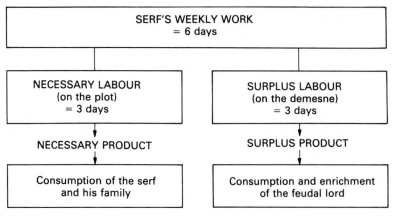

B. In a capitalist society

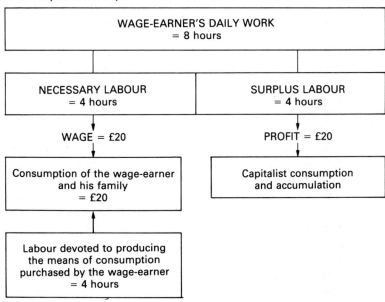

Figure 1.2 Necessary labour and surplus labour under feudalism and capitalism.

labour' is equal to 4 hours: at the end of this period, the wage-earner has 'produced as much labour as he consumes'. But the wage-earner works for longer than this (he works 8 hours in our example) and consequently he 'produces more labour than he consumes': this difference between the total labour-time and the 'necessary labour' constitutes the surplus labour given free to the capitalist.

The second difference arises from the fact that, contrary to what takes place in the feudal system, the division between necessary labour and surplus labour is not visible in the capitalist system. On the one hand, the wage-earner spends all his working time in the same enterprise, while the serf works partly on his plot of land and partly on the demesne. On the other hand, a daily wage of £40 is expressed in practice in the form of payment for 8 hours at a rate of £5 an hour (all the hours appear therefore to be paid and no particular hours to be given free). Finally, and above all, the only visible phenomena (apart from the total labour-time) are the wages (equal to the price of the means of consumption to be purchased) and the profit, both expressed in pounds: how are we to grasp the reality in terms of labour (necessary and surplus labour) behind the phenomena expressed in prices (wages and profits)?

The Proof (in Three Stages)

How are we to grasp the reality in terms of labour behind the phenomena expressed in prices? We come here to the fundamental originality of Marxist political economy. This consists in proving that *the apparent division between wages and profits conceals a more fundamental division between necessary labour (paid) and surplus labour (unpaid, free)*. This division of labour is not directly visible, it cannot be 'shown' as in the case of the feudal system. It is therefore a question of 'proving' the reality by means of a rigorous scientific analysis. How should this analysis proceed? Three types of proof will be put forward in turn.

Proof by theory

Since wages and profits are expressed in *prices* (pounds), the first stage consists in enquiring into the *phenomenon of price in general*: how is it that all commodities have a price? We must emphasize here an essential difference from non-Marxist political economy. The latter considers prices as a 'self-evident' phenomenon and only enquires into the exact level of the prices of different commodities (why this price rather than that?). The Marxist approach, on the contrary, while providing the whole theoretical apparatus needed to explain the exact level of prices, enquires primarily into the essential meaning, into the basis, of this general phenomenon. The result of this enquiry, as we shall see in chapter 2, can be expressed as follows: behind the phenomenon of *price*, there is concealed the reality of *labour* devoted to producing the commodities (the reality of 'value').

Once the connection between labour and price is established, it is possible to demonstrate the reality of free surplus labour in the capitalist system. Chapter 3 will show that, behind the phenomenon of the wage, there is concealed the reality of necessary labour and behind the phenomenon of *profit*, the reality of *surplus labour* (the reality of '*surplus value*').

Proof by fact
The next stage of the analysis consists in showing the practical implications of the state of affairs which has been thus demonstrated: in what way is this surplus labour or this surplus value helpful for our understanding of the observable tendencies of the capitalist system? A comparison with psychoanalysis can be useful here. Psychoanalysis attempts to locate a 'deep core' of the personality in the unconscious: to the extent that it is successful, a whole series of seemingly inconsistent exterior aspects of the personality can be given a coherent explanation. In the same way, Marxist political economy claims to locate the 'deep core' of the capitalist system in surplus value: if this is the case, we should then be able to understand and explain, in a coherent way, a whole series of visible phenomena and tendencies of the system: resistance to the reduction of working hours, increase of productivity, state intervention, export of capital, crises and inflation etc. We will actually see in chapters 7–10 that Marxist theory proves rewarding in the analysis of numerous essential aspects of contemporary capitalism; this, in its turn, confirms the validity of the theoretical proofs (chapters 2 and 3) put forward by Marxist political economy.

Proof by statistics
A final way of bringing out the reality of surplus labour in capitalism consists in documenting it with actual statistics. Although current statistics conceal the reality we are referring to (the data on hourly wages suggest on the contrary that all working hours are paid) it is none the less possible to use them to isolate the surplus labour and assess its importance. This will be the object of chapter 11, which will provide an empirical assessment for five European countries for the years 1966–78.

GENERAL STRUCTURE OF THE BOOK

Three intermediate chapters (4, 5, 6) are inserted in the middle of the proof of the book's central theme, which is that capitalist profit arises from the surplus labour of the wage-earners. These intermediate chapters, like chapters 2 and 3, present basic concepts of Marxist economic theory: several of them will be used in the second and third stages of the proof.

Chapter 4 presents the basic ratios of Marxist political economy (rate of surplus value, composition of capital, rate of profit) and studies in detail the factors affecting each of these ratios.

Chapter 5 presents briefly the 'reproduction schemes', which aim to clarify the *interdependence* between the different branches of capitalist production.

Chapter 6 presents an original and systematic analysis of the 'surplus revenue transfer schemes', which bring out the *competition* among capitalists to appropriate for themselves the surplus revenue created by the surplus labour of the wage-earners.

The logical structure of the book as a whole can be set out in the following way.

PART I: The basic concepts of Marxist economic theory

(1) The theoretical proof of the central thesis: the concepts of value and surplus value.

Chapter 2:   The basis of the price of commodities: value (labour)
Chapter 3:   The basis of capitalist profit: an increase of value (surplus labour, the exploitation of labour-power)

(2) Other basic concepts of Marxist economic theory
Chapter 4:   The basic ratios of Marxist political economy
Chapter 5:   Reproduction schemes
Chapter 6:   Surplus revenue transfer schemes

PART II: The application of Marxist economic theory to the analysis of capitalism

(1) The factual proof of the central thesis
Chapter 7:   Capitalist competition for the appropriation of surplus revenue
Chapter 8:   Some essential tendencies of capitalist growth
Chapter 9:   Capitalist growth and crises
Chapter 10: Capitalist growth, money and prices

(2) The statistical proof of the central thesis
   Chapter 11:   An empirical estimation of the rate of surplus labour
                 in five European countries 1966–78

Conclusion: The reproduction of capitalism

The conclusion goes beyond the essentially economic approach of
the analysis, to bring out the political and ideological elements which
contribute to the reproduction of capitalism.

NOTES

1. To avoid all ambiguity, it is helpful to add some further details to these
   definitions.
(1) Domestic labour (from the Latin *domus* = home, house) relates
    essentially to labour carried out in the home (hence its name).
    Domestic labour and labour in the home are not, however, synony-
    mous: on the one hand, the concept of domestic labour does not
    include *professional* activities carried out in the home (e.g. the labour of
    a paid servant, office work done at home); on the other hand, it does
    include *non-professional* activities carried on outside the home (outdoor
    hobbies, mutual 'helping out' between neighbours). We could have
    used the term 'private labour' but this will be given a specific meaning
    later on.
(2) Social labour is not the only type of labour to be useful to society:
    domestic labour contributes just as much to the reproduction of
    individuals and of society, it is therefore just as useful and as necessary.
(3) The same activity, defined by its content, can come under the heading
    both of social labour and of domestic labour: thus the preparation of a
    meal comes under the heading of social labour if it is carried out
    professionally (e.g. in a restaurant) and of domestic labour if it is not
    (e.g. at home).

2. We are not considering here the question of the capacity in which the
   workers produce or help to produce these goods or services: whether as
   wage-earners, capitalists, self- employed etc. We will come back to this
   when we examine the third distinctive criterion.
3. On the distribution between capitalists and self- employed, see below p.
   6.
4. Chapter 2 will distinguish more precisely, within the market production
   sector, *production* activities themselves and *circulation* activities.
5. Here too, some observations on terminology will be useful, to avoid all
   ambiguity.
(1) As we have already pointed out in the text, the *administration* sector

includes, apart from administration itself, various other *non-market professional activities* (e.g. education).

(2) The administration sector does not constitute the whole of the non-market production sector. As we shall see later in this chapter, the *non-market production* sector includes, on the one hand, the *administration* sector (non-market *professional* activities or non-market social production) and, on the other, the *domestic* production sector.

6. Since labour-power and labour are two distinct things, the market on which workers offer their labour-power should be called 'labour-power market' rather than 'labour market'. As to the offer of labour-power, we will speak interchangeably of its *'hiring out'* or its *'sale'*. (We will return later to the concept of the *sale* of labour-power. See chapter 3, p. 58, n. 13.)

7. We have already noted (p. 6) that the wage-earner, unlike the serf, *sells* his labour-power on a *'labour market'*.

PART I
The Basic Concepts of Marxist Economic Theory

2

The Basis of the Price of Commodities: Value

The aim of this chapter is to gain an understanding of the general phenomenon of price. Commodities are bought and sold at such and such a price: How is it that they all have a price? What do these prices mean? To answer these questions, we are going to proceed in four stages.

(1) The first stage consists in making clear what we are talking about, that is, in *defining commodities* and *pointing out their visible features*. This will give us the opportunity to answer such questions as: Are all goods commodities? Are services also commodities?

(2) The second stage consists in enquiring into the *role* and *basis* of the exchange of commodities: What function is carried out by commodity exchange? What are the conditions which make this exchange possible? This stage will bring up the key concept of *value*, or labour devoted to the production of a commodity which is sold.

(3) The third stage then enquires into the *meaning of price* in general. It shows how the *price* of commodities (expressed in pounds) is the necessary expression of their *value* (expressed in hours of labour).

(4) The fourth and final stage approaches the question of the *level of particular prices* and goes on to place what has been said about value and prices in the context of the whole of Marxist theory.

COMMODITIES

The Concept of Commodity

Commodities are defined here as *goods or services* which are *produced for the market*, that is, produced for the use of the purchaser rather than for the use of the producer/vendor. Thus chairs made by a joiner and steel produced in a steelworks are commodities, for these are objects produced for sale; these goods will be used by the purchasers and not – except to a very limited extent – by the enterprise which has produced them.

The producers of commodities therefore produce for sale; the payment they receive permits them to purchase in exchange other commodities produced by other producers.

The three criteria laid down in the above definition enable us to specify which things count as commodities and which do not.

The market
The most obvious condition for goods and services to be commodities is that they should be *sold on the market*.

The following are, therefore, *not* commodities:

(1) Goods and services *intended for the personal use of the producer* (e.g. farm products consumed by the farmer himself).
(2) Goods and services which, while intended for the use of persons other than the producer, are *not passed on to them by means of the market* (where a price is paid).

This second category of non-commodities essentially includes the two kinds of goods and services belonging to the sector of non-market production (see Figure 1.1, p. 8):

(1) Collective goods and services resulting from *directly social labour*: these are financed by the community and passed on without charge to the users (e.g. a public park, free transport services, police services etc.).
(2) Private goods and services resulting from *domestic labour*: these are produced and consumed within the family circle (or the non-professional sphere in general), and are not sold (no price is paid).

Production
A second condition for goods and services to be commodities is that they should be *produced*, that is, that (unlike 'gifts of nature') they

should be *the result of human labour being applied to 'production'* (as opposed to 'circulation').

This condition leads us to exclude from the concept of commodities two quite distinct categories of goods and services.

The following are *not* commodities:

(1) 'Gifts of nature' or natural resources: these are goods and services provided free by nature, *without the intervention of human labour.* Thus fresh air, natural rain, river water, virgin soil, iron ore under ground, fruit growing wild etc., involve no human production and so are not commodities. (However, air in cylinders, artificial rain, water piped into houses, tilled soil, iron ore after extraction, fruit from orchards etc., all involve some human activity and will be commodities if they are sold.)

(2) Services which, while involving some human labour, consist in *circulation* and not in production.

What is the distinction between production and circulation? A society in which production takes place for the market presupposes activities of two types: activities devoted to producing something (no matter what) and activities devoted to selling (or hiring out) what one has produced and buying (or hiring) what others have produced. While the former activities create something new, the latter merely transfer rights of ownership (or of use) over things which are already in existence. Thus the building of a house, its upkeep and its repairs create something new (this is obvious in the case of the building; in the other two cases, the new product is the well-maintained or renovated house, compared with the same house when in need of repair); on the other hand, the sale or lease of a house creates nothing new, but merely transfers the ownership or use of an already existing building from one person to another. Similarly, the production, transport and storage of fruit creates something new (the newness, in the case of transport and storage, is fresh fruit within reach of the consumer, compared with fruit which is either spoilt or too far away); but the successive sales, from the producers through the wholesalers and retailers to the consumers, create nothing new: once again, they merely transfer, from one person to another, the ownership of an already existing product.[1] Similarly, the mining of gold or the printing of banknotes creates something new; but the financial operations dealing with gold and currencies, the lending and borrowing of money, merely transfer, from one person to another, the rights of ownership or of use over certain quantities of gold, dollars, francs etc.

These examples enable us to give a general definition of circulation activities. Circulation activities are all activities which secure *the transfer, from one person to another, of the rights of ownership or use over products (commodities or money) which are already in existence.* The activities concerned essentially consist of *buying and selling, hiring and letting, borrowing and lending.* As for production activities, it is impossible to specify their content, otherwise than in contrast to circulation activities: to produce is to work at any activity that is not a circulation activity.[2]

Let us be clear that circulation activities, though producing nothing new, are just as useful and indispensable as production activities: in a market-based society, selling (or letting or lending) is the necessary complement of production: the transfer of the product to the purchaser (or hirer or borrower) is the proof of the social utility of the product that has been created and enables the producer to acquire, in his turn, the products created by others.

Goods or services

The distinction between goods and services can be made as follows. 'Goods' are products of labour which are separable from their producer; they can be stockpiled and their consumption takes place after their production (for example: cars, books, medicines, hairbrushes); services, on the other hand, are products of labour which are inseparable from their producer: they cannot be stockpiled and their consumption is simultaneous with production (for example: transport, education, medical care, a haircut).

Are services commodities in the same way as goods? In our view, services should be classified in the same way as material goods: to the extent that they involve production and are sold, they are commodities. Thus, the services of the taxi-driver or the barber are commodities, because they are produced for sale. But services performed in the family circle are not commodities, because they are not intended for sale; commercial and financial and hire services are not commodities either, because they do not involve production.

The Two Visible Features of Commodities

All commodities necessarily possess two visible features: a price and a use-value.

The *price* of a commodity is the quantity of pounds (or of francs, marks, dollars etc.) for which it can be exchanged; it is *the amount of money which the producer hopes to receive or actually receives from the sale of the commodity*.

In order to be sold, the commodity must be useful to the purchaser, it must be of some use or other to him (otherwise he would not buy it): in other words, the commodity must have a *use-value* for the purchaser. The use-value of goods or services can be defined as their *capacity to be of some use or other* – or again, as their usefulness. Thus the use-value of water is to be of use for cleaning or for quenching thirst; the use-value of a bomb is to be of use for destruction; the use-value of morphine is to be of use for relieving pain, and so on. No moral judgement is made on the use which is made of goods or services, or on the needs they are meant to satisfy. But we must make clear, when speaking of commodities, that the use-value must be appreciated from the point of view of the purchaser and not from the point of view of the producer: the producer of commodities produces goods or services which have a use-value for the purchaser and acquires in exchange other goods or services which have a use-value for him.

If all commodities have in this way a price and a use-value, *goods or services which are not commodities can also have one or other of these two qualities*. This is clear for use-value: products which are not intended for the market and gifts of nature obviously have a usefulness for those who benefit from them: we may call 'use-values' (as distinct from 'commodities') those goods and services which are of some use or other without being commodities.[3] This is equally true for *price*: circulation services imply the payment of a certain price (commercial profit margin, interest, rent) and gifts of nature can also be exchanged at a certain price, in so far as they admit of private ownership (thus an area of land or of sea, admitting of private ownership, may be sold or leased out at a certain price; but not the air, which nobody can normally own).

Summary

Table 2.1 sums up the distinctions which have just been set out in order to explain the concept of commodity. It also shows that the notions of *use-value* and of *price* cover a field much wider than that of commodities.

TABLE 2.1   *Classification of goods and services according to the criteria of commodity, use-value and price*

Goods and services	Commodity	Use-value	Price
1. *Resulting from human labour*			
(production, as opposed to consumption)			
(a) In the market sector			
(goods and services sold)			
Products	Yes	Yes	Yes
Circulation services	No	No	Yes
(b) In the non-market sector			
(goods and services not sold)			
Collective goods and services	No	Yes	No
Domestic products	No	Yes	No
2. *Provided by nature (natural resources)*			
(a) Not appropriated	No	Yes	No
(b) Appropriated and sold	No	Yes	Yes

THE HIDDEN FACE OF
COMMODITIES: VALUE

The Social Function and Basis of the Exchange of Commodities

Each producer of commodities produces for the market rather than for himself and buys in exchange on the market, with the proceeds of his sale, the commodities he needs for his consumption (food, clothing etc.) or for his work (raw materials, machines etc.). The exchange of commodities (through sales and purchases) is thus a necessary condition of social life in a market society, based on the division of social labour and on the interdependence of the producers.

But how is it that the producer of a given commodity (clothing, for example) can exchange his product for other dissimilar commodities (for example: food, drink, transport)? What is it that makes possible the exchange of commodities which are so different in their physical and technical properties and in their utility (in their 'use-value')?

If two dissimilar commodities (shoes and tables, for example) can be exchanged through sales and purchases on the market, there must then be in these two kinds of objects a *common element* relevant to the market, a common denominator which makes it possible to relate them (to each other) on the market. In a similar way, if one can exchange eggs for meat in a diet, it is because the two foodstuffs contain a common element relevant to diet (for example, the fact that both are sources of protein). What can be the common relevant element which enables us to relate two items which are to be exchanged on the market?

The first answer which comes to mind is no doubt to say that this common denominator is the price: two pairs of shoes can be exchanged for a table, because their common price is, say, £50. But this answer will not do, for it implies that two puzzling questions have been already resolved. For what is this notion of price? Why is the price of a table specifically £50? Before we can examine these questions, we must find the true common denominator of commodities.

This true common denominator of commodities is in fact the *indirectly social labour*, typical of a market society, which we have already introduced in chapter 1. To make this clear, let us recall that every society must carry out a precise allocation of social labour in order to satisfy a series of needs: so much labour for the production of item X, so much for item Y, etc. But this allocation of social labour – which constitutes a universal requirement – can come about in two totally distinct ways (which can, however, be combined in a particular society).

Either a central authority decides *consciously* and *a priori* the types of production to be carried out and the distribution of workers between these various types of production. In such a case the actual labour of any producer is immediately recognized as useful to society: it is called *directly social labour*.

Or else the producers decide separately, and on their own initiative, the type of labour they are going to carry out and so the type of product they are going to make. In this case the labour of any producer cannot be recognized directly as social labour, as labour useful to society. It appears first as *private labour*: this can be defined as labour based on the free initiative of the individual and devoted to the production of goods or services intended for sale. The private labour of each individual producer is only recognized as *socially useful labour* at a second stage, when (and in so far as) his products find a purchaser, that is, when they are sold on the market. If this is the case, the private labour performed by the individual producer is called *indirectly social labour*. If it is not the case, that is, if an article does not find a purchaser, this means that the private labour of the producer is not recognized as socially useful labour. If the producer wishes to survive, he must redirect his labour, so as to produce goods which meet the needs of other producers.

The *social function* of commodity exchange thus becomes apparent. Commodity exchange is the means by which the *allocation of social labour* is brought about *in a society based on private labour* (on the free initiative of the producers). *The common element* contained in the various commodities exchanged also becomes apparent. This common element is *indirectly social labour*, i.e. *private labour recognized as useful to society by means of the market* (by virtue of the fact that the producer finds a purchaser on the market). This indirectly social labour, typical of commodity production, is also called *abstract labour* or *value*. We can thus say – very briefly – that the necessary common denominator of the commodities exchanged is their value.[4]

The Value of Commodities

We have just defined value (or abstract labour) as *indirectly social labour*, that is, labour resulting from the free initiative of the producers and recognized as useful to society by virtue of the fact that the commodity finds a purchaser on the market. Bearing in mind all that this definition implies, we can define this same value more briefly as *private labour recognized as social labour by means of the market* or again *as labour devoted to producing a commodity which is then sold*.

Moving on from there, we must now make some more detailed observations concerning the value of commodities. A first set of observations is related to the *production* aspect, to the labour of the producers. We then stress the *market* aspect, or the essential role of the sale of the goods or services produced. We finally make a few comments on the *changes in value* over time.

The production aspect

Past value and new value   The labour devoted to producing any commodity (tables, shoes etc.) comprises in reality two distinct types of labour.

(1)   The labour-time needed for the making of the commodity itself (for the processing of the raw material into a finished product).

(2)   The labour-time which was needed to produce the means of production (that is, the raw material as well as the tools, machines, buildings, and so on.).[5]

If the producers themselves had to produce the means of production (raw material, tools) which they use, it is clear that we should include in the value of their respective commodities, not only the labour-time spent in carrying out the actual processing, but also the time spent in carrying out the 'preliminary' operations required to produce the means of production.

In practice, due to the division of social labour, the 'preliminary' operations are carried out by other producers, from whom the means of production are bought; but the time spent by these other producers should also be counted in the value of the commodities in question.

Let us suppose, for example, that 15 hours are required to produce the materials and tools used in making a table and only 5 hours to produce the materials and tools used in making a pair of shoes, while the work of processing takes 5 hours for both commodities. We will have in this case:

Value of the table: 15 hours + 5 hours = 20 hours
Value of the pair of shoes: 5 hours + 5 hours = 10 hours

The labour-time required to produce the means of production purchased (material and tools) is known as *past labour* (or *dead labour*); the labour-time spent in the processing operation is known as *present labour* (or *living labour*).[6]

In the course of the processing operation, the producer actually carries out two simultaneous functions:

(1)   He *transfers* to the commodity (tables, shoes) a *past value*, that is, the value of the means of production purchased. (We can also say that he *conserves* this past value: if the joiner did not carry out the processing operation, his raw material and the tools would eventually deteriorate and the labour previously expended in producing them would be lost.)

(2)   Moreover, the producer *adds*, to this past labour, his present labour: he creates a *new value* (or added value).

From the above, we deduce the following principle: *the value of any commodity is the sum of the past labour and the present labour necessary to its production* or *it is the sum of the past value transferred and the new value created by the producer.*

Regarding the past value (or value of the means of production bought), we must further explain that it is transferred in different ways, according to whether we are dealing with means of labour or with raw material. Let us consider for example the production of a wooden table, which involves the utilization of 20 kg of raw material (requiring 14 hours of labour) and of various tools and machines (requiring 10 000 hours of labour). The 20 kg of raw material can be used only for the production of a single table: all 14 hours of past value thus reappear in the table. In contrast, the tools and machines can be used for the production of a whole series of tables: let us suppose they are intended to secure the production of 10 000 tables (after which they would have to be replaced because they would be physically worn out or technologically out of date). In this case, the 10 000 hours of past value are only transferred in their totality in the complete series of 10 000 tables produced: so each single table only includes 1/10 000 of the total value of the machines and tools, say 1 hour. The total past value of a single table will therefore be 14 hours + 1 hour, say 15 hours. As a rule, we can say that *the value of the materials used is transferred 'in one go' to the finished product, whereas the value of the means of labour used is only transferred gradually* (in inverse proportion to their anticipated use-life).

Social value and individual value   Taking up the preceding example, let us suppose that, for the majority of producers, the value of a table is equal to 20 hours, broken down into 15 hours of past labour and 5 hours of present labour.

It is inevitable that, in reality, certain manufacturers expend more time than the majority, and others less, in making a similar table. These differences can apply to past labour as well as to present labour. Let us take for example a relatively inefficient producer Z, who produces in 30 hours instead of 20. These 30 hours could correspond, for example, to 15 hours of past labour and 15 hours of present labour: this means that producer Z uses the same tools and the same quantity of material as the other manufacturers but he is much slower in the work of processing. These 30 hours could also correspond, for example, to 25 hours of past labour and 5 hours of present labour: this means that Z works as fast as the other manufacturers but that he uses more antiquated and more expensive tools or that he wastes the raw materials. These differences in the quantities of labour,[7] required by different producers, help to bring out the concept of *social value*, as opposed to the concept of *individual value*.

The *social value* of a commodity is the quantity of labour necessary *on an average* to produce this commodity, that is, the quantity of labour required in average conditions of *technique*, *skill* and *intensity*, prevailing at a given time.

In contrast, the *individual value* of a commodity is the quantity of labour required by a *particular producer* to produce this commodity.[8]

One problem arises here: does not the labour of a particular producer, relying on more advanced technology, on greater skill or intensity, create more value than the labour of another producer, whose labour is less advanced on the technological side, less skilled or less intensive? The point of view adopted here is that there is no difference: provided that commodities are sold, an hour of labour (whatever the special characteristics of this labour) creates an hour of value, neither more nor less than any other hour of labour. However, we will see further on that labour which is technologically more advanced, as well as labour that is more skilled and more intensive, while not creating any more value, is none the less more remunerative to the producer who carries it out.[9]

Unit value and total value   By *unit value*, we understand the value of a unit (a litre, a ton, a piece etc.) of a given commodity. By *total value*, we understand the value of a *set* of commodities produced (by one or several producers) during a certain space of time.

In the preceding example, the figure of 20 hours represents the *unit* social value of the table, the figure of 30 hours, the *unit* individual value for producer Z. If the production sold daily is 1000 tables for the producers as a whole, the *total* social value (of the commodities produced by the industry) is 20 000 hours; if it is 10 tables for Z, the *total* individual value (of the commodities produced by Z) is 300 hours.

Summary   Table 2.2 brings together the main distinctions which we have just set down.

TABLE 2.2   *Distinctions concerning the concept of value (the production aspect)*

Labour (past and present) required ⟶ to produce	on an average	by a particular producer
one unit of a commodity	unit social value	unit individual value
a set of commodities	total social value	total individual value

In the continuation of this chapter and in subsequent chapters, the word 'value' used without other specifications will designate the unit social value, that is, the quantity of labour (past and present) required on an average to produce one unit of a commodity.

The market aspect: the realization of value

We have defined value as *labour devoted to producing a commodity which is sold* or as *private labour, recognized as social labour by means of the market*. After making some detailed observations regarding the labour of the producers and production, it is important to emphasize here the role played by the sale on the market.

As long as a commodity is not sold, it is not established that the labour expended in producing it is labour that is useful to society: the labour embodied in the finished product is therefore only a *potential* value. When the commodity finds a purchaser, it appears that the labour of the individual who has produced it is labour useful to society; value, which until then is a mere potentiality, becomes a *reality*. The *realization of value* can therefore be defined as the *recognition by the market of the social character of the private labour* expended in producing a commodity.

Let us stress that value implies both production *and sale*. Production by itself is not sufficient: before the commodity is sold, the labour-time embodied in it does not count as value, but simply as private labour expecting social recognition. Only the sale of the commodity grants this social recognition and transforms into value the private labour embodied in a commodity. Thus, while it is correct to assert 'no production, no value', it is equally necessary to add 'no sale, no value'.

Changes in value over time

The value of a commodity changes over time according to changes in the productivity of labour. A *decrease in labour productivity* means that less commodities are produced by a given quantity of labour, or again that more labour is needed to produce one unit of a commodity: this results in an *increase in the unit value* of the commodities. Conversely, an *increase in labour productivity* means that more commodities are produced by a given quantity of labour, or again that less labour is needed to produce one unit of a commodity: this results in a *decrease in the unit value* of the commodities.

The most normal tendency consists of increases in labour productivity and of consequent decreases in the unit value of commodities. Increases in labour productivity may be due to various factors: improved natural conditions (the discovery of more fertile soils, for instance), improved work organization, higher skill and efficiency of the workers, improved technology and greater mechanization of the production process (use of more and/or better machines). Most influential among all these factors are technical progress and mechanization: their *raison d'être* and impact will be analysed in detail at a later stage.[10]

We know that the unit value of a commodity includes past value transferred and new value created. A change in productivity may affect either of them, or both. To illustrate this, let us take up the example of p. 29 where the unit value of the table is 20 hours = 15 hours (past value) + 5 hours (new value). An increase in productivity will depress the unit value (from 20 hours to, say, 18 hours) but this result may be achieved in various ways: it may be that only the new value per unit decreases (for instance, 18 hours = 15 hours + 3 hours or 18 hours = 16 hours + 2 hours); it may be that only the past value per unit decreases (for instance, 18 hours = 13 hours + 5 hours); and it may be that both of them decrease (for instance, 18 hours = 14 hours + 4 hours).

We have stressed that value becomes a reality only if and when the product of private labour is sold. This fact is relevant to the present analysis of changes over time in productivity and unit values. Suppose for example that a joiner intending to produce a table buys the necessary means of production (for example, wood) in a given year (t_0) and that their value at t_0 is 15 hours; suppose next that the joiner produces his table only 5 years later (in t_5), spending 5 hours of present labour; suppose finally that productivity increases in the production of wood between t_0 and t_5 have reduced the time necessary to produce the same quantity of raw material from 15 hours to 10 hours. In that case, the unit value of the table produced (provided it is sold) is only 15 hours (10 hours + 5 hours), despite the fact that the table incorporates (embodies) 20 hours of labour (15 hours + 5 hours). This example illustrates a general principle which may be stated as follows: in the same way as value is realized only when the product is sold, the magnitude of past value transferred depends on the average conditions of production (of the means of production) prevailing at the time the final product is sold.[11]

PRICE AS THE EXPRESSION OF THE VALUE OF COMMODITIES

The Meaning of Prices

The preceding section identified the element which different commodities have in common, namely, *value*. The question we must now look at is this: How does it come about that this value of commodities is expressed, not as a certain quantity of labour, but as a certain price, as a certain quantity of pounds (here the exact quantity is not important)? Why do we say for example that a table is worth x pounds (and not x hours of labour)? So the question here is of the *meaning of the price-phenomenon*.

The answer can be given in three propositions: (1) the value of a commodity only appears when the latter is sold and purchased; (2) the sales and purchases of commodities have to be made through the medium of money; and (3) the value of commodities therefore appears (is expressed) as a certain quantity of money, that is, as a certain price.

1. The value of a commodity only appears when the latter is sold and purchased. Under a system of commodity production, the labour devoted to producing commodities is not recognized *a priori* as value, as socially useful labour. To be so recognized, the commodities produced must each find a purchaser, they must be sold, on the market. The exchange of commodities on the market (through sales and purchases) is therefore the necessary condition for the value of commodities to appear: it is the only proof that the labour devoted to producing the commodities is socially useful labour.

2. The sales and purchases of commodities have to be made through the medium of money. A system of commodity production is based on the private initiative of a multitude of *autonomous* producers producing different commodities (different as regards their use-value). These autonomous individuals must of necessity enter into mutual *relations*, whatever the actual nature of the production they are engaged in. It is therefore necessary for there to be, between these different private producers, a *specific social bond*, recognized and accepted by all of them: this bond is provided by money (by the pound, for example).[12] The exchange of commodities does not therefore constitute a widespread form of barter: it assumes the existence of a currency common to all producers, for which each of them can exchange his own particular commodity.

3. The value of commodities is expressed as a certain price. The private labour devoted to producing a commodity is recognized as value by virtue of the sale of this commodity for money: consequently, the value of the commodity appears (is expressed) as a certain quantity of money (for which the commodity can be exchanged). This quantity of money (for example, this number of pounds) constitutes the price of the commodity: consequently, the value of every commodity appears (is expressed) as a certain price.

The Magnitude of the 'Monetary Expression of Values'

We have just seen that the *value* of every commodity (the *labour* devoted to producing a commodity actually sold) is expressed as a certain *price* (as a certain number of pounds). If this is so, there must always exist, in every market society, a certain relation between the sum total of *prices* (in *pounds*) and the sum total of *values* (in hours of *labour*). This quantitative relation between the sum total of prices and the sum total of values is called the 'monetary expression of values' and is represented by the symbol E:

$$E = \frac{\text{sum total of prices}}{\text{sum total of values}}$$

As an example, let us take a market society where the producers provide together, in the course of a year, 1 million hours of labour and where the total price of commodities sold is £10 million. In this case, the quantitative relation between the sum total of prices and the sum total of values is equal to £10 million per 1 million hours or £10 per hour.

The monetary expression of values can also be obtained by making the quantitative relation between the sum total of monetary *revenues* and the sum total of values. In fact, the price of all the commodities sold constitutes the aggregate monetary revenue of a market society: in the example above, in selling their commodities at an aggregate *price* of £10 million, the producers create an aggregate monetary revenue of £10 million.

We can therefore write

$$E = \frac{\text{sum total of prices}}{\text{sum total of values}} = \frac{\text{sum total of revenues}}{\text{sum total of values}}[13]$$

The quantitative relation E therefore represents two things simultaneously:

(1) It gives the *'translation' into price of 1 hour of value*: it shows by
     what price (what quantity of money) 1 hour of value (1 hour
     of labour devoted to the production of commodities) is
     expressed. Thus in the example, to say that E equals £10 per
     hour amounts to saying that 1 hour of value is 'translated', is
     expressed, by a monetary magnitude of £10.

(2) It represents the *monetary revenue created per hour of value*: it
     shows the quantity of monetary revenue created by each of
     the hours devoted to the production of com modities (in so
     far as these are sold on the market). In the example, to say
     that E = £10 per hour amounts to saying that 1 hour of value
     creates a monetary revenue of £10.[14]

Knowing the magnitude of E, we can express the value of
commodities in *hours* of labour as well as in prices (in *pounds*). If for
example we consider three commodities (A, B, C) whose social
values are taken as equal to 40, 20 and 4 hours of labour, we can
write (if E = £10 per hour)

    1 commodity A = 40 hours = £400
    1 commodity B = 20 hours = £200
    1 commodity C = 4 hours = £40

In these relations, the different quantities of labour constitute the unit
social values of the commodities; the different prices represent the
same values but expressed as a certain amount of money, as a certain
price.[15]

Value and price: summary of the approach
After these observations on the magnitude of the monetary
expression of values, it may be helpful to summarize the steps we
have so far taken in this chapter.

The first section (pp. 22–6) defined commodities and pointed out
their most obvious features, namely, price and use-value: commodities, we could say, are use-values (useful goods or services)
produced and sold at a certain price.

The second section (pp. 26–33) started from this 'visible' phenomenon (the exchange of commodities at a certain price) to identify a
hidden reality, namely, *value*. The exchange of commodities (through
sales and purchases) presupposes an element common to all of them:
this element resides in the fact that all the commodities exchanged are
the product of private labour recognized (*a posteriori*, at the time of sale)
as labour useful to society. In other words, *the common element in all*

the commodities exchanged resides in their value (or the indirectly social labour devoted to producing them).

The third section (pp. 34–6) proceeded in the opposite direction: starting from the hidden reality (value), it explained how this was necessarily manifested in the 'visible' form of a *price*. The social character of private labour only becomes apparent at the time of the sale of the commodity, at the time of the exchange of this commodity for a certain quantity of money, for the payment of a certain price. In other words, *the value of a commodity is only manifested through the price at which it is sold.*

At this point of the exposition, the essential object assigned to this chapter has been achieved: we have discovered that behind the *price* of commodities (in *pounds*) is hidden the reality of the *value* of commodities (in *labour*-time).[16] We could therefore move on straightaway to the next stage of the analysis, which consists in discovering, behind *wages* and *profits* (in pounds), the reality of *necessary labour* and of *surplus labour*. Before doing so, however, we will examine a related question which concerns, not the nature or the basis of price, but its magnitude: if the price of commodities manifests the value of commodities (if value is the hidden basis of the price of commodities), can we say that the prices of commodities will be proportional to their value? The study of this question is useful from different points of view.

(1) It will enable us to explain the mechanism through which the allocation of social labour is brought about in a society founded on the free initiative of individuals.
(2) It will enable us to deal with a current objection claiming precisely that, according to Marxist theory, prices are proportional to values.
(3) It will enable us at the same time to indicate more clearly the content and aim of the Marxist theory of value.

VALUE, PRICES AND EXCHANGE RATIOS

Simple Prices and Market Prices

Having examined the social function and the basis of commodity exchange and having then perceived how the value of commodities is expressed by a certain price in pounds, we can now consider the question of the exchange ratio between commodities.

Let us take for example the numerical relationships set out above (p. 36). The exchange ratio between commodities B and C (which we will assume to be a television set and a chair) will be five chairs to one television set. Such an exchange ratio is determined by the price of the two commodities (one television set = £200, one chair = £40) and, more basically, by their respective values (one television set = 20 hours, one chair = 4 hours). Can we conclude from this that the exchange ratio between the commodities is determined by the relationship between their respective values or, in other words, that the commodities are exchanged according to their respective values?

The answer *would be* yes *if* the prices at which the commodities were bought and sold were indeed equal to the theoretical prices in the example. But the latter are *theoretical* prices in many respects for, as we shall see, they assume the existence of various conditions which in practice are never fulfilled. Indeed, the theoretical prices of the previous example are nothing more than the monetary expression of the social value of the commodities: *these theoretical prices which correspond exactly to the monetary expression of the value of commodities* are called *simple prices*.[17] On the other hand, *the prices which actually prevail on the market*, the prices at which commodities are bought and sold, are called *actual prices* or *market prices*.

The hypothetical conditions which are necessary for market prices to coincide with simple prices can be summarized as follows.

(1) The commodities must be produced in such quantities that *supply is equal to demand*.

(2) The commodities must be produced either by *independent self-employed producers* or by *capitalist branches* characterized by a *similar degree of mechanization*.

(3) There must be *free competition among producers* (which excludes both monopoly agreements between producers and intervention by the public authorities).

(4) The various producers within the same branch must only turn out a *single type of commodity* (thus excluding 'joint products') and this type of commodity must be *homogeneous* and *reproducible*.

Let us now see why market prices differ from simple prices, once one or other of these conditions is not fulfilled.

Reasons for the Differences Between Simple Prices and Market Prices

Imbalances between supply and demand

We spoke earlier of the social function of the exchange of commodities: commodity exchange has the function of bringing about the allocation of social labour in a society based on the free initiative of producers. To see how this function is actually carried out, we can consider the two following problems.

(1)   What is necessary for a given distribution of labour to be stable?
(2)   What is necessary for the producers, while remaining free agents, to effect, if required, a change in the distribution of social labour?

1. For any distribution of labour to be considered as stable, every producer (at least, every producer working under average conditions of technology, skill and intensity) must obtain the same revenue for the same period of labour – and this whatever the branch of production he is working in: if this is the case, it is not in the interest of any producer to redirect his activity and to move from one branch of production to another. And for each (average) producer to obtain the same revenue for the same period of labour, the market price of each commodity must be equal to its simple price.

Let us illustrate this by taking up the example of the television set and the chair. Let us assume that the social value of these two commodities is broken down in the following way between past value and new value:

value of television set = 20 hours = 12 hours + 8 hours
value of chair   = 4 hours = 2 hours + 2 hours

In a working day of 8 hours (present labour), the maker of television sets produces one set, while the joiner produces four chairs. The value of what each of them produces daily is therefore:

value of one television set = 20 hours = 12 hours + 8 hours
value of four chairs   = 16 hours = 8 hours + 8 hours

If the monetary expression of values is £10 per hour, the price of the two daily products is broken down thus:

price of one television set = £200 = £120 + £80
price of four chairs   = £160 = £80 + £80

The daily turnover (or gross takings) will vary from one producer to the other,[18] but, once the cost of the means of production has been deducted, the revenue of each producer is identical (£80).[19]

The revenue being the same, it is not in the interest of either producer to change his line of production: it is not in the interest of the producer of chairs to become a producer of television sets or vice versa.

Consequently, in the context of the hypothetical conditions set out above, we can draw up the first proposition: *simple prices, which ensure equality of revenue for all (average) producers, ensure stability in the allocation of social labour*; in other words, simple prices constitute a norm of equilibrium (or stability) in the allocation of social labour.[20]

2. But the distribution of social labour can never be decided once and for all. It has to be constantly modified under the pressure of technological progress (reducing the quantity of labour necessary to produce the same number of goods or services) and of changes in demand (requiring changes in the quantities to be produced). Let us assume for example that the demand for chairs increases more rapidly than their production: a reallocation of social labour becomes essential, in the sense that a greater quantity of labour should be devoted to the production of chairs. How will this requirement be met in a society based on the free initiative of producers?

In such a society, the mechanism of reallocation will be put into operation by a rise in the price of chairs, which will go up for example from £40 to £50: such a rise will result in an increase in the revenue of producers of chairs (from £80 to £120); this increase will cause a certain number of producers to go in for the production of chairs rather than other commodities; when the production of chairs levels up with the demand, the price of chairs will revert to its previous level[21] and the revenue will again be the same as in other branches of production.

Consequently, in the context of the hypothetical conditions set out above, we can state two additional propositions.

(1) Market prices fluctuate according to the variations of the relations between supply and demand, and these *fluctuations of market prices constitute the means of ensuring the necessary reallocations of social labour.*

(2) *Market prices* do not, however, fluctuate *in vacuo* but *oscillate around simple prices*, which constitute the norm of equilibrium (or stability) in the allocation of social labour.

Capitalist production and inter-branch differences in mechanization
Simple prices only produce a norm of equilibrium in the allocation of
social labour if the other hypothetical conditions set down above
obtain in reality. One of these conditions is that production must be
carried out by independent self-employed producers and not by
capitalist enterprises. What becomes of the norm of equilibrium and
of the reallocation of social labour, if the production is of a capitalist
nature?

1. As we shall see in chapter 3, the purpose of capitalist production is
not the pursuit of a revenue (intended for consumption) but the
pursuit of a profit in relation to the capital expended (a profit
intended essentially for accumulation). The norm of equilibrium in
the allocation of social labour is consequently modified: equilibrium
is achieved, not when every capitalist (producing in the average
conditions of his particular branch) obtains the same revenue, but
when each of them obtains the same *rate of profit* in relation to the
capital invested. Every average capitalist must therefore obtain the
same rate of profit whatever branch of production he has invested his
capital in and whatever the degree of mechanization in this branch.
We will study in chapter 6 the problem of equalization of average
rates of profit between the different branches of production when the
latter are unequally mechanized: let us merely observe here that, in
order to ensure this equality of average rates of profit, the market
price in each branch should be equal, not to the simple price, but to
what is called the *price of production*. This may be defined as a
*theoretical price ensuring in a capitalist system the equality of average rates of
profit between different unequally mechanized branches of production.*[22]
   Consequently, under capitalism and in the context of the other
hypothetical conditions set out above, we can state this new
proposition: *prices of production, which ensure equality of rates of profit for
the (average) capitalists in the different branches, ensure stability in the
allocation of social labour under capitalism*; in other words, prices of
production constitute a norm of equilibrium in the allocation of
social labour under capitalism.[23]

2. As for the reallocations of social labour (made necessary by
changes in the relationships between supply and demand), they will
always be brought about by variations in market prices. Variations in
market prices (diverging from the prices of production) will
determine changes in the rates of profit (increases in some branches
and decreases in others), and these variations in the rates of profit will

bring about changes in the allocation of social labour (as capitalists tend to leave the less profitable branches and to enter the more profitable ones). This process will go on until a new balance is reached between demand and supply in all branches: when this point is reached, the market price in each branch is again equal to the price of production, and the average rates of profit are again equal in all branches. Hence the following two propositions.

(1)   Under capitalism, *fluctuations of market prices* (according to changes in the relationships between supply and demand) *ensure the necessary reallocations of social labour.*

(2)   Under capitalism, *market prices fluctuate around the prices of production*, which constitute the norm of equilibrium (or stability) in the allocation of social labour.

Restrictions on free competition

Whether commodities are produced by independent producers or by capitalists, reallocations of social labour assume that *producers are in a position to move freely* to more remunerative branches of production and that *market prices can fluctuate freely* in response to changes in the relations between supply and demand.

In reality, there may be *obstacles to the entry of producers* into a number of branches of production: these may be protected against the competition of outsiders, either by hard facts (the amount of investment required) or by legal restrictions (regulations restricting entry to various professions). In both cases, existing producers (directly or through the intervention of the public authorities) may fix their *sale price above the norm of equilibrium* (simple price or price of production): in this way they enjoy a revenue or a rate of profit which is higher than the average, and continue to enjoy it to the extent that the restrictions to the entry of competitors prove effective.

These considerations lead us to distinguish two types of market prices.

(1)   *Competitive market prices*: these are the market prices which, under free competition, *fluctuate around the theoretical norm of equilibrium* (simple prices or prices of production) *according to changes in the relationships between supply and demand.*

(2)   *Regulated market prices* (or *monopoly prices*): these are the market prices *maintained, by the producers or the authorities* (through circumstantial or legal restrictions to the entry of

new competitors), *at a level higher than would result from free competition.*

The existence of restrictions on free competition thus has a twofold effect, one on the level of the market price, the other on the allocation of social labour.

(1) The *market price* does not simply oscillate around the norm of equilibrium (simple price or price of production): it is maintained at a different level.

(2) The *reallocation of social labour* between branches are made less easily: to the extent that restrictions prove effective, higher revenues or profit rates do not lead to reallocations of social labour.

Heterogeneous products, multiple products, non-reproducible products
We have assumed up to now that the commodities produced within each branch of production had some very definite characteristics: they were *homogeneous* commodities (in the sense that rival producers produced commodities that were exactly similar and of the same quality); they were *single* commodities (in the sense that each producer produced only a single, well-defined, type of commodity); and they were of course *reproducible* commodities (in the sense that they could be produced again and again, and by different producers).

Reality very often does not reflect these assumptions and the level of *market prices* is affected accordingly (though the *reallocation of social labour* is not necessarily affected).

First of all, it is clear that competitors within the same branch of production produce *relatively heterogeneous commodities* rather than commodities that are exactly similar and of the same quality: whether dealing with motor cars or hairdressing, each in his own field tries to differentiate his product from the product of his competitors and to make known the specific qualities (real or imaginary) of his particular product. The products thus differenti-ated may very well embody the same quantity of labour; their *market prices* will vary according to the specific qualities attributed to and recognized in each of them. These differences in market prices will give rise to differences in the revenues or profits of the various producers; as previously, these differences will determine *reallocations* of social labour: producers will be directed by preference towards the most remunerative product qualities.

Again, from choice or from necessity, producers frequently produce a *variety of commodities*: the automobile firm offers a range of cars and of lorries, the butcher's shop sells ham as well as bacon (joint products). Here again, *market prices* will no longer correspond to simple prices; thus two joint products (1 lb of ham and 1 lb of bacon) obviously embody the same quantity of labour, but their market prices will differ depending on the qualities recognized by the consumers. As for the *reallocations* of social labour, these will still be determined by comparisons of revenue or of rate of profit between branches of production; the only difference is that here the revenue or rate of profit depends on a variety of products rather than on a single product.[24]

Finally, *non-reproducible commodities* (original works of art, rare postage stamps, plots of land) also command *market prices* unconnected with the quantity of labour embodied in them, but directly dependent on the relations between supply and demand: an artist of genius will get a lot of money for little work. To the extent that a commodity is not reproducible, one cannot talk of a branch of production, of social value, nor of *reallocation* of social labour towards a more remunerative 'branch'. The producer of an unreproducible commodity which is highly valued on the market is in a monopoly situation: he benefits from a revenue higher than the average and he may continue to benefit from it permanently, as his commodity cannot be reproduced by competitors.[25]

Conclusion

Contrary to a current opinion (shared as much by most of Marx's detractors as by a number of his supporters), *Marxist theory in no way claims that the prices of commodities are proportional to the values of commodities*; in a *capitalist society*, in which there are *differences in mechanization between branches, obstacles to free competition, inevitable imbalances between supply and demand*, etc. such a connection between values and prices could only be fortuitous.[26]

The contribution of Marxist theory regarding price is a double one. On one hand, the *theory of value* (the main subject of this chapter) points to the *true meaning of the general phenomenon of prices*: behind the visible phenomenon of prices (expressed in pounds, in francs, in dollars etc.) it uncovers the hidden reality of value. In this sense, Marxist theory can be justly considered as a theory of *the basis of prices*.

On the other hand, upon this theory of value are grafted the theoretical developments (rapidly touched on in the last section) which specify the various *reasons why market prices do not correspond to simple prices*: values are necessarily expressed in terms of prices, but market prices, while deriving from values and simple prices, necessarily diverge from them.[27]

How does the theory of value fit into the body of Marxist theory? Let us recall that one of the essential aims of Marxist political economy is to prove that the total profit of the capitalist class rests on the exploitation of wage-earners, who are obliged to supply unpaid surplus labour. More precisely, Marxist theory aims at proving that the visible division between wages and profits hides a more basic division between necessary labour (paid for by wages) and surplus labour (unpaid, free). Since wages and profits are visible amounts expressed in pounds, and since behind them one claims to uncover invisible realities expressed in hours of labour, the proof assumes that one has previously brought to light the general connection between the visible phenomenon of prices expressed in pounds and the hidden reality of value expressed in hours of labour. Such was the aim of the theory of value outlined in this chapter. The theory of surplus value constructed on this basis will enable us to establish the link between profit and surplus labour: this is the aim of the next chapter.

NOTES

1. One difficulty in making the distinction can arise from the fact that the same people can carry out the two types of activity simultaneously; this is especially the case of tradesmen, who at the same time carry out operations of production (transport, packaging, storage, bulk packing and delivery) and of exchange (purchase/sale in the strict sense).
2. Thus activities such as public relations and advertising belong to production and not to circulation.
3. We should note incidentally that *circulation* services cannot be called commodities or use-values specifically; they merely transfer, from one person to another, the right to the use of a commodity (simple use or ownership).
4. More precisely, we ought to distinguish between value (which is a property of *commodities*) and abstract labour (which is a specific type of *labour*). We ought to say that two commodities have a common denominator (their value) because the labour that produced both of them is recognized as abstract labour. Abstract labour may be considered as the *substance* of value of the commodities, the other constituent aspects of value being its *magnitude* and its *form (or expression)*. The latter two aspects will be examined presently.
5. In Marxist terminology, *means of production* are subdivided into *objects of labour* (the materials on which the labour of processing is carried out)

and *means of labour* (all the means utilized directly or indirectly to carry out this labour, i.e. tools, machines, buildings etc.).

6. The 'processing operation' actually includes all the operations carried out by the producer himself (as opposed to the operations carried out by the other producers from whom he buys the means of production). Where the producer himself produces part of the means of production he needs, the labour-time he spends in this production is included in the 'processing operation' and counts as present labour.

7. The *quantity* of labour is measured by its *duration* (expressed here in hours).

8. Obviously, we are assuming – and we will come back to this in a moment when speaking of the *realization of value* – that the producer succeeds in selling his commodity: if this is not the case (if, for example, he puts in more time than his competitors and does not find a purchaser), his product is not a commodity and has no value (his private work is not recognized as socially useful). Let us observe that Marxist literature is reluctant to follow Marx in the use of the concept of *individual value*: it prefers to employ the expression '*individual labour-time*'. The concept of *social value* is used currently but, to describe the same concept, authors also speak of 'socially necessary labour-time'.

9. This will be demonstrated in chapter 3, in the framework of capitalist production: it could apply just as well, *mutatis mutandis*, to non-capitalist market production. Many writers consider that skilled labour (called complex labour) creates more value than average labour (called simple labour). The problem of 'reducing complex labour to simple labour' then consists in establishing to what extent the former creates more value than the latter.

10. See especially chapter 8, pp. 160–73.

11. The problem will be taken up later on, in the analysis of obsolescence and inflation in contemporary capitalism. (See chapter 10.)

12. The evolution of concrete *forms* of money (metallic coins, bank notes, current account money) will be examined in chapter 10.

13. As we shall see in chapter 11, the sum total of values and the sum total of prices or revenues can in theory be understood in two different senses: *either* the sum total of *total* values (incorporating the past values transferred) and the sum total of *gross* prices or revenues (incorporating the cost of the means of labour and materials used); *or* the sum total of *new* values (excluding the past values) and the sum total of *net* prices or revenues (after deduction of the cost of means of labour and materials). It is the latter sense which is employed here: the denominator of E is the sum total of *present* labour devoted to producing the commodities and therefore represents the sum total of *new* values (excluding the past value of the means of production); similarly the numerator is the sum total of the *net* prices of commodities or of the producers' *net* revenues

(after deduction of the cost of means of production used).

14. The monetary expression of values, expressed by a certain number of pounds per hour, should not be confused with the hourly wage which is also expressed by a certain number of pounds per hour. In the context of this chapter, we are not considering the wage concept. We will see later that the monetary expression of values, which is equal to the *revenue created* per hour of labour, is necessarily greater than the *wage earned* per hour of labour (see chapter 4). We will see, in a more general way, that the *revenue created* and the *revenue earned* do not generally coincide: in a market society, the revenue created is redistributed in a number of different ways (see chapter 6 for the analysis of these redistributions or transfers in a capitalist society).

15. In this example, *we take the values as known* and translate them into prices by multiplying them by E. We will examine in the final chapter to what extent we may reverse the process: that is, *start from known prices* and divide them by E to obtain values.

16. *Value* and *price* should be distinguished from a third concept which we have not dealt with, namely *exchange-value*. *Exchange-value* is the *ratio of exchange between two commodities*: as exchange in a market society necessarily takes the form of sales and purchases for money, exchange-value necessarily takes the form of a price, that is to say, of a ratio of exchange between a commodity and a certain quantity of money. Current usage confuses the three concepts of value, exchange-value and price, as does prevailing economic theory.

17. We can write: simple price of a commodity = unit social value of the commodity × E (the monetary expression of values). The concept of simple price does not belong to classical Marxist terminology. It can be found in an article by Bullock and Yaffe ('Inflation, the Crisis and the Post-War Boom', *Revolutionary Communist*, 3–4, Nov. 1975) and is used systematically by M. De Vroey, who describes, in various places, the exact nature of the relationships between values and prices (see for instance 'Value, Production and Exchange' in *The Value Controversy*, Verso and NLB, 1981).

18. We can see that the turnover is higher in the case where there is a higher ratio of past labour to present labour.

19. We assume here that the state levies no tax (or that taxation affects every branch to the same extent).

20. Note that simple prices cannot be observed, any more than values: all that can be observed (apart from the market prices) are the producers' revenues.

21. We are assuming in this argument that there is no increase in productivity in the production of chairs nor any change in the monetary expression of values (E). If the producers (new or old) improve productivity, the value of chairs falls and the new price level will be lower than the old one (assuming that E remains constant).

22. Prices of production would only coincide with simple prices if all branches of production were characterized by the same degree of mechanization.
23. Note that prices of production are not observable, any more than simple prices: all that can be observed (apart from the market prices) are the capitalists' profits and rates of profit.
24. In the example of the cars, the producer can modify the range of products on offer; in the case of joint products, this is hardly practicable.
25. Regarding those goods and services which can have a price without being commodities (such as privately appropriated 'gifts of nature' and circulation services), their price has no connection with their (non-existent) value but depends directly on the relations between supply and demand: this is so for the price of virgin soil, for rates of interest, commercial margins, rents, etc.
26. The idea of proportionality between prices and values was defended by Marx's predecessors, the classical economists (Smith, Ricardo).
27. To the extent that it sets out the theoretical reasons which make market prices diverge from simple prices, Marxist theory provides a theoretical framework enabling us to explain the exact level of market prices. But research actually carried out by Marxist economists does not emphasize this particular problem, which to most of them appears a secondary one.

3

The Basis of Capitalist Profit: Surplus Value

Chapter 2 focused on the *price of commodities*: behind the visible phenomenon of price (expressed in pounds), it revealed the hidden reality of value (expressed in hours of labour). This chapter is focused on the *revenue of producers* and more precisely on wages and profits; it aims to reveal, behind these visible magnitudes expressed in pounds, the hidden realities of *corresponding value* (or necessary labour) and of *surplus value* (or surplus labour).

In the same way as the preceding chapter dealt essentially with the phenomenon of prices *in general* (rather than with the exact level of particular prices), the present chapter attempts to convey an understanding of the phenomena of profit and of wages *in general*: the actual differences in profits and wages (earned in a particular enterprise or branch of production, by a particular category of workers) will only be dealt with in subsequent chapters.

However, this chapter does not proceed directly to a study of the basis of wages and profits. It begins by examining the basis of revenues, in the *hypothetical* case where all production is carried out, not by wage-earners working on the capitalists' account, but by *simple commodity producers*, that is to say, by independent producers, working on their own account and not employing any wage-earners at all. The hypothesis of generalized simple commodity production is entirely theoretical: it does not correspond in any way to any existing social system. But this first approach is of a pedagogic nature; it will enable us, as the chapter unfolds, to reach a more exact understanding of the necessary source of capitalist profit.

The whole of the chapter is based, *for the sake of simplicity, on the assumption that market prices are equal to simple prices*. As we saw in the preceding chapter, this assumption implies among other things, that there is *generalized free competition* (which excludes the existence of 'monopolistic' branches of production, protected by restrictions on the entry of outside competitors) and that there is an equilibrium *between supply and demand.* The revenues of the producers (simple commodity producers, wage-earners, capitalists) cannot therefore be explained by a special 'market power', by an advantageous position resulting from restrictions on competition or from conditions of scarcity. More basic explanations will have to be found.

THE BASIS OF THE REVENUE OF THE SIMPLE COMMODITY PRODUCER

Form and Purpose of Simple Commodity Production

Let us consider, by way of example, a craftsman joiner producing tables for sale. Like every commodity producer, this joiner earns his living from the sale of his product; but in order to be able to produce, he must initially purchase the means of production (materials and tools). Let us symbolize the commodities purchased initially (that is, the means of production) by C_0, the process of making the tables by P, the new commodity (the finished product) by C_1 and the money spent on the purchase or received from the sale by M. We can then represent the complete cycle of the craftsman's operations of purchase, production and sale in this way:

$$M - C_0 \ldots P \ldots C_1{}^+ - M^+$$

This formula allows us to distinguish the three following categories of operations:

First category of operations $(M - C_0)$: with the money available, the craftsman purchases his means of production (materials and tools).

Second category of operations $(\ldots P \ldots)$: this is the process of production which turns out a new commodity, the finished product, C_1 (the tables). This new commodity is marked with a + sign, $(C_1{}^+)$ to show that it has a value higher than the value of the commodities the producer has purchased: for the value of the tables (like that of any other commodity) includes, besides the past value (or the labour-time needed to produce the means of production he has purchased), the new value added by the present labour of the producer.

Third category of operations $(C_1{}^+ - M^+)$: the new commodity is sold to another producer in exchange for a sum of money M^+. The sign + means that the sum of money obtained by the sale (M^+) is larger than the sum of money expended on the purchase of the means of production. By selling his finished product for a sum of money M^+, the producer gets back what he requires to repeat the purchase of the necessary means of production and obtains in addition a net revenue equal to the difference $M^+ - M$.

We can illustrate these operations by giving a quantified example. Let us assume that the value of a table is 5 hours, broken down into 3 hours of past value plus 2 hours of new value; that the daily labour-time is 8 hours (so the value of the daily production will be 12 hours + 8 hours = 20 hours): and that the monetary expression of values is equal to £10 per hour. In this case, the general formula, for one day's production, becomes:

$$£120 - 12 \text{ hours} \ldots \text{P} \ldots 20 \text{ hours} - £200$$

The joiner therefore obtains £200 from the sale of his product. What would he use this sum of money for?

A part (£120) must be used to *repeat the purchase of the necessary means of production*, to purchase the same means of production as before (or possibly other means of production involving the same monetary cost).

The other part (£80) constitutes a net revenue. What will he do with it? The hypothesis of simple commodity production implies that this net revenue must be entirely 'consumed', that it must be used exclusively for the purchase of means of consumption: the independent producer cannot purchase supplementary means of production (for example, he cannot double the size of his enterprise), as he can only count on his own labour-power.[1] The craftsman who succeeds in his branch of production can only materially increase his scale of production by combining, with the purchase of supplementary means of production, the purchase and employment of outside labour-power: but the craftsman employing wage-earners in this way would in fact turn himself into a capitalist.

Consequently, in the case of simple commodity production, the successive cycles

$$M - C_0 \ldots P \ldots C_1^+ - M^+$$

will repeat themselves with figures which will be identical from one cycle to another:

$$£120 - 12 \text{ hours} \ldots \text{P} \ldots 20 \text{ hours} - £200$$

The sum of money obtained at the end of each cycle (M^+) is indeed larger than the sum spent at the start (M). But, the assumption being that of generalized simple commodity production, the purpose of the production cannot be to obtain the maximum monetary revenue with a view to accumulation (with a view to the purchase of supplementary means of production, which would require at the same time the purchase of additional labour). The purpose of typical simple commodity production is the exchange of commodities with different use-values: each craftsman produces and sells a certain type of commodity with the aim of purchasing (besides the required means of production) the means of subsistence he wishes to consume.

To illustrate this purpose of simple commodity production, the preceding formula can be transformed into another of the following kind:

$$C_1 - M - C_0, C_2$$

where C_0 and C_1 represent, as before, the means of production and the finished product and C_2 the means of subsistence purchased. We could simplify the formula still further by writing:

$$C - M - C$$

where C represents the commodities sold or purchased and M the money involved in the exchanges.

These last two formulae have the advantage of explicating two specific features of a (hypothetical) system of simple commodity production. In such a systém:

(1) the purpose of production is *the obtaining of actual commodities* rather than the increase of a sum of money (the obtaining of use-values rather than the increase of value);
(2) *money* is only involved as a *medium of exchange* and not as capital to be increased.

Basis of the Monetary Revenue of the Simple Commodity Producer

Having thus perceived the specific purpose of simple commodity production (and we will see in the following section the quite different purpose of capitalist production), it may be rewarding to return to the first formula in order to analyse the source of the simple commodity producer's monetary revenue: the results of this analysis will prove useful for a clearer perception of the necessary source of capitalist profit.

The question we must examine here is the following: in the formula

$$M - C_0 \ldots P \ldots C_1^+ - M^+$$

how does it come about that M^+ is larger than M? What is the source of the producer's monetary revenue $(M^+ - M)$?

The answer is clear enough if we go back to the quantified example given earlier:

$$£120 - 12 \text{ hours} \ldots P \ldots 20 \text{ hours} - £200$$

The producer's revenue (£80) is the monetary expression of the new value created by him in one day of labour (this new value is added to the past value of the means of production he has purchased). In other words, the *source of the producer's revenue is the present labour devoted by him to the production of the commodity.*[2]

It is also interesting to indicate where our producer's revenue *does not come from*.

It does not come from the past labour required to produce the means of production he has purchased. This past value (equal to 12 hours or £120) is simply transferred by the producer to the final product and is to be found unaltered, without the slightest increase, in the value of the final product. The fact that C_1^+ has a greater value than C_0 (20 hours or £200) does not, therefore, derive from past labour but solely from the producer's present labour (8 hours).

The producer's revenue is not created either in the first category of operations $(M - C_0)$ or in the third category of operations $(C_1^+ - M^+)$. These operations ensure the circulation of commodities, as opposed to the operations of production $(\ldots P \ldots)$. As we indicated when we defined commodities,[3] *circulation activities do not create any use-value*, they do no more than transfer rights of ownership (or of usage) over things already in existence: the transaction $M - C_0$ makes the craftsman the owner of the means of production he has purchased (while the seller of the means of production becomes the owner of the sum of money paid by the craftsman) and the transaction $C_1^+ - M^+$ makes the purchaser the owner of the final product which is sold (while the craftsman becomes the owner of the sum of money paid by the purchaser). *Circulation activities do not create any value either*, they do no more than modify for each exchange the form in which the same quantity of value appears: the craftsman who purchases his means of production hands over a sum of money (£120), *expressing* a value of 12 hours, in order to acquire commodities *'embodying' the same quantity of value*; when he sells his daily production, he hands over a commodity *'embodying'* a value of 20 hours in order to obtain a sum of money (£200) *expressing the same quantity of value*.

Circulation activities do not therefore create any value, though their performance may require a fair amount of time (waiting for the customer, negotiations, possibly the drawing up of an agreement, transfer of sums due etc.).

As they create no value, they cannot, any more than past labour, be the source of the craftsman's revenue. The commodity producer's revenue has no source other than present labour devoted to the *production of the commodity*, that is, the labour carried out in the course of the production process (. . . P . . .).

This process must, however, be understood in a wider sense than the actual making of the product: it also covers the transport of the means of production to the workshop, the upkeep of the workshop and of the means of production, possibly the stocking and care of the product. All these technical operations are clearly distinct from circulation operations (purchase – sale) and form part of production.[4]

We may conclude from the above – and on the assumption that all commodities are produced by simple commodity producers – that the total amount of their revenues corresponds to the total amount of new value created by them in *production*. This fundamental principle does not exclude, however, that *circulation* may give rise to certain *special* categories of revenue, levied on the sum total of revenues.

Two cases should be considered here. First of all, different circumstances (scarcity, cunning, an advantageous position) may enable certain producers to purchase their means of production at a market price lower than the simple price or to sell their final product at a market price higher than the simple price. In the example, this would be the case if the joiner purchased his means of production for less than £120 or sold his tables for more than £200. This producer would obviously benefit from a revenue higher than the norm (£80) but it would be at the expense of other producers (those producing the means of production or those buying the tables), who would see a shortfall in the revenue at their disposal. The *ups and downs of circulation* (resulting in market prices different from simple prices) do not, therefore, create any new revenue in the aggregate: they simply cause a redistribution of aggregate revenue, which still corresponds to the total amount of present labour performed by the producers.[5]

The second case to consider is that where the circulation of commodities between producers is carried out, no longer solely by the producers themselves, but through *agents specializing in the circulation of commodities: the merchants* (whether wholesalers or retailers). While the producers sell in order to buy, these specialized agents buy in order to sell (without producing anything themselves) and try to obtain a sum of money larger than the sum of money they start with. Instead of a cycle C — M — C, the final purpose of which is the obtaining of actual use-values, the merchant's cycle of operations begins and ends with money and only serves any purpose if the sum of money is greater at the end of the cycle than at the beginning: it is represented by $M - C - M^+$.

The question is to know what is the source of this merchant's revenue ($M^+ - M$). We have seen that the circulation activities carried out by a producer do not create value but simply modify the form under which the same quantity of value appears. Similarly, when these same circulation activities are carried out by specialized agents: these activities do not create commodities and value, they merely transfer the ownership over certain values (commodities or money).[6] Consequently, the merchant's income can only stem from a transfer of revenue from the producers. The merchant, for example, will purchase the producers' commodities at a market price *lower* than the simple price and will resell them at a market price equal to the simple price: this difference constitutes the commercial margin (in the strict sense), taken by the merchant from the producers' revenues.

We can set out an analogous argument with regard to the *agents who specialize in the circulation of money: the money-lenders.* The money-lender's cycle of operations is represented by the formula $M - M^+$. It begins and ends with money, but does not pass through either production or even the exchange of commodities. At the first stage, the money-lender transfers a money capital M; at the second stage, the borrower retransfers a sum M^+, equal to the capital plus interest. For the same reasons as for the merchant, the moneylender's income can only stem from a transfer of revenue from the producers: those of them who have recourse to the moneylender's services repay him by a deduction from their revenues.[7]

THE BASIS OF CAPITALIST PROFIT

Form and Purpose of Capitalist Production

Formally, the complete operational cycle of purchase, of production and of sale, carried out in the framework of capitalist production, is analogous to that of a simple commodity production.

$$M - C_0 \ldots P \ldots C_1^+ - M^+$$

The capitalist purchases various commodities (C_0); he combines them in a process of production (P), from which comes a final product (C_1^+), which has more value than the commodities he has purchased; selling the finished product, he gets back a sum of money (M^+) larger than the sum initially laid out.

However, substantive differences separate these two types of production. The most obvious is that capitalist production is carried out essentially by wage-earners, whose labour-power is hired by the capitalist. To make this point explicit, the formula above should be written:

$$M - C_0 \quad \begin{cases} M.P. \\ L.P. \end{cases} \ldots P \ldots C_1^+ - M^+$$

where M.P. and L.P. represent the means of production and the labour-power which the capitalist obtains.

The second difference is that the profit obtained ($M^+ - M$) does not have to be intended exclusively for the purchase of means of consumption, as is the case in typical simple commodity production. Nothing prevents the capitalist from devoting a part of his profit to the purchase of supplementary means of production *and* of the supplementary labour-power which will operate them. Indeed, the competition between capitalists, as we shall see, encourages each of them to act in this way. Only a relatively small fraction of the profit will therefore be consumed: the greater part will be reinvested in supplementary means of production and labour-power. This *purchase of supplementary means of production and labour-power* is called capitalist *accumulation*. Due to this accumulation, the successive cycles of capitalist production go on repeating themselves on an ever increasing scale.[8] If we disregard the fraction of profit destined for capitalist consumption, then the whole sum M^+ reappears at the starting point of the following cycle. This will enable the capitalist to recover a larger sum of money (M^{++}) according to our formula:

$$M^+ - C_0^+ \quad \begin{cases} M.P.^+ \\ L.P.^+ \end{cases} \ldots P \ldots C_1^{++} - M^{++}$$

The sum M^{++} will in its turn constitute the starting point of a new cycle, which will call on further means of production and labour-power and will procure for the capitalist an even larger sum of money.

The original formula

$$M - C_0 \quad \begin{cases} M.P. \\ L.P. \end{cases} \ldots P \ldots C_1^+ - M^+$$

therefore correctly describes the specific character of capitalist production. It expresses the three following characteristics:

(1) Capitalist production is based on the *purchase of labour-power* (and not only on the purchase of means of production, as in the case of simple commodity production).

(2) The purpose of capitalist production is *profit as such* ($M^+ - M$) (and not the production and exchange of commodities, sought for their actual use-values).[9]

(3) Money intervenes both as a *medium of exchange* (for the purchase of means of production and of labour-power and for the sale of the finished product) *and* as *capital to be increased* (M must be transformed into M^+).

The Basis of Capitalist Profit: Setting out the Problem

If capitalist production is correctly represented by the formula:

$$M - C_0 \quad \begin{cases} \text{M.P.} \\ \text{L.P.} \end{cases} \quad \ldots P \ldots C_1{}^+ - M^+$$

it remains to specify the source of capitalist profit: how is it that, at the end of the cycle, we obtain a sum M^+ larger than M?

The preceding analysis regarding the source of the simple commodity producers' revenue should enable us to size up the problem straightaway by a process of elimination.

First of all, capitalist profit *cannot be derived from the operation* $M - C_0$ (purchase of means of production and of labour-power) *nor from the operations* $C_1{}^+ - M^+$ (sale of finished products). These operations come under circulation; as we have said, they create neither use-value nor value but merely transfer rights of ownership and modify the form under which the *same quantity of value* appears. It is true that some capitalists can profit from favourable circumstances and buy at a market price lower than the simple price (in the transaction $M - C_0$) or sell at a market price higher than the natural price (in the transaction $C_1{}^+ - M^+$). But, as shown earlier, what is gained by some is lost by others (that is, there is a transfer of revenue).[10] So we cannot explain the *general* phenomenon of capitalist profit in this way. The explanation of capitalist profit must therefore be sought, as before, on the production side. Commodities are bought and are sold on average at their simple price, but *capitalist production leads to the creation of an increase of value*: the commodities produced (C^+) have a value greater than the value of the commodities purchased (C_0).

Moreover, the profit *cannot*, any more than before, *be derived from the past labour* required to produce the means of production which have been purchased. This past value is simply transferred to the final product and can be found unchanged, without the slightest increase, in the value of the final product.

Consequently, *the increase of value created in production* (the fact that C^+ has a value greater than C_0) *can only be derived from the present labour of wage-earning producers.*[11] It remains for us to see *how* the wage-earners' labour can thus create an increase of value, the source of capitalist profit. In this, we should first of all pause to consider this particular 'commodity' sold to the capitalist by the wage-earners, namely, their *labour-power.*

Labour-Power as a 'Commodity'

General principles

We indicated in chapter 1 the difference between *labour* and *labour-power.*[12] *Labour-power* is the sum of the physical and intellectual faculties which fit a man for work, it is his capacity to work. *Labour* itself consists in the employment of these faculties, of this capacity to work.

Is labour-power always a commodity? Is it ever a commodity? Let us recall the initial definition, according to which commodities are goods or services *produced* for the *market* (where they are sold at a certain price). From this we can infer two propositions.

1. Labour-power is not necessarily a commodity, as it is *not necessarily sold on a market.* The simple commodity producer does not sell his labour-power; he uses it for his own account and lives from the sale of his product. The capitalist does not sell his labour-power; on the contrary, he purchases the labour-power of the wage-earners and lives from the sale of the product of his enterprise. Only the wage-earner sells his labour-power, which he puts at the capitalist's disposal.[13]

2. Strictly speaking, labour-power (even that of the wage-earner) is not a commodity, as it is *never produced.* Labour-power is not a factory product. It must rather be considered as a natural resource (or 'gift of nature'), which is maintained in existence through the consumption of a variety of goods and services (either domestic products, or collective goods and services, or commodities).

Like every natural resource, labour-power has a certain *use-value.* Like every natural resource owned privately, labour-power can be sold at a certain *price.* However, not being a commodity, labour-power, strictly speaking, has no *value.* Therefore, if in subsequent pages we speak of the wage-earners' labour-power as a 'commodity' and of the 'value of labour-power', we simply conform to a current but mistaken usage, which focuses on the sale of the labour-power and forgets the fact that labour-power is *not produced*.[14]

Use-value, price and 'value' of labour-power
The use-value of a natural resource or of a commodity is its capacity to be of some use, to respond to some need or other on the user's part. *The use-value of labour-power* is *its capacity to provide a certain amount of labour*, to respond to the need, on the capitalist's part, to bring into operation means of production which are too large for him to operate on his own.

The price of a natural resource or of a commodity is the sum of money for which it is sold. *The price of labour-power* is *the wage* which the worker obtains for the sale of his labour-power.

The value of a commodity is the quantity of labour required to produce this commodity. Let us modify this definition slightly, so as to make it applicable to the case of labour-power (which is not a factory product). The value of a commodity is the amount of labour required for this commodity to exist, to be available to the purchaser. In order for labour-power to exist in this way, available for the capitalist, the wage-earner must consume a certain number of the necessaries of life (the 'means of subsistence'): in a commodity society, most of these are commodities purchased from other producers. Hence the following definition: *the 'value of the labour-power' of a wage-earner is the quantity of labour required to produce the means of subsistence purchased by the wage-earner: it is the value of the means of subsistence purchased* by him.

Let us set down the elements of this definition more precisely.

1. Means of subsistence. These can be broken down into *means of consumption* (food, clothing, housing, leisure activities etc.) and *means of training* (studies, books etc.). The first cover the general needs of the worker, the second cover the specific need to obtain a degree of skill, such as will attract possible purchasers of labour-power.

On the other hand, these various means of subsistence are intended to cover both the needs of the wage-earner and those of his family: for the *reproduction* of labour-power must be ensured from one generation to another.

2. Means of subsistence purchased. Most of the means of subsistence consumed by the wage-earner and his family are *commodities*

purchased from other producers. This is not the case, however, for all of them: *domestic goods and services* (produced within the family circle), as well as *collective goods and services* (provided free of charge, such as parks, administrative services, compulsory education, etc.) are not commodities and have no 'value'. We are touching here on the problem of the relations between commodity production and non-commodity production, a problem to which we will return later on. For the moment, let us just assume that all the means of subsistence consumed by the wage-earner are actually purchased by him, that is, that they are commodities.

3. Value of the means of subsistence purchased. The value of the means of subsistence purchased, and thus the 'value of labour-power', depends on two things: (a) *the number of means of subsistence purchased*, and (b) *the value of each of them* (the quantity of labour required on average to produce each of them). What do these two elements depend on?

The value of each of the means of subsistence depends on the *degree of productivity* achieved in their production and therefore varies, depending on the country and period under consideration. If the degree of productivity is high, the quantity of labour required to produce each commodity is relatively low (in comparison with other times or other countries). This reduced value will be reflected in a similarly reduced price.[15]

The number of the means of subsistence consumed, as well as their *nature*, also varies depending on the country and period under consideration. This is due partly to differences in natural conditions: thus the type of housing and of clothing depends in part on the climate. But the variations are mainly due to differences in economic and social conditions: the type of housing and clothing depends as much on fashion as on climate; cinema and television have replaced the traditional leisure activities; the increasing number of private cars is bound up with factors such as the fall in their relative price, the systematic effect of advertising, the distance from the place of work and the inadequacy of public transport; the duration of 'required' studies to obtain such and such a 'required' degree constitutes another 'social fact'. We could multiply the examples. Let us rather pinpoint the essential factors which explain these variations in the quantity of means of subsistence which are consumed.

The *degree of productivity* achieved, in so far as it is reflected in a fall in the value and price of commodities, makes a greater number of commodities accessible to the mass of wage-earners. However, within the limits made possible by the degree of productivity achieved, it is the overall *balance of forces* between wage-earners and capitalists which determines the level of consumption of the masses.[16] This overall balance of forces depends on different factors, particularly on the relations between supply and demand of manpower (variable according to the state of the economy), on the degree of organization of the working-class, on the political power of the capitalist class, etc. The level of consumption of the masses will in any case be found within two limits, an upper and a lower one. The lower limit is the level of consumption which would threaten the actual survival of the workers.[17] The upper limit is the level of consumption which threatens capitalist profit to such a degree that there is no further advantage in continuing production (in this case, as we shall see later, the workers are thrown out of work, which threatens their living standards and enables the capitalist to get back into profit).[18]

Function, level and form of the wage
The cycle of operations carried out by the wage-earner is formally identical to that of the simple commodity producer

$$C - M - C.$$

Both sell a commodity C, to obtain a sum of money M, intended for the purchase of other commodities C. The substantive difference resides in the nature of the commodity which is sold: the simple commodity producer sells the *product* of his labour while the wage-earner sells his labour-*power*. But in both cases, the money obtained from the sale only comes in as a medium of exchange and not as capital to be increased. In both cases, the money obtained serves to purchase actual commodities: the purpose of the cycle of operations is *the purchase of means of subsistence*.[19]

The formula C — M — C shows clearly the *function* of the wage, which is *to enable the wage-earner to purchase his means of subsistence*: the wage-earner sells a 'commodity' C (his labour-power) for a certain sum of money M (the wage) which he uses to purchase other commodities C (his means of subsistence).

The same sum of money represents the price of the labour-power sold (the wage obtained) and the price of the means of subsistence purchased (the wage spent). Just as every price depends basically on the value of the commodity in question, the wage depends basically on the 'value of the labour-power', that is to say, the value of the means of subsistence purchased.

Let us assume for example that it takes 3 hours to produce the means of subsistence purchased daily by an average wage-earner;[20] the daily 'value of his labour-power' is thus equal to 3 hours. If the monetary expression of values is equal to £10 per hour, the price of his means of subsistence will be £30: his daily wage will also be equal to £30.[21]

If the *function* of the wage is clearly to enable the wage-earner to purchase his means of subsistence, the payment of the wage can take different *forms*, in particular the form of *hourly wages* and that of *piece rates* (piecework payment). If the normal length of a working day is 8 hours, the wage of £30 will be expressed in the form '£3.75 an hour'; if the normal output of a worker is 150 pieces per day, the same wage of £30 will be expressed in the form '20p per piece'. In both cases, we have the impression that the wage is the price of *labour provided* (calculated in hours or on piecework), when the wage is in reality the price of the *labour-power* (the rates of hourly wages or piecework are obtained by simply dividing the price of the means of subsistence – that is to say, the price of the labour-power – by the normal number of hours or the normal output). We will soon see the advantage, from the capitalist point of view, of making the wage appear as remuneration of the labour provided rather than as the price of labour-power.

The Creation of Profit by Labour-Power

In our search for the basis of capitalist profit ($M^+ - M$), we concluded that this should correspond to an increase of value created in the course of production (C_1^+ having a greater value than C_0) and that this increase of value could only be derived from the wage-earner's present labour. We are now in a position to understand *how* the wage-earner's labour can thus create an increase of value: we will see that *labour-power creates more value than it consumes*.

This general principle can be demonstrated by means of an extremely simplified example, in which we will consider *one* capitalist enterprise employing one wage-earning producer. The limited character of the example should not suggest, however, that we are interested in such and such a wage or in a particlar profit: in fact, the wage-earning producer considered in the example and also the capitalist enterprise in which he works, are taken as representative of all wage-earners and of all capital enterprises respectively.[22]

Let us assume that the daily 'value' of the wage-earner's labour-power is 3 hours: in other words, the value of the means of subsistence purchased daily by this wage-earner is 3 hours, or again the production of his means of subsistence requires each day 3 hours labour on the part of other producers (distributed among the various branches of production which contribute to the production of these means of subsistence).[23] If the monetary expression of values is £10 per hour, the price of the means of subsistence and the price of the labour-power will be £30. In paying out £30 to purchase the labour-power of the wage-earner for one day, *the capitalist purchases this labour-power 'commodity' at its simple price, corresponding to its 'value'*; at the same time, this sum of £30 enables the wage-earner to purchase his daily means of subsistence at their simple price, corresponding to their value.

But in purchasing the labour-power for a daily wage of £30, *the capitalist acquires the right to use this commodity for the whole duration (legal or customary) of the working day*. Let us assume that the normal working day is 8 hours.[24] The wage-earner must therefore provide 8 hours of labour (present labour), during which he creates a new value equal to 8 hours: *this new value created in using the wage-earner's labour-power for the whole day is therefore higher than the 'value of the labour-power' itself, higher than the value of the means of subsistence consumed*. In monetary terms, the new value of 8 hours is equal to £80. From this new revenue of £80 only one part has to be paid to the wage-earner (£30) and the other part constitutes a profit for the capitalist (£50).

The wage-earner's working day can therefore be divided into two parts. The first part (3 hours) is equal to the 'value of the labour-power' and is called *necessary labour-time* or necessary labour. This can be defined as *the quantity of labour corresponding to the labour devoted (by others) to produce the means of subsistence* of the wage-earner in question. During this space of time (3 hours), the wage-earner 'provides as much labour as he consumes', he produces a value equal to that of the means of subsistence he consumes; we can also say that he creates a *corresponding value*, that is, *a value equal to the 'value of his labour-power'*.

The wage received (£30) relates to this first part of the labour-time, to this necessary labour: it is nothing other than the expression in monetary terms (in pounds) of the value of the means of subsistence, of the 'value of the labour-power', of the corresponding value.

The second part (5 hours), the difference between the total labour-time and the necessary labour-time, is called *surplus labour-time* or surplus labour. This can be defined as the *labour performed in excess of the labour devoted (by others) to produce the means of subsistence* of the wage-earner in question. During this space of time, the wage-earner *creates a surplus value*, that is to say, *an amount of value which exceeds the 'value of his labour-power'*.

It is this increase of value, this surplus value, which is the source of capitalist profit. Returning to the formula synthetizing capitalist production,

$$M - C_0 \quad \begin{cases} M.P. \\ L.P. \end{cases} \quad \ldots P \ldots C_1{}^+ - M^+,$$

capitalist profit ($M^+ - M$) is derived from the fact that the finished product intended for sale ($C_1{}^+$) has more value than the commodities purchased at the start (C_0). This increase of value is derived from the particular 'commodity' which is the labour-power of the wage-earning producers: the latter have in fact the ability to create an amount of value greater than the value of their own labour-power, greater than the value of the means of subsistence they consume. Consequently, *the source of capitalist profit is the increase of value created by the wage-earning producers, it is their surplus labour.*

The foregoing argument is summed up by Figure 3.1. In it, we compare *the 'value of labour-power'* and *the value created by labour-power*, breaking down the latter into its two components: *the corresponding value* (which underlies the wage) and the increase of value or *surplus value* (which underlies the capitalist surplus revenue). We see clearly that the wage-earner's present labour *creates a new value and a net revenue* as in the case of the simple commodity producer; but in this case, *it creates a surplus value and a surplus revenue* for the benefit of the capitalist.[25]

We can now understand the analogy, suggested in the introduction, between the feudal serf and the wage-earning worker. Both are obliged to work more than is necessary to produce their means of subsistence,[26] and the surplus labour thus provided free of charge is the source of profit and of enrichment of the dominant class.

We see also how the form of hourly wages hides the reality of surplus labour under capitalism: if we consider the wage of £30 as the payment of 8 hours of labour at £3.75 an hour, we actually have the impression that *all* the working hours are paid and that the wage-earner gives no surplus labour free of charge. Incidentally, the advantage of the form of hourly wages is not only *ideological* (hiding the reality of surplus labour) but also *pecuniary*. For this formula enables the capitalist to pay the wage-earner 'by the hour' and to pay

(a) 'Value of labour-power'

Value of means of subsistence
=
3 hours

┌─────────────────────────┐
│   │
└─────────────────────────┘

£30
=
Price of means of subsistence

(b) Value created by labour-power

8 hours = total labour = new value created

┌───┐
│   │
└───┘

£80 = net revenue created

Necessary labour =	surplus labour =
Corresponding value	surplus value
=	=
3 hours	5 hours

┌─────────────────────┬───────────────────────┐
│   │   │
└─────────────────────┴───────────────────────┘

£30	£50
=	=
wage	surplus revenue

FIGURE 3.1   *Comparison of 'value of labour-power' and value created by labour-power.*

him less than £30 if he works for less than 8 hours: the wage-earner then earns a wage *lower* than the price of the usual means of subsistence, which for the capitalist partly makes up for the lower amount of surplus value created.

Three Objections to the Theory of Surplus Value

The preceding paragraph explained how capitalist profit results from the surplus labour of wage-earning producers. This explanation — known as the theory of surplus value — usually meets with several objections of varying cogency. We will reply here to two of them, and will return later to the third.

Surplus labour depends on the figures given in the example
The existence of surplus labour in capitalist society was demonstrated above *on the assumption* that the 'value of labour-power' was equal to 3 hours. Hence this objection: if we assume the 'value of labour-power' to be equal to the labour-time (8 hours), the surplus

labour disappears and the source of profit has to be looked for elsewhere!

We can answer this objection by at least two lines of argument, one logical, the other statistical.

If we assumed that each wage-earner's labour-time coincided with the 'value' of his labour-power (with the time required for the production of his means of subsistence), this would mean that the total labour-time of all wage-earners would be devoted to producing their means of subsistence and nothing else. But a part of the social labour-time is obviously devoted to producing things other than the means of subsistence for the wage-earners: one need only think of the production of armaments, of goods and services for the capitalists' consumption. This must mean that the total labour-time worked by the wage-earners is greater than the 'value' of their collective labour-power or, in other words, that they are all obliged to provide surplus labour.

The reality of surplus labour can also be highlighted with the help of concrete statistics: chapter 11 will show that in five European countries, since 1970, the surplus labour of the wage-earners is of the order of 3–4 hours per working-day of 8 hours.

Machines also provide 'surplus labour'

According to this objection, capitalist profit can just as well be explained by the 'surplus labour' of machines: for example, 10 000 hours are needed to produce a machine which will be able to work for 25 000 hours.

In reality, we are comparing here two things which are not comparable: 25 000 hours of *machine* 'labour' (it would be better to speak of the machine's 25 000 hours of *operation*) and 10 000 hours of *human labour* (present and past) required to produce the machine (10 000 hours of *value*). In the previous analysis, on the contrary, we compared things which were actually comparable: *human* labour (present) performed by labour-power (the *value* created by the labour-power) and *human* labour (past and present) required to produce the wage-earners' means of subsistence (the '*value* of the labour-power').

If we wish to make a relevant comparison involving machines, we can only compare the *value* they have with the *value* they transmit to the finished product. But the value transmitted cannot be greater than the value they have. Though indispensable to the process of production, machines cannot in any way create an additional value which would form the basis of profit.

The most highly mechanized enterprises make the most profit

This objection – the most serious – brings out an apparent contradiction between the Marxist theory of surplus value and the reality of the world of business. According to the theory, waged labour alone is the source of profit. But in actual fact, it is the most highly *mechanized* enterprises (those which employ relatively few wage-earners) which make the highest profits! And how do we explain the profit of capitalist enterprises or industries which are entirely *automated*, where there is no longer any living labour?

The answer to this objection will be provided further on.[27] We will prove that the total surplus revenue or profit of the capitalist system is always really *created* by labour-power, and by labour-power alone; but different degrees of mechanization or automation result in a *redistribution* of this total mass of profit or surplus revenue among *particular* capitalist enterprises or branches of production. It is this redistribution of the total surplus revenue created by the wage-earners which explains the higher profit of particular enterprises or branches of production which are highly mechanized or even automated.

THE QUESTION OF 'NON-COMMODITY' MEANS OF SUBSISTENCE

When analysing the 'value of labour-power' earlier on, we assumed that all the wage-earners' means of subsistence were *commodities* which had to be *purchased*.

We thus overlooked the fact that wage-earners are consumers of various *collective goods and services* (which are provided free of charge), as well as of various *domestic goods and services*. How ought we to treat these two categories of non-commodity products, which form part of the means of subsistence consumed by the wage-earner? Let us begin by examining the simplest case, that of domestic products.

Domestic Products

These can be defined as *products made by and for members of a non-commodity community*, whether a family community or some other type.[28] Just taking the family as an example, domestic products include goods and services as varied as meals prepared by the housewife, the clothes she knits or runs up, repairs and odd jobs around the house, looking after and bringing up the children, work in the garden etc. These domestic products call for different means of production, which can be either commodities (purchased) or goods and services actually produced within the setting of domestic production: thus a meal may be prepared with *purchased* electric household appliances and *purchased* vegetables or tinned foods, or with the produce of the garden and home-made tools.

Domestic products constitute a variable part of the means of subsistence of the wage-earner and his family and they demand a variable amount of their labour. But these domestic means of subsistence are not commodities, they have neither value nor price. They are not products intended for sale; thus the labour which is put into them creates no value and the resulting goods and services have no price. Conversely, these means of subsistence do not have to be purchased by the wage-earner: he does not have to pay a price in order to obtain them. And since domestic products do not have to be purchased, the capitalist does not have to pay a wage for this part of the wage-earners' means of subsistence.

The situation can therefore be described schematically in the following way. The *means of subsistence* consumed by the wage-earner and his family are made up of two parts: purchased commodities and domestic goods and services.[29] The *labour-time* devoted to producing them is also divided into two parts: the labour embodied in the purchased commodities and the labour put into the domestic products. But the '*value of labour-power*' incorporates only the labour-time devoted to the production of the purchased commodities (which alone creates any value) and not the labour-time put into the domestic products (which creates no value). As for the *price of labour-power*, the *wage*, it only corresponds to the price of those means of subsistence which are purchased: the capitalist does not therefore have to pay out any money in respect of domestic activities, which, from his point of view, are free of charge.[30]

Collective Goods and Services

Apart from *domestic* products and the means of subsistence they *purchase*, wage-earners also consume various *collective goods and services*, which are provided entirely or almost entirely free of charge. Let us give as examples the roads and the motorway network, public parks, medical care, social, administrative and judicial services, education, civil and national defence etc. All these goods and services are intended for and are in principle available to all members of society.[31]

Collective goods and services are provided free of charge, but involve a considerable monetary cost. This is where the difference from domestic products can be observed. Domestic activities cost nothing in monetary terms (apart from the price of the means of production *purchased* in order to perform them). Collective goods and services, on the contrary, involve a considerable monetary cost: not only the *means of production* have to be paid for (school buildings, government offices, machines, office equipment) but also the *labour force* which produces these collective goods and services (officials, magistrates, teachers, police, social security employees etc.).

In practice, products for collective use, intended in principle for *all* members of society, are financed by deductions from *all* incomes (National Insurance contributions and taxes, paid by wage-earners and capitalists alike). Hence the question: does the wage-earners' share in the *financing* of collective goods and services correspond to their share in the *consumption* of these goods and services?

Within the limits of this exposition and for the sake of simplicity, we are going to *assume* quite simply that the wage-earners' share in the financing of collective products is *equal* to their share in the consumption of them. Under these circumstances, the wage-earners themselves finance their own (apparently 'free') collective consumption (the consumption which they do not 'purchase' in the strict sense).

The wages paid by the capitalists have therefore on the one hand to allow for the *purchase* of the wage-earners' *individual* means of subsistence and, on the other, for the *financing* of the *collective* means of subsistence the wage-earners consume. The wage which fulfils this double function is the *gross direct and indirect wage,* corresponding to the *wage-cost* (that is, the cost to the enterprise). As we see in Figure 3.2, this wage comprises three distinct elements:

a) *The net direct wage* obtained by the wage-earner (which he actually gets each week, month or year).

b) *Taxes on income* he must pay (for the most part deducted at source).[32]

c) *National Insurance contributions* (unemployment, sickness, accident, pension) deducted partly from wages and partly from profits. These constitute the *social wage,* also called the *indirect wage* or the *deferred wage* (as it is only utilized in the event of sickness, retirement, etc.).

FIGURE 3.2   *Different concepts of wages*

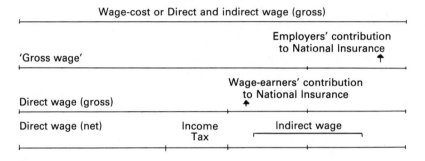

'PRODUCTIVE' AND 'UNPRODUCTIVE' LABOUR

A Restatement of Some Theoretical Principles

In order to place the question of productive and unproductive labour in context, we should take another look at various distinctions, concepts and principles which have been discussed in the course of the last two chapters. Table 3.1 has been designed for this purpose: to present a synthesis of all the relevant distinctions.

The first column takes up the three main types of activity which we have been able to single out: *commodity production, circulation* and *non-commodity production*. A commodity society must necessarily be involved with the first two types of activity: by definition, it presupposes the activity of production – of goods and services intended for the market – and the activity of circulation – effecting the transfer, between economic agents, of rights of ownership or use over commodities or money. A commodity society is also involved in a certain number of activities which produce goods and services which are not intended for the market: these comprise domestic activities and the production of collective goods and services, which we have just been discussing.

The second column distinguishes between waged and non-waged labour for each category of activity. Some observations may help to explain more fully the contents of the six lines (1–6) we have set out.

As regards *non-waged* labour (lines 1, 3, 5), the activities of *commodity production* are those of the *simple commodity producers*, dealt with at the beginning of the chapter. The *circulation* activities (line 3)

TABLE 3.1 A classification of activities and of results produced

ACTIVITIES			RESULTS PRODUCED				
			In terms of use-value	In terms of labour		In terms of value and price (productive labour)	
By content and commodity character of products	By commodity character of labour-power		Creation of use-value	Provision of labour	Provision of surplus labour	Creation of value and revenue	Creation of surplus value and surplus revenue
(a)	(b)		(c)	(d)	(e)	(f)	(g)
Commodity production	Non-waged	1	Yes	Yes	No	Yes	No
	Waged	2	Yes	Yes	Yes	Yes	Yes
Circulation	Non-waged	3	No	Yes	No	No	No
	Waged	4	No	Yes	Yes	No	No
Non-commodity production	Non-waged	5	Yes	Yes	No	No	No
	Waged	6	Yes	Yes	Yes	No	No

are those of *merchants* and *moneylenders* (whose cycles of operations have been represented by $M - C - M^+$ and $M - M^+$ respectively) as well as a part of the activities of the producers themselves, in so far as they have to purchase their means of production ($M - C_0$) and sell their final products ($C_1^+ - M^+$). As for the activities of *non-commodity production* (line 5), these comprise *domestic* activities, as well as some internal activities (e.g. book-keeping) performed both by producers and by merchants and moneylenders.

As regards *waged labour* (lines 2, 4, 6), the *activities of commodity production* are obviously those of wage-earners involved in process P in production enterprises, carrying out the cycle of operations

$$M - C_0 \ldots P \ldots C_1^+ - M^+.$$

What is the position of waged labour performed in circulation activities or in non-commodity production?

Wage-earners employed in *circulation* (line 4) normally work in capitalist enterprises. These may be enterprises devoted essentially to production or specializing in circulation. The former (that is, production enterprises) have in fact to devote a certain minimum of labour and therefore of wage-earning personnel to circulation activities, belonging to $M - C_0$ (financial provision, recruitment of personnel and payment of wages, purchase of means of production etc.) and of $C_1^+ - M^+$ (sale of products). The latter on the other hand are not involved in production but specialize in the circulation of commodities (commercial enterprises) or in the circulation of money (financial enterprises: banks and insurance companies).

Wage-earners employed in *non-commodity production* (line 6) produce goods and services which are not intended for sale. They work, either within capitalist enterprises (commercial, financial or production enterprises), or in specialized administrative departments. The former – the capitalist enterprises – employ a staff of variable size who produce goods and services for *internal use*: such staff would include book-keepers, doormen, supervisors, telephonists, social workers, cleaners etc., employed by a firm for its own internal requirements.[33] The latter – the administrative departments – produce goods and services for *collective use*, which are not intended for sale on the market: officials of various public and semi-public bodies, members of teaching staff, etc. belong to this sector which we call 'administration'.

Table 3.1 then specifies the nature of the results produced by the various distinct types of activities and of labour. These results are considered from three points of view: in terms of use-value (column (c)), in terms of labour (columns (d) and (e)) and in terms of value and price (columns (f) and (g)).

As regards *use-value*, we saw that activities of production (commodity or non-commodity) create use-value, while circulation activities do not.[34] The distinction between waged and non-waged labour is immaterial here.

As regards *labour*, the issue is whether all labour gives rise to *surplus labour*. We saw in this chapter that wage-earners, in (capitalist) commodity production, do provide surplus labour for the capitalists' benefit: they work for a longer period than the time corresponding to the labour required to produce their means of subsistence. The same thing can be said of wage-earners employed in circulation or in non-commodity production (administration): bank clerks, civil servants, a firm's book-keepers etc. also work for a period (for example, 8 hours) longer than the time required to produce their means of subsistence (for example, 3 hours). The characteristic of all waged labour (the use-value of labour-power as a commodity), is precisely to provide such surplus labour. The characteristic of non-waged labour, of independent labour, by contrast, is not to provide any surplus labour: the independent worker does not sell his labour-power, he does not work for the benefit of an employer, who would utilize his labour-power for a period of time greater than its (presently non-existent) 'value'.

As regards *value* and *price*, the question is about what type of labour creates *value* and *revenue* and what type of labour creates, more precisely, *surplus value* and *surplus revenue*.

We saw that only labour employed in the *production of commodities* creates value and revenue: this is true both of waged labour and of non-waged labour. But *waged* labour employed in commodity production has the special characteristic of creating surplus value and surplus revenue for the capitalists' benefit: the value created by the wage-earner can be broken down into corresponding value (equal to the value of the means of subsistence purchased) and surplus value (due to the wage-earner's surplus labour); the revenue created can be broken down into a wage for the wage-earner and surplus revenue for the capitalist. In other words, *waged* labour employed in commodity production creates more value than it consumes, creates more revenue than it receives and spends. By contrast *non-waged* labour *in principle* does not create more value than it consumes, does not create more revenue than it receives and spends.[35]

As for other activities (circulation and non-commodity production), they create neither value nor revenue (although they involve an expenditure of labour): if they are carried out by wage-earners, they can therefore create neither surplus value nor surplus revenue (although they do involve surplus labour).

The Two Concepts of Productive Labour

1. In a broader sense, *productive labour* is *labour which creates value and revenue*. In this sense, *all labour (whether waged or not)* devoted to the *production of commodities* is productive and all labour (whether waged or not) assigned to circulation or to non-commodity production is unproductive (see Table 3.1, column (f)).

2. In a narrower sense, which is specific to capitalism, *productive labour* is *labour which creates surplus value and surplus revenue*. In this sense, only *waged* labour devoted to the *production of commodities* is productive. All labour (whether waged or not), assigned to circulation or to non-commodity production, is unproductive; *non-waged* labour devoted to the production of commodities is also unproductive (see Table 3.1, column (g)).[36]

Importance of these Distinctions

1. Let us first consider the distinction between unproductive labour and productive labour *in the broader sense*. The importance of this distinction is that it enables us to grasp the extent of those activities which create revenue, in order to assess the potential for financing activities which do not create revenue.

To make this clear, we must first of all consider the source of the income of unproductive workers. We have seen that activities of circulation and of non-commodity production create neither value nor revenue. These activities, however, are indispensable to the functioning of a commodity society and the economic agents who perform them must earn an income (without one, these indispensable activities would not be performed): thus merchants and moneylenders have to make a profit, as well as capitalists specializing in trade or finance; in the same way too, wage-earners employed in circulation activities (trade, banking or insurance) or in administration (whether or not within a firm) have got to receive a wage. Since these incomes (wages and profits) are not created by the activities in question (circulation and non-commodity production), they must be derived from revenues created elsewhere, namely in the activities of commodity production. This is obvious as regards the payment of wage-earners working in the sector of 'administration' (civil servants, teachers, etc.): these workers are paid from taxes or contributions levied on all incomes. It is equally true – though less obvious – for wages and profits in trade and finance: these incomes are derived from the commercial or financial profit margins which the firms concerned take from the profits of production enterprises who have recourse to their services.

The importance of the distinction between productive labour (productive of value and revenue) and unproductive labour (unproductive of value and revenue) therefore appears in the following way. Since the incomes of some economic agents (the unproductive ones) are taken from the revenues created by other economic agents (the productive ones in the broader sense), it is important to specify which are productive activities (productive of value and revenue) and which are not. In fact, it is only possible to develop the financing of unproductive activities if productive activities are themselves sufficiently developed, if the revenues created by the latter are sufficient to provide what is required to pay the unproductive workers.

2. Let us now consider in a more detailed way the distinction between unproductive labour and productive labour *in the narrower sense*. The point of this distinction is to single out those activities which produce what capitalism aims at producing, namely surplus value and surplus revenue.

The importance of the distinction can be illustrated in the following way. We know that capitalism tends at present to develop a whole series of 'services' (whether of tourism, insurance, office cleaning, etc.) and, more generally, that the 'tertiary' sector (the production of services) is taking an increasing part in the whole of economic activity, at the expense of the 'primary' sector (the production of agricultural or mineral raw materials) and of the 'secondary' sector (the production of industrial goods). Are the wage-earners engaged in this tertiary sector productive of surplus value and surplus revenue? If they are, if they create surplus value, the capitalist system finds there a new source of nourishment for its perpetuation and its growth. If they are not, if profit and wages in the tertiary sector are a burden on the existing total surplus revenue, the capitalist system comes up against new limits to its total scope for profit and accumulation (taken to extremes, the whole surplus revenue created would be financing unproductive activities and nothing would remain available for accumulation).

The answer to this question leads us to distinguish three 'sub-sectors' within the tertiary activities: the tertiary sector of *circulation* (commercial and financial business), the tertiary sector of *administration* (production of collective goods and services, such as education, justice, defence etc.), and the tertiary sector of *commodity production* (tourism, catering, leisure activities, garages, laundries etc.).

The development of the tertiary of commodity production contributes to the renewal of capitalist profit: the wage-earners working in these enterprises constitute an extra source of surplus value for the whole of the capitalist system. By contrast, *the development of the tertiary of circulation and of administration involves a growing levy on surplus revenue.* Such a development is only possible if the aggregate of surplus revenue increases, that is, if the number of wage-earners employed in commodity production increases and/or if the degree of exploitation of these workers (the rate of surplus value) increases as well.[37]

The distinction between unproductive and productive labour in the narrower sense, as it specifies those activities producing surplus value and surplus revenue, is therefore of prime importance if one wishes to analyse the scope and the limitations of the capitalist system, in so far as profit and accumulation are concerned. Does this mean that the distinction between unproductive and productive labour in the broader sense (productive of value and of revenue) is without importance in an assessment of the potential for profit and accumulation in the capitalist system? Not at all, and for two reasons.

First, in so far as a (non-waged) activity is productive of value and of revenue, it is 'self-financing': it involves *no levy on surplus revenue* and can in principle contribute to the financing of other (unproductive) activities. Let us consider, for example, the activity of doctors in the private sector: is their work productive of value and revenue or not? If it is, the doctors' incomes derive from the value created by their labour. If not, these incomes derive from a levy on the wages and the surplus revenue created in society as a whole: they thus reduce the profit available for the capitalists and the capitalists' scope for accumulation.

Next, in so far as a (non-waged) activity is productive of value and revenue, it can indirectly *increase capitalist profit* and thus help finance capitalist accumulation. We will see[38] that the market mechanism brings about transfers of revenue from the 'weak' (less mechanized or less protected) producers to the 'strong' (more mechanized and more protected). Non-capitalist producers find themselves caught up in this market mechanism and in the transfers of revenue involved: if they are less strong than their capitalist competitors, their labour (provided it is productive in the broader sense, that is, devoted to commodity production) will create value and revenue, but a part of that revenue will be lost to them and will feed an increase in capitalist profits and in the potential for accumulation.

A further word on the distinction between productive and unproductive wage-earners, to clear up a frequent misunderstanding. We have seen that the distinction between productive and unproductive waged labour is important in so far as it helps to define the capacity of the capitalist system to create surplus revenue and to renew its sources of surplus revenue. We must emphasize that this distinction is not in any way aimed at dividing the wage-earners into two social classes, whose interests could be considered as contradictory (some creating surplus revenue, the others living off the surplus revenue created).

In this respect, we should remember that *unproductive wage-earners perform surplus labour in the same way as productive wage-earners*: as in the case of productive wage-earners, the duration of their working day normally exceeds the working time necessary for the production of their means of subsistence. If a steel worker and a civil servant work 8 hours and get the same wage, representing 3 hours labour (necessary labour), both of them provide 5 hours surplus labour (the difference is that the steel worker's 5 hours surplus labour will create a surplus revenue for the capitalist, while the civil servant's 3 hours necessary labour will be paid for by a levy on the surplus revenue). Unproductive wage-earners do therefore provide surplus labour and the capitalist class has an interest in increasing both this surplus labour and the surplus labour of productive wage-earners: to increase the surplus labour of productive wage-earners is to increase the creation of surplus revenue; to increase the surplus labour of unproductive wage-earners is to reduce the levy on the surplus revenue and so to increase the profit available.[39]

Though distinct from the point of view of the creation of surplus revenue, productive and unproductive wage-earners do not, however, constitute two opposed classes. All of them share the following features: they are obliged to sell their labour-power, they carry out activities which are indispensable to the functioning of the capitalist system, they are subject in their labour to the capitalists' orders and they perform surplus labour which it is in the capitalists' interests to maximise.[40]

NOTES

1. To illustrate this point by way of another example: an independent
   typist cannot devote her net income to buying a second typewriter, as
   the latter could only be used by *another* typist.
2. We can also say that the producer's present labour creates *a new value
   and a net income* (which he realizes on selling the commodity). We will
   also observe that the *hourly revenue* of the simple commodity producer
   (£80 for 8 hours of labour, or £10 an hour) is equal to the monetary
   expression of values. (We will come back to this point in chapter 4; see
   p. 86.)
3. Chapter 2, pp. 23–4.
4. The distinction between circulation and production is less apparent in
   certain cases, such as in trades where operations of purchase and sale
   overlap with operations of transport, storage, etc.
5. The same idea can be expressed in other terms. We could say that the
   differences between market prices and simple prices correspond to an
   exchange of unequal values (the joiner obtaining a revenue of £100 for a
   working day of 8 hours will be able to acquire consumer goods costing £100 and representing 10 *hours* of labour). *But this exchange of unequal
   values does not create new value, any more than the exchange of equal values*
   (when market prices and simple prices coincide): the exchange of unequal values merely causes a redistribution of the total revenue, which corresponds to the total value created by the present labour of all producers.
6. Let us state once again that we are talking about circulation operations
   in the strict sense (transfer of rights of ownership or of usage). The
   other operations carried out by a merchant (transport, storage of
   products) go beyond this transfer of rights: they are a part of
   production (in the wider sense) and so create value.
7. Can we say that the merchant and the moneylender enrich themselves
   at the expense of the producers? It is true that the commercial and
   financial margins come out of the producers' revenues. But it is equally
   true that the moneylender frees the producers from the obligation to
   find the finance required for production (if it is needed) and that the
   merchant frees the producers from the obligation to find buyers; both
   therefore allow the producers to devote themselves fully to the
   production of commodities, of value and of revenue. In a dynamic
   view, the commercial and financial margins will therefore be collected
   on an *increased* total revenue.
8. This continuous increase in the scale of capitalist production is only
   strictly true if we consider the whole of capitalist production; obviously
   there is nothing to prevent certain capitalist enterprises from stagnating
   and failing altogether.
9. Note that the pursuit of profit is not the effect of the capitalists' *conscious
   will*: it is the result of a *compulsion* that bears down on all of them within

Capitalist Profit: Surplus Value

the capitalist framework (the capitalist who does not make a profit is doomed to elimination).

10. In other terms, the sum of the *circulation profits* of some and of the *circulation losses* of the others equals zero.

11. To which we should add the labour of the capitalist himself if he takes a part in production (whether as engineer, planner etc.). As this (possible) labour of the capitalist does not constitute in any case more than a minimal fraction of the total present labour, we can disregard it in the course of this argument.

12. See chapter 1, p. 5.

13. A terminological observation regarding the 'purchase' or the 'sale' of labour-power. Juridically speaking, wage-earners obviously remain owners of their labour-power (they do not become slaves): they only transfer to the capitalist the right to make use of, to dispose of this labour-power (in this sense, the term *'hiring out'* of labour-power would be more correct). The same applies, incidentally, to the means of production or the money obtained by the capitalist. The borrowed money, the leased building, land or plant remain the (juridical) property of the lender or lessor. But the essential point is not whether there is or is not transfer of *juridical ownership*: the essential point resides in the transfer of *real ownership*, in the fact that the capitalist acquires *the right of use and of disposal to his advantage* over means of production and labour-power. (We will bring up again the distinction between juridical ownership and real ownerhsip when we come to the subject of the ownership of assets in enterprises (see chapter 8, p. 174, n. 13).

14. It should be stressed immediately that the inadequate use of the concepts of 'commodity' and 'value' in connection with labour-power does not affect the Marxist analysis of the source of profit, as developed in the following pages.

15. The reduction in price is only observable if the reduction in value is not counterbalanced by a greater increase in the monetary expression of values, as in a period of inflation. In this case, the reduction of value most often only appears in the form of *a fall in the 'relative price'*, that is to say, of a rise in price, relatively smaller than the rise in other prices. Even in a period of inflation, however, we can observe certain *falls in absolute prices* in response to increases in productivity; consider the price of many electronic goods in the last 20 years.

16. The difference in consumption *between particular categories of wage-earners* depends also on their relative positions of strength or weakness; these in turn are dependent on factors such as the scarcity of manpower, the degree of unionization, the degree of profitability of the enterprise or the branch of production etc.

17. Obviously, the disappearance of an *individual* worker is not important, if he can be easily replaced: what is important for capitalism is the existence and renewal of the working *class*.

18. Here too, we must consider *average* capitalist profit rather than the profit of such and such an *individual* capitalist: the disappearance of an individual capitalist is not important as long as the continuity of the capitalist system as a whole is not threatened.

19. The purchase of means of subsistence does not always have to be immediate: a part of the wages or of the income can be saved up in view of *deferred consumption* (especially for the purchase of durable goods such as a house or a car).

20. Those means of subsistence, which are not the object of daily purchase, are reduced here to a daily base (for example, if the wage-earner buys one pair of shoes a year, we calculate that he buys 1/365 of a pair a day).

21. Instead of saying that the level of the wage depends in this way on the value of the labour-power or on the value of the commodities purchased, could we not say on the contrary that it is the wage paid which determines the number of commodities that can be purchased and thus the value of the labour-power? This only *seems* to be true. We have just seen that the value of labour-power depends on the number of commodities purchased and on the *average value* of these different commodities. The level of the wage obviously does not determine the average value of the commodities purchased, that is, the quantity of labour required to produce each of them. Does it determine the number of commodities purchased? Apparently yes: a higher wage allows a higher consumption and wage-earners express their immediate wage-claims in terms of wage increases. More basically, the relationship goes the other way: what wage claims aim for is an increase in what is called the 'real wage', that is, an increase in *the number of means of subsistence they can purchase*: to the extent that these claims are successful, they are normally reflected in a rise in the nominal wages actually paid.

22. This involves making two distinct assumptions:
    (1) All capitalist enterprises are productive enterprises (we exclude for the moment commercial and financial enterprises) and all wage-earners are involved in productive activities (we exclude for the moment wage-earners involved in circulation or administrative activities, within or outside the enterprise).
    (2) Within the production sector, the wage-earner and the enterprise under consideration are 'average' in all respects (in degree of mechanization, intensity and skill of labour, etc).
    These two assumptions will be relaxed at a later stage, particularly in chapter 6.

23. These various branches of production are on the one hand, those which produce the actual means of subsistence (for example, textile, food and car industries) but also, on the other, those which produce the means of production used by them (for example, agriculture and metallurgy).

24. For the purposes of the demonstration, it is sufficient that the working day should be more than 3 hours.

25. Two observations on terminology are required here, regarding surplus value:

    (1) In standard Marxist terminology, the concept of surplus value designates both the surplus labour of wage-earning producers (expressed in hours) and the income of capitalists (expressed in pounds). In the text which follows, the concept of surplus value is reserved for the wage-earning producers' surplus labour (in hours), while the concept of surplus revenue is applied to the capitalists' revenue (in pounds). To be precise, we can say that *the surplus revenue is the surplus value expressed in pounds.*

    (2) Surplus revenue so defined does not correspond necessarily to the capitalist's actual profit. In reality, we can say that *the surplus revenue is the theoretical amount of profit exactly equal to the monetary expression of the surplus value created by waged labour* (in the same way that the simple price is the theoretical price exactly equal to the monetary expression of the social value of a commodity). We will see, in chapter 6, the different reasons which make *the actual profit differ from this theoretical amount which is equal to the surplus revenue* (in the same way that the market price of commodities differs from the theoretical price, which is the simple price). Until then, the simplifying assumptions of this section and of chapters 4 and 5 enable us to establish the equation: surplus revenue = capitalist profit.

26. The means of subsistence are produced by the serf himself in the feudal system; they are produced by other wage-earners in the capitalist system (because of the division of social labour).

27. Chapter 6, pp. 110–15.

28. In the literal sense, domestic products are those made by and for the members of the household (domus = house) (including products which a single person makes for himself). In a wider sense, they include products made by and for members of a larger community (for example: an African clan, an Indian settlement, a monastic order).

29. This description excludes for the moment the *collective* goods and services consumed by the wage-earners.

30. If the wage does not have to cover domestic products, it ought on the other hand to allow for the possible purchase of means of production (for example electric household appliances) used in the domestic circle but not produced in it.

31. It is important to note that we are not discussing the *social function* of all these collective products. As we will see later, the public expenditure on education, justice, law and order, defence, the road network, etc. is *not neutral*: their function is to perpetuate capitalist domination and to ensure the reproduction of capitalist society. But this function does not prevent collective goods and services from being available to all members of society, workers and capitalists alike: thus the motorways are used for the transport of capitalist commodities as well as for the

individual recreation of wage-earners; justice serves to defend the private ownership of means of production as well as to resolve the conflict of responsibilities between neigbours or between victims of road accidents; between two capitalist wars, national defence ensures a capitalist peace, enjoyed by workers and employers alike. Of course the accessibility of collective goods or services may be limited on statutory grounds (thus social services are intended only for the needy) or simply by hard facts (thus motorways are not accessible to wage-earners who cannot afford a car, universities are closed to all the victims of the educational and social selection process, justice is too distant for the common run of mortals).

32. Taxes on income are *direct taxes*. *Indirect taxes* (VAT, taxes on consumption) are paid as and when the income is spent; when the wage-earner buys his consumer goods (at a price incorporating VAT), part of the money spent becomes the income of the producers of the consumer goods, the other part (the VAT) merely passes through their hands and is passed on to the state. The amount of indirect taxes which the wage-earners have to pay is therefore incorporated in the net direct wage. Let us remember that the taxes (direct and indirect) paid by the wage-earners are supposed to be used, like the National Insurance contributions, for the financing of collective products consumed by the wage-earners.

33. It is a different case where a firm engages the same type of staff (book-keepers or cleaners for example) not for its own internal requirements but in order to provide specialized services to other firms or individuals: thus a firm specializing in company accounts or in office cleaning. Such firms are capitalist production enterprises (carrying out the complete cycle $M - C_0 \ldots P \ldots C_1^+ \overset{\cdot}{-} M^+$ and the wage-earners employed in type P activities within these firms create a new value (including a surplus value) and a net revenue (including a surplus revenue).

34. See chapter 2, pp. 22–4 and chapter 3, pp. 53–4.

35. This principle applies perfectly in the case of an average producer within the framework of a (hypothetical) generalized simple commodity production (see pp. 51–2). We shall see later that independent producers competing with more efficient capitalist enterprises normally do create more value and revenue than they consume: this fact will lead us to reconsider applying the concepts of surplus labour, surplus value and surplus revenue to those independent producers (see chapter 7, p. 148).

36. Whether we take the strict view of productive labour or the wider view, we will observe that unproductive labour is far from constituting a homogeneous whole: it embraces waged activities and other non-waged activities; it embraces also both circulation activities and activities of *non-commodity production* (see Table 3.3).

37. As we shall see shortly, it is in the interest of the capitalist system to increase the rate of surplus labour of *unproductive* wage earners too.
38. Chapter 6, pp. 110–22.
39. As we shall see in chapters 4 and 8, a wage-earner's surplus labour increases as his labour-time is lengthened and as his level of consumption (and therefore his wage level) decreases. The longer the working time of each unproductive worker, the smaller the number of unproductive workers which need be employed and the smaller the total amount of wages needed to pay them; the lower the wage of each unproductive worker, the smaller the total amount of wages to be levied on the surplus revenue.
40. Once we grant that the distinction between productive and unproductive labour is not bound up with the question of social classes, we will recognize a capitalist's labour as productive (of value and revenue) when he actually takes part in commodity production (as an engineer or as an organizer but not as a 'coupon clipper').

4

The Basic Ratios of Marxist
Political Economy

In this chapter, we are going to break down the value and the price of commodities into their different components. From there, we will be able to deduce and analyse the basic ratios of Marxist political economy.

For simplicity's sake, we are making three general assumptions which underlie all the developments which are to follow.

(1) We assume that all activities belong to *commodity production* (ignoring activities of circulation and non-commodity production) and that all these activities of commodity production are carried out solely by *wage-earners* (ignoring the possible existence of simple commodity producers).[1]

(2) We conduct our arguments on a *macro-economic level*: the wage-earners or enterprises considered in the examples are 'average' in all respects and representative of all wage-earners and enterprises.

(3) We assume that the means of production (means of labour + materials) as well as the labour-power are purchased 'in one go' at the the beginning of the period of time considered (1 day, 1 year) and that their purchase has to be renewed 'in one go' at the end of this same period. As far as the means of labour (machines, tools) are concerned, this implies that their value and price must be transferred completely to the value and price of the product created during the period under consideration.

The first two assumptions enable us to establish an *equivalence* between the *surplus revenue created* by the wage-earners (the surplus value expressed in monetary terms) and the *profit obtained* by the capitalists (we will see in chapter 6 that the profit differs from the surplus revenue once one or other of these assumptions is withdrawn). The third assumption, as we shall see later in the chapter, enables us to establish an *equivalence* between the *cost of production* and the *money-capital invested* at the start.

THE COMPONENTS OF VALUE AND OF PRICE

A Restatement of Some Theoretical Principles

In order to analyse the value and price of commodities, we will restate four theoretical principles which have been brought out in previous chapters and illustrate them by means of a numerical example.

1. First principle: the value of a commodity consists of *past value* (that is, the value of the means of production purchased or past labour) and *new value* (created by the present labour of the producer).

   Example: a commodity produced in a day of 8 hours (present labour) and with means of production worth 12 hours (past labour) has a value of 20 hours.

2. Second principle: the value of a commodity is expressed as a certain *price*, constituting the gross revenue of the producer; this price or gross revenue consists of the *price of the means of production* and the producer's *net revenue*.

   Example: if the monetary expression of values is £10 per hour, the price of the commodity considered above is £200; this price or gross revenue consists of £120 (price of the means of production) and £80 (net revenue).

Past labour or Value of means of production	Present labour or New value created	Value of daily production
=	=	=
12 hours	8 hours	20 hours
£120	£80	£200
=	=	=
Price of means of production	Net revenue created	Price of daily production

3. Third principle: the net revenue created arises from the producer's present labour: it represents the new value expressed as price.

In the example above, the producer's net revenue (£80) corresponds to the new value expressed in pounds (8 hours × the monetary expression of values).

Note that the producer's hourly revenue (revenue *created* and *earned* per hour of labour) is identical with the monetary expression of values (£10 per hour).

4. Fourth principle: in the capitalist system, the new value and the net revenue created are divided into two parts: the *new value* consists of *corresponding value* (necessary labour) and *surplus value* (surplus labour); the net revenue created consists of *wages* and *surplus revenue*.

Working from the data of the previous example, but assuming this time that we are dealing with a capitalist enterprise employing waged labour, we must break down the value and the price of the production into three parts (the figures in parentheses apply to the *annual* production of an enterprise employing *100* wage-earners for *250* days).[2]

Past labour or	Present labour		Value of the production
	Necessary labour or	Surplus labour or	
Value of means of production	Corresponding value	Surplus value	
=	=	=	=
12 hours	3 hours	5 hours	20 hours
(300 000 hours)	(75 000 hours)	(125 000 hours)	(500 000 hours)
£120	£30	£50	£200
(£3 million)	(£750 000)	(£1 250 000)	(£5 million)
=	=	=	=
Price of means of production	Wages	Surplus revenue	Price of the production

Net revenue created

Note that the net revenue *created* per hour of labour (£80: 8 hours = £10 per hour) is, as before, identical with the monetary expression of values; but the hourly wage *obtained* by the worker (£30 : 8 hours =

£3.75 per hour) is less, the difference representing the surplus revenue (per hour) appropriated by the capitalist.

On the basis of the data in the quantified example, the value and the price of the annual production of the enterprise in question can therefore be broken down in the following way:

(1) Value of the = Value of the means + corresponding + surplus
    production   of production   value   value
    500 000 hours = 300 000 hours + 75 000 hours + 125 000 hours

(2) Price of the = Price of the means + wages   + surplus
    production   of production   revenue

    £5 million   = £3 million   + £750 000 + £1.25 million

The Successive Forms of Capital and the Distinction between Constant and Variable Capital

Let us return to the general formula, which synthetizes the complete cycle of capitalist operations $(M - C_0 \ldots P \ldots C_1^+ - M^+)$. This formula can be rewritten applying the data of the above example.

M = money-capital invested initially
    = £3.75 million = £3 million + £750 000

C_0 = means of production and labour-power purchased
    (value = 375 000 hours = 300 000 hours + 75 000 hours)
    (price = £3.75 million = £3 million + £750 000)
:
:
P = process of production
:
:
C_1^+ = commodities produced
    (value = 500 000 hours = 300 000 hours + 75 000 hours +
                                              125 000 hours)
    (price = £5 million = £3 million + £750 000 + £1.25 million)
M^+ = money-capital recovered
    = £5 million = £3 million + £750 000 + £1.25 million)

From this breakdown it is possible to specify the various forms that capital successively takes in the complete cycle of operations (money-capital, productive capital, commodity capital and again money-capital) and to introduce an essential distinction, within money-capital, between constant and variable capital.

Money-capital invested: constant and variable capital
We call *money-capital* the *sum of money invested initially with the object of obtaining a profit.* This money-capital is divided in two parts, called respectively constant capital and variable capital.

Constant capital is the *part of money-capital used for the purchase of the means of production* (£3 million in the example). The means of production merely transfer their own value (which remains constant) to the product, without creating any increase of value.

Variable capital is the *part of money-capital used for the purchase of the labour-power (of productive wage-earners)* (£750 000 in this example): it is so called from the fact that this productive labour-power creates a surplus value, an increase of value in relation to its own value.[3]

Productive capital
In purchasing means of production and labour-power, the capitalist transforms his money-capital into productive capital.

Productive capital can be defined as *the set of means of production and labour-power brought together in a capitalist production process.*

Commodity capital
In the production process, the capitalist utilizes and consumes labour-power and means of production (which therefore have to be renewed from time to time). In doing this, he causes his capital to undergo a new transformation: it sheds the form of productive capital and assumes the form of *commodity capital* ready for sale.

Money-capital recovered: constant capital, variable capital, profit
The last metamorphosis results from the sale, which restores to the capital its initial form of money. The sum of money recovered through the sale – the 'turnover' – is broken down into three parts.

The first two parts (£3 million and £750 000) enable the capitalist to renew (on the same scale) the purchase of the means of production and of the labour-power consumed in production. In selling the finished product, the capitalist *recovers* the capital he laid out in order to acquire the necessary means of production and labour-power and this will enable him to purchase afresh the same means of production and labour-power (or others costing the same price).

The third part (£1.25 million) is the *profit* or *increase of money* obtained in relation to the capital initially laid out. This profit will be used partly for the capitalist's *consumption*, but essentially for *accumulation*, that is, for the purchase of *additional* means of production and labour-power.[4]

The Components of Value and of Price as Expressed in Symbols

Table 4.1 brings together the principal concepts of the previous analysis and symbolizes them by means of letters. The symbols *in italics* represent magnitudes expressed in hours of labour; the same symbols in *plain type* represent magnitudes expressed in prices (in pounds). The connection between the two categories of symbols is made through the monetary expression of values (E): thus

$$C = C \times E,$$

that is, the constant capital (or the price of the means of production) is equal to the value of the means of production (expressed in hours) multiplied by E (expressed in pounds per hour).

TABLE 4.1 *Symbolization of the basic concepts of Marxist political economy.*

1. *In terms of price*
    C = constant capital (= price of means of production)
    V = variable capital (= price of
        labour-power, or of the means of subsistence purchased)
    S = surplus revenue created
    P = profit obtained

2. *In terms of value*
    C = past value (= value of means of production)
    V = corresponding value created by labour-power (= value of
        labour-power or of the means of subsistence purchased)
    S = surplus value created by labour-power

With the aid of these symbols, the total value and the total price of the production considered in the previous example can be expressed concisely:

Total value of the product = $C + V + S$
Total price of the product = $C + V + P = C + V + S$

Two remarks have to be made concerning the total price of the product.

(1)   The equation

$$C + V + P = C + V + S$$

is only true if the *profit obtained* by the capitalist is equivalent
to the *surplus revenue created* by the wage-earners. As we
mentioned at the beginning of the chapter, such an equivalence implies that we conduct the argument on a macro-
economic level, that is, that we consider capitalist production
as a whole (and not the production of a particular enterprise
or branch, for which this equivalence does not hold).

(2)   The sum C + V represents both the *money-capital invested*
initially (the money-capital laid out) and the total *production
cost* (as incorporated into the price of the annual product and
recovered through the sale of this product). At the beginning
of the year, the capitalists have laid out a sum of money (C +
V) necessary for the purchase of the means of production and
labour-power; since the purchase of the means of production
and labour-power has to be renewed at the end of the year
(see the third assumption on p. 84), this same sum (C + V)
must be incorporated as production cost into the selling price
of the annual product (so that the capitalist recovers it
through the sale).

THE BASIC RATIOS OF MARXIST POLITICAL ECONOMY

From the formula

$$C + V + P \ (= C + V + S),$$

and considering the data of the previous example, we can set out and
analyse the three basic ratios of Marxist political economy: the rate of
surplus value (S') the composition of capital (C') and the rate of
profit (P'). Before doing so, we must again draw attention to the
scope of the present analysis.

1. We are conducting our argument in this chapter on the aggregate,
macro-economic level. Consequently, the magnitudes C, V and S (=
P) refer to the whole of capitalist production and the three ratios in
question are considered here as average ratios. (In later chapters we
will consider these same ratios at particular, micro-economic,
levels.)

2. We continue to assume that the purchases of means of production and of labour-power are made and renewed 'in one go' at the beginning of each year, so that C + V represents both the money-capital laid out and the annual production cost. (In the theoretical appendix we will consider what the basic ratios become when this assumption is abandoned.[5])

The Rate of Surplus Value

The *rate of surplus value* (S′) relates the surplus value or surplus revenue created by the labour-power (S or S̄) to the value of the labour-power or the variable capital spent on its acquisition (V or V̄)

$$S' = S/V = \bar{S}/\bar{V}$$

Thus, in the previous numerical example:

$$S' = \frac{125\ 000\ \text{hours}}{75\ 000\ \text{hours}} = \frac{\pounds 1.25\ \text{million}}{\pounds 750\ 000} = 1.66 = 166\%$$

The rate of surplus-value expresses the *degree of exploitation* of the wage-earners, the degree in which surplus labour is extracted from them (and thus surplus value and surplus revenue if the wage-earners produce commodities, as is assumed here).[6]

The Composition of Capital

The *composition of capital* (C′) relates constant capital (C) and variable capital (V): it relates the part of money-capital used for the purchase of means of production (which produce no increase of value) and the other part used for the purchase of labour-power (productive of an increase of value):

$$C' = C/V$$

In our numerical example, we have

$$C' = \pounds 3\ \text{million}/\pounds 750\ 000 = 4 = 400\%$$

The composition of capital reflects approximately the *degree of mechanization* of the production process, the ratio between the number of means of production used and the number of wage-earners.[7]

The Rate of Profit

The *rate of profit* (P′) relates the profit obtained (P) to the *total* (constant and variable) capital laid out in order to acquire the means of production and the labour-power required for the process of production. If we represent the total capital expended by K (K = C + V), we can write

$$P' = P/(C + V) = P/K$$

Thus in the example:

$$P' = £1.25 \text{ million}/£3.75 \text{ million} = 0.33 = 33\%$$

The rate of profit expresses the *degree of realization of the capitalist aim*, which is to obtain an increase of money (a profit) in relation to the capital initially laid out.

FACTORS AFFECTING THE BASIC RATIOS

This section aims at an analysis of the main factors which affect the three basic ratios described above. In order to make the analysis clear, some new symbols will be introduced. They are all set out in the following list, prior to being presented separately as and when required:

M: number of means of production used
pm: value per instrument of production
pm: price per instrument of production (= *pm*.E)
L: number of productive wage-earners
x: number of means of subsistence purchased per wage-earner, or *real* wage per worker
px: means of subsistence: value per item
px: means of subsistence: price per item (= *px*.E)
w: value of one wage-earner's labour-power (= value of the means of subsistence purchased by a wage-earner)
w: average money wage per worker (= *w*.E)
d: labour-time per wage-earner (= new value created by a productive wage-earner)
D: total number of hours of labour (productive of value)
r: new revenue created per (productive) wage earner (= *d*.E)
R: new revenue created by all (productive) wage-earners (= *D*.E)

Factors Affecting the Rate of Surplus Value

We defined the rate of surplus value as the ratio between the surplus revenue created by the wage-earners and the variable capital (the mass of wages) laid out to acquire their labour-power.

$$S' = S/V$$

Now the surplus revenue is equal to the difference between the new revenue *created* by the wage-earners and the variable capital (or the revenue *spent* on the wage-earners)

$$S = R - V$$

The formula for the rate of surplus value can therefore be written:

$$S' = \frac{R - V}{V}$$

$$\text{or } S' = \frac{R}{V} - 1$$

Working from this formula, two types of transformation can be carried out in order to analyse the factors affecting the rate of surplus value.

The rate of surplus value as a function of the monetary expression of values and of the hourly money wage.

Let us divide the numerator and the denominator of the above formula by D (total labour-time of productive wage-earners):

$$S' = \frac{R/D}{V/D} - 1$$

Let us then divide the two terms of the denominator by L (number of productive wage-earners):

$$S' = \frac{R/D}{(V/L)/(D/L)} - 1$$

The numerator R/D is in fact the *monetary expression of values* (E): it is the ratio of the new revenue created (in monetary terms) to the number of hours of labour which is productive of value (that is, devoted to the production of commodities); in other words, it is the revenue created per hour of (productive) labour. As for the denominator, it represents the *hourly money wage* or the wage obtained per hour of (productive) labour: it is the ratio of the variable capital spent per wage-earner to the labour-time per wage-earner.

We can therefore express the rate of surplus value by the following formula:[8]

$$s' = \frac{E}{w/d} - 1$$

Thus, in the example at the beginning of the chapter:

$$s' = \frac{\text{£10 per hour}}{\text{£3.75 per hour}} - 1 = 1.66 = 166\%$$

What does this formula tell us? We noted in the preceding chapter, in the hypothesis of a non-capitalist production, that the *hourly revenue* of the simple commodity producer is *equal to the monetary expression of values*.[9] We see here, in the context of capitalist production, that the *hourly wage is necessarily less than the monetary expression of values* (otherwise the rate of surplus value would be zero or even negative). The difference between E and w/d arises precisely from the fact that the capitalist seizes a part of the revenue created by the wage-earner; this part corresponds to the surplus revenue appropriated by the capitalist.[10]

The last formula also shows that, for a given monetary expression of values, *the lower the hourly wage, the higher the rate of surplus value or of surplus labour* and vice versa. We can thus see the significance of the workers' struggles over the hourly wage. Although the form of the hourly wage conceals the reality of capitalist exploitation, what is at stake in these disputes is nothing other than the degree of exploitation of the wage-earners: when they demand increases in the hourly wage, the workers are merely demanding, more fundamentally, a decrease in the rate of surplus value or of surplus labour to which they are subjected.

The rate of surplus value as a function of productivity and of the real hourly wage.

Returning to the initial formula, we now divide the numerator and the denominator by L (the number of productive wage-earners).

$$S' = \frac{R/L}{V/L} - 1$$

or $s' = \dfrac{r}{w} - 1$

The numerator represents the new revenue created per wage-earner, and the denominator represents the revenue obtained per wage-earner (no longer by the hour but over a certain period: 1 day, 1 month, 1 year).[11]

We know that the new revenue created per wage-earner is the new value created (or the number of hours of productive labour) expressed in monetary terms ($r = d.E$) and that the wage is the value of the labour-power expressed in monetary terms (w = w.E). We have then

$$s' = \frac{d.E}{w.E} - 1$$

and $s' = \dfrac{d}{w} - 1$

Now the value of labour-power (w) is equal to the value of the means of subsistence purchased by the wage-earner. It is therefore equal to the *number* of means of subsistence purchased (represented by x), multiplied by the *average value* of each of these means of subsistence (represented by px, or price of one unit of x expressed in hours of labour): $w = x.px$.

So we finally get

$$s' = \frac{d}{x.px} - 1$$

Thus in the example at the beginning of the chapter (where $d = 8$ hours per day and w (= $x.px$) = 3 hours per day):

$$s' = \frac{8 \text{ hours}}{3 \text{ hours}} - 1 = 1.66 = 166\%$$

What does this formula tell us? It shows us the contradictory factors affecting the rate of surplus value or the rate of surplus labour: this tends to *fall* when the labour-time per wage-earner (d) decreases; it also tends to *fall* when the wage-earners' level of consumption, their real wage (represented by x), tends to increase,[12] but it tends to *increase* when the average value of the means of subsistence (px) decreases, that is, when the production of these consumer goods registers rises in productivity.[13] We now see — and we will come back to this more fully in chapter 8 and the following chapters – that *the rate of surplus labour can remain constant, and even increase, in spite of an increase in the wage-earners' level of consumption* (x). If we assume labour-time (d) to be constant, it is necessary – and sufficient – that *the real wage* (x) *should increase relatively less than productivity in the production of the wage-earners' means of subsistence*: in this case, px falls relatively more than x increases, and so $x.px$ (the value of the means of subsistence or of labour-power) decreases and s' increases.

The last formula for the rate of surplus revenue can be rewritten in a slightly different form (placing d in the denominator and px in the numerator):

$$s' = \frac{1/px}{x/d} - 1$$

The numerator is now the reciprocal of the value per 'means' of subsistence (the reciprocal of the number of hours per 'means' of subsistence): it therefore represents the number of means of subsistence produced per hour of labour (present and past), that is, *hourly real productivity* in the production of the means of subsistence. As for the denominator, this represents the number of means of subsistence which can be purchased per hour of labour, that is to say, the *hourly real wage*.

This formula allows us therefore to conclude that the rate of surplus value tends to *increase* when hourly real productivity increases and to *fall* when the hourly real wage increases. We see once again that the rate of surplus value can remain constant, and even increase, in spite of an increase in the wage-earners' standard of living: it is sufficient that the real wage should increase relatively less than productivity in the production of the means of subsistence.[14]

Factors Affecting the Composition of Capital

We defined the composition of capital as the ratio of constant capital (used for the purchase of means of production) to variable capital (used for the purchase of labour-power):

$$C' = C/V$$

The constant capital laid out is equal to the number of means of production used (M), multiplied by their average price (pm): C = M.pm.

On the other hand, the variable capital laid out is equal to the number of wage-earners, multiplied by their average wage: V = L.w. Since the whole of the wage (w) is devoted to the purchase (present, deferred or anticipated) of the means of subsistence, it is clear that the wage is equal to the total price of the means of subsistence purchased, that is, to the number of necessaries of life (x) multiplied by their average price (px): w = x.px.

Consequently, the C' ratio can be expressed in the following way:

$$C' = \frac{M.pm}{L.x.px}$$

or again:

$$C' = \frac{M}{L} \cdot \frac{pm}{px} \cdot \frac{1}{x}$$

Moreover, we know that the price of the means of production and of the means of subsistence is equal to their value, expressed in monetary terms: pm = pm.E and px = px.E. Hence we have:

$$C' = \frac{M}{L} \cdot \frac{pm}{px} \cdot \frac{1}{x}$$

This last formula shows us the different factors which affect the composition of capital: C' tends to *increase* when the M/L ratio increases, that is when the number of means of production employed per worker increases;[15] C' tends to *increase* when the pm/px ratio increases, that is, when the number of means of production employed in the production of the means of subsistence than in the production of the means of production (which causes px to fall proportionately more than pm); finally C' tends to *decline* when there is a rise in the number of means of subsistence consumed per wage-earner, that is, when there is a rise in the real wage.

We see that the composition of capital only reflects the degree of mechanization of the production process, or the M/L ratio, very roughly: the evolution of C' is affected, not only by the evolution of M/L, but also by the comparative evolution of productivity in the two production sectors (means of production and means of subsistence), as well as by the evolution of the wage-earners' living standards.[16]

We should also observe that the composition of capital does not express the relation between past labour ('embodied' in the means of production) and present labour (provided by the wage-earners' labour-power). Present labour is equal to $V + S$ (necessary labour + surplus labour), while the denominator of C' is equal only to V (necessary labour, or value of the wage-earners' means of subsistence, equal to L.w or L.x.px.).

Factors Affecting the Rate of Profit

We defined the rate of profit as the ratio P/(C + V). *If we retain the initial hypotheses* of this chapter (*macro-economic level and absence of unproductive wage-earners*), the profit coincides exactly with the surplus revenue created by all wage-earners (P = S).

The relation P′ = P/(C + V) can now be transformed in the following way (replacing P by S, then dividing all the terms by V):

$$P' = \frac{S}{C + V}$$

$$P' = \frac{S/V}{C/V + V/V}$$

$$\text{and } P' = \frac{S'}{C' + 1}$$

This formula shows that the average rate of profit for the whole of the economy depends both on the (average) rate of surplus value and the (average) composition of capital. *The higher the rate of surplus value, the higher the average rate of profit; the higher the composition of capital, the lower the average rate of profit.* The two relationships are logical:

(1)   A high rate of surplus value means that the surplus revenue created by labour-power is relatively high in comparison with the capital spent to acquire the labour-power; for a given composition of capital, the average rate of profit will therefore be so much higher.

(2)   A high composition of capital means that the capitalists spend proportionately more on means of production (which create no surplus revenue) and proportionately less on labour-power (which alone creates surplus revenue): for a given rate of surplus value, the average rate of profit will therefore be so much lower.

We should emphasize the fact that the last formula is only applicable on the macro-economic level (and also not taking into account the existence of non-productive workers).

On the *micro-economic* level (that is for a particular enterprise or a particular branch of industry), a composition of capital higher than the average is not reflected in a lower rate of profit; this comes about due to the transfers of surplus revenue which benefit the most-mechanized enterprises or branches, transfers which enable them to obtain a higher profit than the surplus revenue created by their wage-earners. This is what will be dealt with in chapter 6.

On the *macro-economic* level, the formula enables us to bring out the constraints and lines of action which the capitalist system must take into account: the constraint is the increasing mechanization imposed by competition, which tends to reduce the rate of profit; the possible line of action is the increase of the degree of exploitation of the wage-earners, in order to restore the rate of profit. These different tendencies, which are at the heart of the capitalist system, will be dealt with in chapter 8.

NOTES

1. This assumption amounts to saying that *all the workers are productive in the strict sense*, that is, creators of surplus value and of surplus revenue.

2. As we said at the beginning of the chapter, the example given here deals with an *average* enterprise. It may be useful to observe at this stage that *differences of mechanization* among enterprises *would normally affect the relative weights of past and present labour* (the volume of the means of production operated per worker is greater in a more mechanized enterprise, so the relation past labour/present labour is normally greater). But *these differences in mechanization would not affect the division of each producer's present labour* as between necessary and surplus labour.

   The respective values of the *daily* production *per wage-earner* would for example break down in this way:

   more-mechanized enterprise: 24 hours + 3 hours + 5 hours
                              = 32ı hours
   less-mechanized enterprise: 6 hours + 3 hours + 5 hours
                              = 14 hours

3. The distinction between *variable* capital and *constant* capital must not be confused with the distinction between *circulating* capital and *fixed* capital. The first distinction divides the elements of the production process according to whether or not they create surplus revenue: the second distinction divides the elements of the production process according to whether they have to be constantly renewed or whether they can be used for several production processes.

   Schematically, the two distinctions overlap in the following way (each arrow means 'is used to purchase').

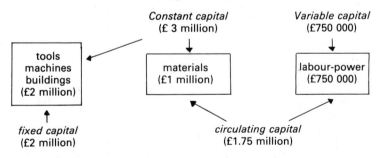

4. This *accumulation* of (part of) the profit gives rise to the *expanded reproduction* of capital, that is to the reproduction of the cycles M — $C_0 \ldots P \ldots C^+ — M^+$ on an ever-increasing scale. On this, see chapter 5 and chapter 8, p. 160.

5. As will be seen in the theoretical appendix, the present assumption implies that the *period of turnover* or the *rate of turnover* is equal to unity, both for constant capital and for variable capital. This assumption, which is intended to simplify the presentation of the argument, will be maintained throughout the book (except in the very few cases where the problem at hand does not allow it: such is the case for the problem of *obsolescence* considered in chapter 10).

6. Two observations on terminology will be useful here:
   (1) Strictly speaking, one should distinguish between the rate of surplus value S' (relating two amounts expressed in hours of value: S/V) and the rate of surplus revenue S' (relating two amounts expressed in terms of money: S/V). As the two ratios are actually identical, we will conform to current terminology and use only the term '*rate of surplus value*' (defining it either by S/V or S/V).
   (2) When considering not (only) productive wage-earners but (also) unproductive wage-earners (who do not create surplus value nor surplus revenue, though they provide surplus labour), the term '*rate of surplus value*' is no longer adequate. We will then use the broader term of '*rate of surplus labour*' (defining it as the ratio between the surplus labour provided and the value of labour-power).

7. We will see in the following section why the C/V ratio can only very *roughly* represent the degree of mechanization. We should observe that Marxist literature generally refers to the C/V ratio as the '*organic* composition of capital' and to the degree of mechanization (the ratio between means of production and number of wage-earners) as the '*technical* composition of capital'. (See p. 97, note 15).

8. The magnitudes expressed *per worker* (including the rate of surplus value) are represented here by lower-case letters. In so far as the wage-earners considered in the numerical example of this chapter are taken as 'average' wage-earners, representative of all wage-earners, we obviously have: $s' = S'$.

9. See chapter 3, p. 53, note 2.

10. In the case of unproductive wage-earners (who do not create surplus value nor surplus revenue), the difference between E and w/d corresponds to the *surplus labour* they provide, and the above formula expresses the '*rate of surplus labour*' to which they are subjected (see p. 91, note 6).

11. The new revenue created per wage-earner (r) is commonly known as 'net value added' per worker or 'productivity' per worker. So we can say that *the rate of surplus value increases when the 'productivity' increases relatively more than the wages* per worker. We will observe that 'productivity' here, just like the wage, is expressed in *so many pounds* per worker: it is a matter of *monetary* productivity and of *money* wages. The later transformations of the formula will enable us to express the rate of surplus value as a function of *real* productivity and of the *real* wage.

12. The *real wage* is merely the level of consumption, the number of commodities which can be purchased for a given *money wage* (what the worker currently receives as his payment). The rise in the real wage can be statistically determined by dividing the rise of the money wage by the appropriate figure in the index of consumer prices.

13. For the rises in productivity result in reductions in the quantity of labour – present and/or past – required to produce the commodities, that is, in reductions in the unit value of commodities. (See chapter 2, p. 32).

14. The last formula suggests that we can approach the evolution of the rate of surplus value by the comparison of statistical series describing respectively the evolution of the hourly real wage (x/d) and the evolution of hourly real productivity in the production of the means of subsistence ($1/px$). The evolution of x/d can be easily obtained by dividing the figures of the money hourly wage by the index of consumer prices. However, it is not so easy to obtain the evolution of $1/px$. In fact, the statistics of real productivity are usually obtained by dividing, by an appropriate price index, the money 'value added' created per worker (or per hour of labour) in industry. These statistics have two defects: first they only deal with industry (while a growing number of necessaries of life are produced in the services sector); secondly they only express at best the productivity per hour of *present* labour (while $1/px$ represents the quantity of necessaries of life per hour of past and present labour). Chapter 11 will present an empirical method making it possible to calculate the magnitude of px more accurately.

15. The M/L ratio (the ratio between the number of means of production and the number of workers) is often called the '*technical* composition of capital'. In contrast, the C/V ratio (which we have referred to as the 'composition of capital' could be called more precisely 'the *value*-composition of capital' or the '*price*-composition of capital'. Marxist literature also refers to the C/V ratio as the '*organic* composition of capital'.

16. Note that the M/L ratio cannot be measured: it is not possible to add together spades, tractors and kilowatts. The only ratios which can be estimated empirically are C/V (in pounds) or $C/(V + S)$ (in hours) or C/L or K/L; but these different ratios often only constitute a *distorted* approximation of the M/L ratio, as they are affected *by the evolution of the value or of the price* of the means of production and the means of subsistence (and also, as regards C/V, by the evolution of the real wage).

5

The Reproduction Schemes

From the *individual* capitalist's point of view, every activity is good as long as it brings him a profit. It is all the same to him, whether he obtains this profit by investing in iron and steel, in agriculture, banking, textiles or tourism.

It is not the same from the viewpoint of the capitalist *system*, taken as a whole. All productions are interdependent, none of them can exist and expand independently of the others. Thus, for example, an expansion of the automobile industry requires a parallel expansion of the iron and steel industry (which provides the sheet metal) and of road construction. The expansion of the iron and steel industry requires in its turn an increase in the production of iron ore and of energy etc. while the extension of the road network requires the opening up of new quarries and so on.

In a capitalist society, this equilibrium in the development of different productions is not thought out *a priori* or consciously organized. As explained in chapter 1 (p. 4) and chapter 2, pp. 26–28, the distribution of social labour between different branches of production rests on the free initiative of thousands of capitalists, who are in competition with each other and are only seeking their individual profit. Equilibrium in the allocation of social labour between different branches of production can only be achieved by trial and error, in response to the indications of the market: if the production of sheet metal does not keep up with the production of cars, the price of sheet metal will increase, which will encourage the capitalists to expand this line of production according to the demands of this general interdependence.

Thus the requirements of general interdependence do not reveal themselves directly, as such, to the eyes of the capitalists: they only appear to them indirectly, by way of the market. The reproduction schemes which we will discuss aim to make these requirements explicit or to spell out the equilibrium conditions of capitalist production. These requirements or conditions will be explicated 'in themselves': we shall disregard the actual conditions under which capitalist production takes place and in particular the competition in which the capitalists are involved. The reproduction schemes may therefore be defined as *schemes illustrating, in a formal manner, the abstract conditions necessary for the (theoretical) equilibrium of capitalist production, taken as a whole.*

The most usual schemes examine the relations of interdependence, not between the multitude of particular branches of production, but between two main sections: the section producing the means of production (department I) and the section producing the means of consumption (department II). These two departments are necessarily interdependent: the first has to produce the means of production for both departments and the second has to produce the means of consumption for both the wage-earners and the capitalists of the two departments. Can we specify the necessary relations between the two departments, for there to be (theoretical) equilibrium between their respective productions? Such is the problem examined through the reproduction schemes.[1]

The problem is first examined in the (unrealistic) case of a *simple reproduction* of capitalist production, that is, on the assumption that all the surplus revenue would be consumed by the capitalists and that, consequently, the cycle

$$M — C \ldots P \ldots C^+ — M^+$$

would constantly be reproduced on the same scale. It is then examined in the (realistic) case of *expanded reproduction*, where a part of the surplus revenue is accumulated and where consequently the cycle

$$M — C \ldots P \ldots C^+ — M^+$$

is reproduced on an ever larger scale.

In both cases, the schemes are based for simplicity's sake on the following assumptions.[2]

(1) All the activities are (capitalist) production activities: we disregard the existence of circulation and administration activities (within and outside the two departments).
(2) The rate of surplus value and the composition of capital are identical in both departments.

(3) In both departments, the means of production have to be renewed at the end of a production cycle assumed to be of 1 year.

(4) The monetary expression of value is £1 per hour, so that the symbols and figures used can represent either values (in hours of labour) or prices (in pounds).

SCHEMES OF SIMPLE REPRODUCTION

In the hypothesis of simple reproduction, *all the surplus revenue is consumed* by the capitalists and there is no accumulation. Simple reproduction therefore appears as a succession of identical cycles of production, a succession which permits the *maintenance of social wealth*, but not its increase.

In such a hypothesis, what do the respective productions of the two departments have to be?

(1) Department I has to produce production goods at a total value $(C_1 + V_1 + S_1)$ exactly equal to the value of the means of production used up annually in *both* departments $(C_1 + C_2)$.

(2) Department II has to produce consumption goods of a total value $(C_2 + V_2 + S_2)$ exactly equal to the consumption of both wage-earners and capitalists of *both* departments $(V_1 + S_1 + V_2 + S_2)$.

In algebraic terms, we ought then to have the two following equations, which express the necessary equality between supply (production) and demand for production goods as well as for consumption goods.

$$\text{Supply} \quad = \text{Demand}$$

Production goods: $C_1 + V_1 + S_1 = C_1 + C_2$

Consumption goods: $C_2 + V_2 + S_2 = V_1 + S_1 + V_2 + S_2$

Each of these equations gives us after simplification:

$$C_2 = V_1 + S_1$$

This equation expresses the necessary relation between the two departments for simple reproduction to take place. We can read the equation in the following way: the demand for production goods coming from the department producing consumer goods has to be equal to the demand for consumer goods coming from the department producing production goods.

We can illustrate these different relations by the following example, where the figures correspond to annual data.

Department I: $4000C_1 + 1000V_1 + 1000S_1 = 6000$

Department II: $2000C_2 + 500V_2 + 500S_2 = 3000$

Total: $6000C + 1500V + 1500S = 9000$

We see that the value of supply and the value of demand are equal both for the production goods ($6000 = 4000C_1 + 2000C_2$) and for consumption goods ($3000 = 1000V_1 + 1000S_1 + 500V_2 + 500S_2$).

The simplified equation gives us:

$$2000C_2 = 1000V_1 + 1000S_1.$$

For simple reproduction, the same data are repeated from year to year.

SCHEMES OF EXPANDED REPRODUCTION

In the case of expanded reproduction, only a part of the surplus revenue is *consumed*, the other part being intended for *accumulation*, that is, for the purchase of supplementary means of production and labour-power. The successive cycles of production will therefore begin each time with a larger capital ($C + V$): they will allow an *increase of social wealth*.

What do the respective productions of the two departments have to be in the case of expanded reproduction?

1. Department I has to produce, in the course of a given annual cycle, production goods of a total value ($C_1 + V_1 + S_1$) to satisfy two demands:

(1)   a *replacement* demand, corresponding to the value of the means of production *used up* in the course of a year in *both* departments ($C_1 + C_2$). These means of production have to be replaced in order for the following cycle to begin at least on the same scale;

(2)   an *expansion* demand corresponding to the proportion (c) of the surplus revenue which the capitalists of *both* departments

decide to invest in *supplementary* means of production $(c_1S_1 + c_2S_2)$. These means of production have to be materially produced for the following cycle to begin on a larger scale.[3]

2.   Department II must produce, in the course of a given annual cycle, consumption goods of a total value $(C_2 + V_2 + S_2)$ to correspond, in this case too, to two demands:

(1)   a '*replacement*' demand, corresponding to the value of the means of consumption purchased annually by the wage-earners and the capitalists in *both* departments. If we represent, by k, the fraction of the surplus revenue which the capitalists devote to their consumption, this first part is equal to $V_1 + V_2 + k_1S_1 + k_2S_2$.[4]

(2)   an '*expansion*' demand, corresponding to the proportion (v) of the surplus revenue which capitalists of *both* departments decide to invest in supplementary labour forces: these will come into action in the following cycle and additional means of consumption must be foreseen for them (which will be purchased by the *additional* wages paid). This second part is equal to $v_1S_1 + v_2S_2$.

In algebraic terms, the necessary equality between supply and demand both for production goods and for consumption goods is expressed in the following equations:

$$\text{Supply} \quad = \text{Demand}$$

Production goods: $C_1 + V_1 + S_1 = C_1 + c_1S_1 + C_2 + c_2S_2$

Consumption goods: $C_2 + V_2 + S_2 = V_1 + v_1S_1 + k_1S_1 + V_2 + v_2S_2 + k_2S_2$

Each of these equations gives after simplification:[5]

$$C_2 + c_2S_2 = V_1 + S_1 (v_1 + k_1).$$

Here too we see that the total demand for production goods coming from the department producing consumption goods has to be equal to the total demand for consumption goods coming from the department producing production goods.

The succession of cycles of production can be illustrated by the following quantified example, where we assume that

$$k_1 = k_2 = 50\%; \; c_1 = c_2 = 40\%; \; v_1 = v_2 = 10\%$$

(the proportion of 40 per cent to 10 per cent reflecting the composition of capital, whch we assume equal in both departments and constant through time).

Department I: $\quad 4400C_1 + 1100V_1 + 1100S_1 = 6600$

Department II: $\quad 1600C_2 + \quad 400V_2 + \quad 400S_2 = 2400$

Total: $\qquad\qquad 6000C + 1500V + 1500S = 9000$

We see that the value of the supply of production goods exceeds the simple replacement demand $(6600 > 4400\ C_1 + 1600\ C_2)$ and that the value of the supply of consumption goods is less than the sum total of wages and surplus revenue $(2400 < 1500\ V + 1500\ S)$.

Of the 1500 of surplus revenue, a half only is used for capitalist consumption (i.e. 750, of which $550 = k_1S_1$ and $200 = k_2S_2$). The rest is used, on one hand, for the purchase of supplementary means of production $(+600,$ of which $440 = c_1S_1$ and $160 = c_2S_2)$, on the other, for the purchase of supplementary labour-power $(+150$ of which $110 = v_1S_1$ and $40 = v_2S_2)$. We thus have the double equation between supply and demand:

Department I: $\quad 6600 = (4400C_1 + 440c_1S_1 + (1600C_2 + 160C_2S_2)$

Department II: $2400 = (1100V_1 + 110v_1S_1) + 550k_1S_1 +$
$\qquad\qquad\qquad (400V_2 + 40v_2S_2) + 200k_2S_2$

The cycle of the following year will then appear as follows:

Department I $\quad 4840\ C_1 + 1210\ V_1 + 1210\ S_1 = 7260$

Department II $\quad 1760\ C_2 + 440\ V_2 + \quad 440\ S_2 = 2640$

Total $\qquad\qquad 6600\ C + 1650\ V + 1650\ S = 9900$

The same process of expansion of all the variables $(C_1, C_2,$ etc.) will recur from year to year.

NOTES

1. As the reproduction schemes disregard the actual conditions in which capitalist production is carried on, they cannot by themselves explain the real tendencies and characteristics of capitalist society: they cannot, for example, explain the increasing mechanization of the production processes, the growth of monopolies, the export of capital, the convergences or divergences of interest within the capitalist class etc. The reader who is not interested in the problem of reproduction schemes

(at least as it is presented here) can, without risk of losing the thread of the argument, move on directly to chapter 6.

2. The first two assumptions enable us to eliminate the problems of transfers of surplus revenue (see chapter 6) and to examine the schemes in their specific characters. Assumptions 3 and 4 enable us to simplify the presentation of the schemes.

3. Since the production of department I has to correspond to *a demand exceeding simple replacement*, we have (in contrast to the schemes of simple reproduction):

$$C_1 \ 1 \ V_1 + S_1 > C_1 + C_2$$

(from which we get $C_2 < V_1 + S_1$).

4. Since a part of $(S_1 + S_2)$ is not consumed by the capitalists, we have (in contrast to the schemes of simple reproduction):

$$C_2 + V_2 + D_2 < V_1 + V_2 + S_1 + S_2$$

(from which we get also $C_2 < V_1 + S_1$).

5. We know that the surplus revenue of each department falls into three parts: c for accumulation in means of production, v for accumulation in labour-power, k for the capitalists' consumption. So we have:

$$c_1 + v_1 + k_1 = 1 \text{ and } c_2 + v_2 + k_2 = 1$$

From here, we obtain:

for the first equation:

$$C_2 + c_2 S_2 = C_1 + V_1 + S_1 - C_1 - c_1 S_1$$
$$C_2 + c_2 S_2 = V_1 + S_1 \ (1 - c_1)$$
$$C_2 + c_2 S_2 = V_1 + S_1 \ (v_1 + k_1)$$

for the second equation:

$$C_2 + V_2 + S_2 - V_2 - v_2 S_2 - k_2 S_2 = V_1 + v_1 S_1 + k_1 S_1$$
$$C_2 + S_2 \ (1 - v_2 - k_2) = V_1 + S_1 \ (v_1 + k_1)$$
$$C_2 + c_2 S_2 = V_1 + S_1 \ (v_1 + k_1).$$

6

The Surplus Revenue Transfer
Schemes

Chapter 3 was concerned with the *general* phenomenon of capitalist profit. In it we proved that the source of the general profit, of the whole profit of the capitalist class, lay in the exploitation of wage-earning workers: the profit has its source in the 'free' surplus labour of wage-earners employed in commodity production, surplus labour which creates a surplus value and a surplus revenue for the benefit of the capitalists.

This proof left unanswered a classic objection to the theory of surplus value. How do we explain the large profit of highly mechanized (even automated) enterprises or branches of production, employing relatively few wage-earners? We will see that *redistributions of surplus revenue take place within the production sector*: the profit of the production sector taken as a whole remains based on the surplus revenue created by the wage-earners, but *a part of the surplus revenue created in the less-mechanized (or less-protected) enterprises or branches of production is redistributed to the more-mechanized (or more-protected) enterprises or branches of production.* Because of this, the less-mechanized enterprises and the less-protected branches will obtain a rate of profit lower than that of the more-mechanized enterprises and the more-protected branches. Hence the drive towards mechanization among the different enterprises, and the rush towards protection among the different branches of production – tendencies to which we will return in subsequent chapters.

The proof in chapter 3, in emphasizing the fact that new revenues are created in *production*, showed indirectly that a part of the total surplus revenue has to be used to finance activities of circulation and of non-commodity production. Bearing in mind the division of social activities into three sectors called respectively *production* (i.e.

commodity production), *administration* (or non-commodity production) and *circulation*, we can say that *a part of the surplus revenue created
in the production sector is redistributed to the administration and circulation
sectors*, where it constitutes the source of specific wages and profits.[1]
Hence certain complementary aspects of the competition between
capitalists, namely the competition between the industrialists (production sector), and the merchants and financiers (circulation sector)
for the share-out of the surplus revenue available and also the
competition between them to lessen the burden of the levies intended
for the administration sector.

This chapter analyses primarily the *mechanisms* of transfers of
surplus revenue: the first section explains *internal* transfers of surplus
revenue within the production sector; the second section explains
external transfers to the circulation and administration sectors, while
the third section illustrates the combined action of the various kinds
of transfer analysed. *Three general assumptions* underlie the analysis of
the mechanisms of transfer.

(1) We assume that the production sector comprises *only capitalist
     enterprises*, to the exclusion of simple commodity producers
     and of public enterprises.
(2) We assume that there is an *equilibrium between supply and
     demand*, and that all goods produced are sold.
(3) We also assume that the purchases of means of production
     and of labour-power have to be renewed at the beginning of
     each year, so that C + V *represents both the money-capital laid
     out* (on the basis of which the profit rate is calculated) *and the
     annual production cost*.

(Chapter 7 will show the *significance* of the surplus revenue transfer
schemes for the analysis of various real-world problems. In doing so,
it will, when necessary, consider the presence of independent
producers or of public enterprises and the possibility of a disequilibrium between supply and demand.)

SURPLUS REVENUE TRANSFERS WITHIN THE PRODUCTION
SECTOR

To simplify the analysis by limiting it to essentials, we will assume,
not only that the production enterprises are all of the capitalist type
but, in addition, that they employ *only productive wage-earners*: we

disregard the group of wage-earners who are employed in circulation or administration activities within the production sector.

Three cases of redistribution (or transfer) have to be distinguished:

(1) Transfers of surplus revenue between *unequally mechanized enterprises* within the same branch of production: the redistributions of surplus revenue take place from the less mechanized to the more mechanized enterprises; their effect is to *differentiate* the *particular* rates of profit within each branch.

(2) Transfers of surplus revenue between *unequally mechanized branches* of production: the redistributions of surplus revenue take place from the less-mechanized to the more-mechanized branches; their effect is to *equalize* the *average* rate of profit of the different branches.

(3) Transfers of surplus revenue between *unequally protected branches* of production: the redistributions of surplus revenue take place from the less-protected to the more-protected branches; their effect is to *differentiate* the *average* rate of profit of the different branches.

In real life, these three types of transfer are in play at the same time, which can offset or reinforce their respective effects as outlined above. But for the requirements of the analysis, we must study each of the causes of transfer separately, abstracting from the other possible causes.

The analysis of the different transfer mechanisms will be illustrated by numerical examples, presented simultaneously in the form of tables and diagrams. To make the presentation of these tables and diagrams easier, we will assume that the monetary expression of values (E) is £1 per hour. This being so, the symbols used (C, V, S, for total magnitudes, c, v, s, for magnitudes per unit produced) express both values (in hours of labour) and prices (in pounds).[2]

Transfers between Unequally Productive Enterprises within the Same Branch of Production

In order to isolate this first type of transfer of surplus revenue, we are going to assume that the branch of production in question (within which various unequally productive enterprises operate) is characterized, by a *degree of mechanization* (the ratio C/V) and also by a *degree of protection* exactly equal to the average.[3] Such is the case of branch II in the quantified example appearing in Table 6.1 and in Figure 6.1.

TABLE 6.1   Transfers of surplus revenue between unequally mechanized enterprises within the same 'average' branch of production

	UNITS	ENTERPRISE 1	ENTERPRISE 2	ENTERPRISE 3	WHOLE OF BRANCH II
Degree of protection					Average
Degree of mechanization (C/V)		9	4	2	4 (= average)
K	(£)	4000	3000	3000	10000
L	(number)	100	150	250	500
C	(£ or hours)	3600	2400	2000	8000
V	(£ or hours)	400	600	1000	2000
S	(£ or hours)	400	600	1000	2000
C + V + S	(£ or hours)	4400	3600	4000	12000
Q	(units)	450	300	250	1000
c	(£ or hours)	8	8	8	8
v	(£ or hours)	0.9	2	4	2
s	(£ or hours)	0.9	2	4	2
c + v + s	(£ or hours)	9.8	12	16	12
S/K	(%)	10%	20%	30%	20%
Simple price	(£)	12	12	12	12
Price of production	(£)	—	—	—	—
Regulated price	(£)	—	—	—	—
p	(£)	3.1	2	0	2
P	(£)	1400	600	0	2000
P/K	(%)	30%	20%	0%	20%
P − S	(£)	+ 1000	0	− 1000	0

Unequally productive enterprises produce the same commodity but with different unit individual values: the more productive enterprises require less labour – past and present – to produce one unit of the commodity in question, the less productive ones require more labour to produce one unit of the same commodity. Productivity and unit individual values may differ between enterprises for several reasons: differences in the degree of mechanization (in the M/L and C/V ratios), difference in natural conditions (varying fertility of soils, for instance), differences in the intensity of labour etc. The most influential among all these possible factors are without any doubt the differences in the degrees of mechanization.

Differences in unit individual values due to differences in mechanization
Table 6.1 and Figure 6.1 describe the situation of three enterprises (or
groups of enterprises) which are taken as constituting an 'average'
branch of production (branch II in the example).

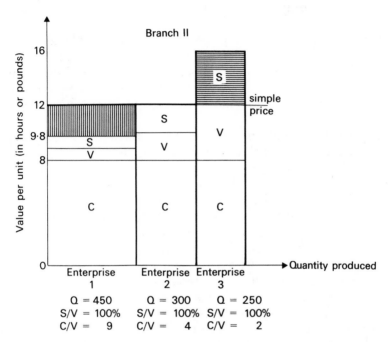

FIGURE 6.1 *Transfers of surplus revenue between unequally mechanized
enterprises within the same "average" branch of production. This figure uses the data
of Table 6.1. The area hatched with horizontal lines represents the surplus revenue
lost in transfer; the area hatched with vertical lines represents the surplus revenue
gained through transfers.*

The three enterprises are characterized by *the same rate of surplus
value* S/V (equal to 100 per cent). The length of the working day is in
each case 8 hours (hence the amount of present labour S + V is in
each case equal to the number of workers L × 8) and the value of the
labour-power is assumed in each case to be equal to 4 hours (hence
V, that is, the corresponding value or the variable capital, is in each
case equal to L × 4).

The technology employed differs from one enterprise to the other:
enterprise 1 is the most mechanized, enterprise 3, the least, while
enterprise 2 operates with 'average' technology within the branch.

Assuming that all other circumstances are equal (natural conditions, intensity of labour, etc.), these differences in the technology employed, in the degree of mechanization, are simultaneously reflected by differences:

(1)   in the composition of capital or C/V ratio (this ratio is highest in 1, lowest in 3);
(2)   in the quantities produced Q (the more highly mechanized the enterprises, the greater their productive capacity);[4]
(3)   in the unit individual values (c + v + s): to produce one unit, 9.8 hours of labour – past and present – are required in enterprise 1, 12 hours in enterprise 2, 16 hours in enterprise 3.

At what level will the sale price be fixed? In a situation of generalized free competition – and assuming the average C/V ratio is equal in all *branches* of production – the sale price in each branch is equal to the simple price, corresponding to the *social value* of the commodity (equal to the labour time required *on average* to produce it).[5] In the example, the sale price is therefore 12 and this sale price applies to all the commodities. Thus, enterprise 1 cannot hope to sell its commodities at 16: potential customers would rather buy from competitors 1 and 2 producing and selling at a lower price. Conversely, it is not in the interest of enterprise 1 to sell its commodities at 9.8: it would make more – and without losing any customers – by selling them at 12.[6]

With the sale price at 12, enterprise 1 obtains a profit per unit (p) of 3.1 (while the surplus revenue per unit (s) is only 0.9). This gives it a total profit of 1400, while the surplus revenue created by its 100 wage-earners is only 400. The additional profit of 1000 is exactly balanced by the fact that, at the other extreme, enterprise 3 makes no profit (the market price enables it barely to cover its production cost C+V), while its 250 wage-earners have created a surplus revenue (have provided surplus labour) equal to 1000. As to the average enterprise, it makes a profit exactly equal to the surplus revenue created by its own wage-earners.

Generalizing these observations, we can say (within the context of the assumptions made to build up this example), that the *total profit* of a branch of industry *is equal to the total surplus revenue* created by the wage-earners in that branch (2000 in the example); but the *differences in mechanization* from one enterprise to another *give rise to a redistribution* among the capitalists *of this total surplus revenue*. This redistribution is brought about automatically by the market: the existence of a uniform price, applicable to all enterprises, penalizes the backward ones (where high unit values reflect a relative waste of human labour) and benefits the most advanced ones (where low unit values reflect a relatively economical use of human labour).

We can consider the extreme case of an entirely automated enterprise, not employing a single wage-earner ($L = 0$). Under this assumption, present labour is non-existent ($V + S = 0$) and so no surplus revenue can be created ($S = 0$). The enterprise will, however, make a profit: as the unit individual value of its commodities (reduced to 'c') is lower than the average, it will benefit indirectly (thanks to the uniform sale price) from the surplus revenue created in the least efficient enterprises.

Differences in unit individual values due to other factors
Before turning to other cases of transfer of surplus revenue, it is important to note that, in the present case, it is the *difference in unit individual values* (together with the existence of a uniform sale price corresponding to the average unit value) which is the cause of the redistribution. This difference in unit individual values is *most often* the result, as in the above example, of differences in the degree of mechanization (in the C/V ratio). We can, however, think of cases where the technology of production is the same in different enterprises but unit individual values differ *for other reasons*: thus, with the same technology, differences in natural conditions (varying fertility in soils) or in the intensity of labour will be reflected in differences in unit values and will give rise to the same phenomenon of redistribution of surplus revenue.

Is value creation affected by differences in mechanization, skill and intensity?
In practice, differences in the degree of mechanization are normally *combined* with differences in *skill* and *intensity* of labour. A more advanced technology does in fact require higher qualifications on the part of the workers (engineers, technicians etc.) responsible for planning, directing and controlling the production process; it also makes it possible to increase the intensity of labour by the mass of workers, subordinated to the machine and to its rhythm.[7]

But these simultaneous differences in technology, in the skill and intensity of labour are not reflected in differences in the creation of value and of surplus value. In fact, the more mechanized, skilled and intensive labour in a particular enterprise has the effect of *reducing the unit individual value of the commodities* produced there, which *brings about a redistribution of the total surplus revenue*: the capitalist employing this type of labour obtains a profit higher than the surplus revenue created by his wage-earners, at the expense of his less efficient competitors. But *the more mechanized, skilled and intensive labour does not create more value* (nor more surplus value) than the more manual, less skilled and less intensive labour.

Transfers Between Unequally Mechanized Branches of Production[8]

Here we have a case that is analogous in principle.

We saw that a less mechanized *enterprise* (where the C/V ratio is lower than the average) suffered a transfer of surplus revenue to the benefit of its more mechanized competitors. Similarly, the relations between *branches of production*, between industries: the less mechanized branches (where C/V ratio is lower than the average of all branches) suffer a transfer of surplus revenue to the benefit of the more mechanized ones (where the C/V ratio is higher than the average).

Why is this so? Let us look at Table 6.2, in which we take up the data relating to the total of branch II and compare the data relating to two other branches (I and III). To isolate the type of transfer we are examining, we disregard the differences between the enterprises within each branch of production and assume besides that none of the branches enjoy any special protection.

The example is built up in such a way that the total capital (K = C + V) is the same for the three branches (K = 10 000) while the composition of capital (C/V) differs from one to the other: it is higher than the average in branch I (C/V = 9), equal to the average in II (C/V = 4) and lower than the average in III (C/V = 2.3).[9] As we assume the rate of surplus value to be identical in the three branches (S/V = 100 per cent), the differences in the C/V ratio are reflected in differences in the quantity of surplus revenue produced and in the 'rate of valorization' S/K.[10] Logically, this ratio is higher in branch III which employs proportionately few machines and many workers (and hence produces a comparatively large amount of surplus revenue in relation to the capital laid out), and it is lower in branch I which employs proportionately many machines and few workers (and hence produces a comparatively small amount of surplus revenue in relation to the capital laid out).

Can the average rate of profit in each branch (P/K) be equal to the rate of valorization (S/K)? This is impossible, if we assume that no branch is protected and that capital can therefore move freely from one to the other. It is impossible, for branch I, the most mechanized, would find itself penalized by a rate of profit of 10 per cent,

TABLE 6.2   *Transfers of surplus revenue between unequally mechanized branches of production.*

	UNITS	BRANCH I	BRANCH II	BRANCH III	BRANCHES I–III
Degree of protection		Average	Average	Average	Average
Degree of mechanization (C/V)		9	4	2.3	4
K	(£)	10000	10000	10000	30000
L	(number)	250	500	750	1500
C	(£ or hours)	9000	8000	7000	24000
V	(£ or hours)	1000	2000	3000	6000
S	(£ or hours)	1000	2000	3000	6000
C + V + S	(£ or hours)	11000	12000	13000	36000
Q	(units)	500	1000	250	—
c	(£ or hours)	18	8	28	—
v	(£ or hours)	2	2	12	—
s	(£ or hours)	2	2	12	—
c + v + s	(£ or hours)	22	12	52	—
S/K	(%)	10%	20%	30%	20%
Simple price	(£)	22	12	52	—
Price of production	(£)	24	12	48	—
Regulated price	(£)	—	—	—	—
p	(£)	4	2	8	—
P	(£)	2000	2000	2000	6000
P/K	(%)	20%	20%	20%	20%
P − S	(£)	+ 1000	0	− 1000	0

compared to a rate of profit of 30 per cent in branch III, the least mechanized. Actually, the equilibrium of capitalist production requires that (average) capitalists get the same rate of profit whatever branch of production they have invested in and whatever the C/V ratio in that branch. Prices in each branch of production must therefore be such as to assure the same average rate of profit in all of them. *These prices, which guarantee the same average rate of profit to all branches, are called prices of production.*

In the example of Table 6.2, taken up in Figure 6.2, these prices of production are respectively £24, £12 and £48 for the three branches in question. They assure a profit per unit produced (p) of £4, £2 and £8 respectively and a rate of profit (P/K) equal to 20 per cent for each branch.[11]

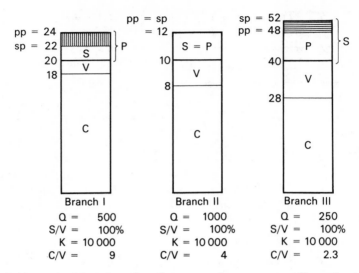

FIGURE 6.2   *Transfers of surplus revenue between unequally mechanized branches of production. This Figure uses the data of Table 6.2. The areas hatched with horizontal lines and vertical lines represent the surplus revenue respectively* lost *and* gained *through transfer.* sp = *simple price;* pp = *price of production.*

Table 6.2 and Figure 6.2 enable us to draw the following conclusions.

1.   When the composition of capital (C/V) varies from branch to branch, the branches where C/V is *lower* than the social average obtain a profit lower than the surplus revenue created (P < S); those where C/V is *higher* than the social average obtain a profit higher than the surplus revenue created (P > S); those where C/V is *equal* to the social average, obtain a profit equal to the surplus revenue (P = S). *Total profit remains equal to total surplus revenue,* produced by the surplus labour of all wage-earners. But *this total profit is redistributed between the different capitalist branches* of production: it tends to be redistributed proportionately to the capital sums laid out in each branch, in such a way that the average profit is the same throughout.[12] (This process is generally referred to as the 'equalization of the rates of profit'.)

However, the fact that the average rate of profit is identical *from branch to branch* does not imply that the *particular* rates of profit are identical *within* the same branch. Within each branch, as we saw earlier, the more efficient enterprises (where the unit value is lower) will benefit from a higher rate of profit than the average, while the less efficient have to be content with a lower rate of profit.[13]

2.   When the composition of capital (C/V) varies from branch to branch, *the equilibrium price is not the simple price* (c + v + s) corresponding to the social value, *but the price of production* (c + v + p) ensuring the equalization of average rates of profit. The price of production is higher, equal or lower than the simple price, according to whether the branch has a higher, equal or lower C/V ratio than the social average.

However, the price of production, just like the simple price under simple (non-capitalist) commodity production, is nothing other than a theoretical equilibrium price and not a market price. The simple price simply ensures a norm of equilibrium in the hypothesis of generalized simple commodity production: when commodities are sold at the simple price in such a model, each producer (providing he produces in average conditions within his branch) obtains a revenue *equal* to that obtained by (average) producers in other branches. In the same way, the price of production ensures a norm of equilibrium in the case of a capitalist production: when commodities are sold at the price of production in such a system, each capitalist (providing he produces in the average conditions of his branch) obtains a *rate of profit equal* to that obtained by (average) capitalists in other branches. But such an equilibrium price is not an actual price, an observable market price. Market prices diverge to various extents from the norm: in a situation of generalized free competition, competitive market prices fluctuate around the norm depending on the short-term fluctuations of supply and demand within each branch; in a situation where protection and regulation prevail, regulated market prices diverge from the norm depending on the degree of protection enjoyed by the different branches. While, in a model of simple commodity production, market prices revolve around an axis constituted by simple prices, *in a capitalist system, market prices revolve around an axis constituted by prices of production.*

Transfers Between Unequally Protected Branches of Production

Besides the differences in the C/V ratio between branches of production, *differences in the degree of protection* enjoyed by different branches can also bring about redistributions of surplus revenue between them.

Marxist Economic Theory

As we saw in the preceding paragraphs, the market price of each commodity tends to move towards its price of production and the average rates of profit of the various branches tend to equal out. But this is only true under the assumption of *generalized free competition*: for this, *capitalists must be in a position to move their capital freely* from one branch to another and *market prices must be able to fluctuate freely* in response to changes in the relations between supply and demand.

Reality is far from corresponding with these two requirements. It is characterized rather by *multiple forms of protection*, due sometimes to market structures, sometimes to interventions by the public authorities: there are numerous branches of production where competition is limited by *restrictions on the entry of new capital*, whether these

TABLE 6.3   *Transfers of surplus revenue between unequally mechanized and unequally protected branches of production.*

	UNITS	BRANCH I	BRANCH II	BRANCH III	BRANCHES I–III
Degree of protection		High	Average	Low	Average
Degree of mechanization (C/V)		9	4	2.3	4
K	(£)	10000	10000	10000	30000
L	(number)	250	500	750	1500
C	(£ or hours)	9000	8000	7000	24000
V	(£ or hours)	1000	2000	3000	6000
S	(£ or hours)	1000	2000	3000	6000
C + V + S	(£ or hours)	11000	12000	13000	36000
Q	(units)	500	1000	250	—
c	(£ or hours)	18	8	28	—
v	(£ or hours)	2	2	12	—
s	(£ or hours)	2	2	12	—
c + v + s	(£ or hours)	22	12	52	—
S/K	(%)	10%	20%	30%	20%
Simple price	(£)	22	12	52	—
Price of production	(£)	24	12	48	—
Regulated price	(£)	26	12	44	—
p	(£)	6	2	4	—
P	(£)	3000	2000	1000	6000
P/K	(%)	30%	20%	10%	20%
P − S	(£)	+ 2000	0	− 2000	0

restrictions are natural or artificial; and there are also numerous branches of production where *regulated prices* prevail, whether these prices are fixed solely by the capitalists or by the intervention of the public authorities. These divergences from free competition are inevitable and cumulative, as we will see in chapter 8. Whether to increase their rate of profit or simply to defend it, all branches feel it necessary to surround themselves with forms of protection. But not all branches are equally successful in this: restrictions to entry appear more or less effective according to different branches; regulated prices are fixed at a higher or lower level according to the (economic and political) strength each of them enjoys. The result is that different branches will have *differentiated average rates of profit* rather than an identical average rate of profit for all: the branches enjoying a higher degree of protection than the average will obtain relatively high average rates of profit, those having to be content with a lower degree of protection will obtain relatively low average rates of profit.

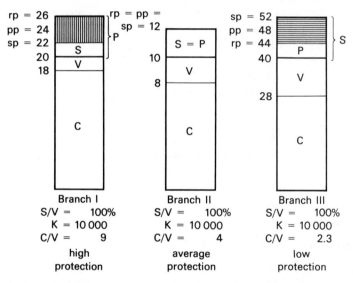

FIGURE 6.3   *Transfers of surplus revenue between unequally mechanized and unequally protected branches of production. This Figure uses the data of Table 6.3. The areas hatched with horizontal and vertical lines represent the surplus revenue respectively lost and gained through transfers. sp = simple price; pp = price of production; rp = regulated price.*

In the example of Table 6.3, taken up in Figure 6.3, we assume that branch I benefits from a higher degree of protection than the average; its regulated price is higher than the equilibrium price of production (£26 instead of £24) and the rate of profit is higher than the average (30 per cent instead of 20 per cent). The situation is assumed to be exactly the opposite in branch III, while branch II is average is all respects.

However, a higher or lower degree of protection, in itself, makes no difference to the labour-time, to the value of the labour-power or to the number of wage-earners employed; so it affects neither the rate of surplus value nor the mass of surplus value created by all branches together and by each of them separately. Thus, the differentiations in the rates of profit involve a redistribution of surplus revenue at the expense of the relatively less protected branches of production and to the advantage of the relatively more protected branches. *Total profit remains equal to total surplus revenue*, which continues to correspond to the surplus labour of all wage-earners. But this *total surplus revenue is redistributed among capitalists according to the degree of protection* which each branch enjoys.[14]

The differences in the degree of protection enjoyed by different branches of production are therefore reflected in differences in the *average* rates of profit for each branch. On these differences between industries are superimposed differences between individual enterprises: within each branch, the *particular* rates of profit vary, as before, according to the degree of efficiency of each enterprise.

SURPLUS REVENUE TRANSFERS FROM THE PRODUCTION SECTOR TO THE CIRCULATION AND ADMINISTRATION SECTORS

Capitalists investing in the production sector carry out the complete cycle of operations

$$M - C_0 \ldots P \ldots C_1 C_1^+ - M^+.$$

Other capitalists specialize in the *circulation* sector: whether in the trade of commodities (cycle $M - C - M^+$) or of money (cycle $M - M^+$). As we have already pointed out on several occasions, the circulation of commodities and of money creates neither use-value nor value; consequently, in this sector, the capitalists' *profits* and the *wages* of the (unproductive) wage-earners involve a charge on the revenues created in the production sector.

The *administration* sector produces a variety of collective goods and services (education, justice, national defence etc.) which are not com-

commodities. These activies produce use-values but they create neither value nor revenue: consequently, the *wages* of the (unproductive) workers of this sector equally involve a charge on the revenues created in the production sector.

A final charge — not mentioned so far and to be touched on rapidly in this section — results from the existence of *land ownership*. The land is a special type of 'good' from several points of view: it is a 'gift of nature' which, in its natural state, involves no human labour (so it has no value, in the strict sense); moreover, it only exists in limited quantities (it is not reproducible, as are the majority of commodities); it admits of private ownership (unlike other natural goods — the air, for example); finally it is indispensable for the exercise of various activities, particularly building and agriculture. These characteristics enable the landowner to demand the payment of a price (the ground-rent) from the builders or farmers to whom he hands over the use of the land. This price does not correspond to any value or to any labour; it has as its origin the sole fact of the private ownership of the land; the owner's revenue, as such, must therefore involve a charge on other revenues.[15]

Table 6.4 illustrates such charges. We have taken the aggregate data (K, L, V, S) concerning the production sector from the Table 6.3; we have added data relating to the other sectors, while — for the sake of simplicity — making the following assumptions.

(1)   The circulation sector does not comprise any productive wage-earners (just as the production sector does not comprise any unproductive wage-earners).[16]

(2)   The wages of the unproductive workers and the ground-rents are entirely charged on the surplus revenue or capitalist profits and not on the wages of the productive workers.[17]

The figures relating to money-capital (K) and to the number of wage-earners (L) are arbitrary, as is the amount of the ground-rent (R), but the figures relating to the wages and to the rates of profit are not. The wages of the unproductive workers in the circulation and administration sectors have to be equal to the wages of the productive workers in the production sector (in the example, each worker (L) receives a wage of 4). Equally, the capitalists have to obtain the same rate of profit (P/K) whatever the sector they specialize in (production, circulation of commodities or of money).

Table 6.4 should be read in the following way. The new value created (in the production sector) is 12 000. One half constitutes the

TABLE 6.4   Transfers of surplus revenue outside the production sector

Sectors			Value and revenue created (in hours or in pounds)			Incomes distributed (in pounds)							Transfers of surplus revenue (in pounds)
	K	L	V	S	V + S	V	V'	R	P	Total	S/K	P/K	
Production	30000	1500	6000	6000	12000	6000	—	—	3000	9000	20%	10%	− 3000
Circulation													
of commodities	2000	100	—	—	—	—	400	—	200	600	—	10%	+ 600
of money	2000	100	—	—	—	—	400	—	200	600	—	10%	+ 600
Administration	—	200	—	—	—	—	800	—	—	800	—	—	+ 800
Landed property	—	—	—	—	⌐	—	—	1000	—	1000	—	—	+ 1000
Total	34000	1900	6000	6000	12000	6000	1600	1000	3400	12000	20%	10%	0

S (Total row): 6000 (boxed)

S (V+S column, Total row): 6000 (boxed)

V' + R (Total row): 6000 (boxed, bracketed)

wages of the productive workers (V = 6000), the other half the surplus revenue created by them (S = 6000). This surplus revenue has to finance the wages of the unproductive workers (V' = 1600) and the ground-rent (R = 1000). Some aggregate profit P remains, equal to 3400 (= 6000 − 1600 − 1000). This aggregate profit is distributed between production, circulation of commodities and circulation of money is such a way that the (equilibrium) rates of profit are equal (at least for the 'average' capitalists) (P/K = 10%). The sum of the incomes distributed is equal to the sum of the revenue created (12 000), but the sum of the surplus revenue (6000) is no longer equal to the sum of the profits (3400): in view of the existence of unproductive workers and of land-owners, *the total surplus revenue is distributed in profits, wages of unproductive workers and ground-rents* (6000 = 3400 + 1600 + 1000).[18] Because of this, the average rate of profit (P/K = 10%) is necessarily lower than the 'rate of valorization' (S/K = 20%).

SYNTHESIS OF THE SURPLUS REVENUE TRANSFER SCHEMES

A Diagrammatic Illustration

Figure 6.4 attempts to illustrate the *combined action* of the different transfers of surplus revenue analysed above. Taking up the main part of the data of the previous tables,[19] it presents them in a *new form*, intended to enable us to compare the transfers between enterprises and transfers between branches as well as the transfers outside the production sector.

The novelty consists in representing, on the horizontal axis, the *number of workers* (and no longer the quantities produced) and on the vertical axis, the data expressed *per worker*: both the value created per worker (corresponding value and surplus value) and the revenue obtained per worker (wage or profit per worker). Each rectangle thus indicates an *aggregate* of value created or of revenue obtained in an enterprise, a branch or a sector.

On the horizontal axis, the wage-earners are distributed between the three sectors (production = 1500 L, circulation = 200 L, administration = 200 L). (As before, we disregard activities of circulation and administration within the production sector, as well as activities of production and administration within the circulation sector). As landed property is not associated with any labour (L = 0), the rectangle representing the rent charged is placed separately from the rest.

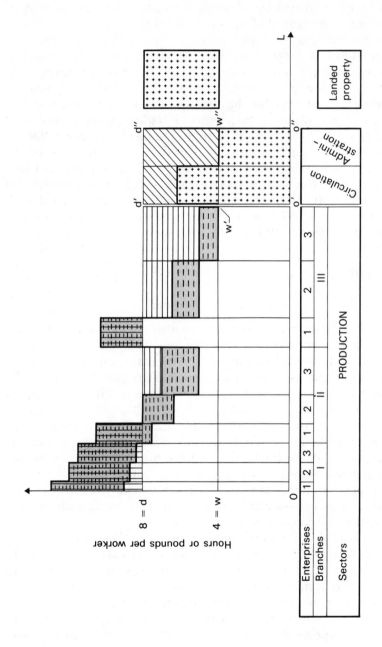

FIGURE 6.4 Synthesis of surplus revenue transfers

On the vertical axis, we first have the daily labour-time of each wage-earner (= 8). The total amount of labour performed by all wage-earners is represented by the rectangle odd"o" (= 1900 × 8 = 15 200); the total amount of new value created (in the production sector) is represented by the rectangle odd'o' (= 1500 × 8 = 12 000). On the vertical axis, we then have the division between necessary labour and surplus labour, assumed the same for each wage-earner (= 4/4). The total amount of surplus revenue (surplus value) is given by the rectangle wdd'w' (=1500 × 4 = 6000), the total amount of wages by the rectangle oww"o" (= 1900 × 4 = 7600, of which 6000 are paid to the productive and 1600 to the unproductive workers).

The *internal* transfers of surplus revenue in the production sector (the only ones to occur, if we disregard unproductive sectors and landed property) are represented by the areas cross-hatched with horizontal lines (representing the surplus revenue lost) or with vertical lines (representing the surplus revenue gained in transfer). The *external* transfers of surplus revenue are represented by the areas marked with − signs (representing the surplus revenue lost by the different enterprises or branches of the production sector) or by + signs (representing the surplus revenue appropriated by the unproductive sectors and by the landowners). The areas which are cross-hatched horizontally must be equal to those cross-hatched vertically, just as the areas marked with − must be equal to those market with +.[20, 21]

If we disregard the unproductive sectors and landed property, the situation for the three branches of industry is as follows. In branch II (where the degrees of mechanization and of protection are equal to the average), the total profit is equal to the total surplus revenue but enterprise 3 loses a part of its surplus revenue to the advantage of enterprise 1, the most efficient. Branch I (with degrees of mechanization and of protection higher than the average) obtains a total profit higher than the total surplus revenue; in the example in Figure 6.4, even the marginal enterprise 3 obtains a profit higher than the surplus revenue created. Branch III (mechanization and protection lower than the average) suffers an overall loss of surplus revenue: this loss is in fact borne by enterprises 2 and 3, while enterprise 1, enjoying a degree of efficiency clearly higher than its competitors, achieves a profit higher than the surplus revenue created.

The financing of the sectors of circulation (wages + profits) and of administration (wages only) reduces the profit available in all the branches and in all the enterprises. This reduction is brought about by the levy of taxes or of National Insurance contributions, by allowing commercial margins, by interest payments on borrowed capital, by the payment of ground-rent. The amount of the reduction depends on the balance of forces existing between each enterprise or branch, on the one hand, and the state, the commercial and financial sector and the landowners on the other. In the example in Figure 6.4, only branch I still makes a profit slightly higher than the surplus revenue created; branches II and III lose surplus revenue and for enterprise 3 in branch III, the profit available is reduced to zero.

Two Conclusions

Having illustrated the combined action of the different transfers of surplus revenue, we will conclude this chapter by emphasizing two essential points. The first one concerns the concrete forms in which transfers of surplus revenue take place. The second one concerns the source of capitalist profit.

The concrete forms of surplus revenue transfers

There is a clear-cut difference in the concrete forms in which redistributions of surplus revenue take place *outside* and *within* the production sector.

Within the production sector, redistributions take place automatically through the mere existence of market prices: if the latter correspond to simple prices, a redistribution is made automatically from the less efficient to the more efficient enterprises; if they correspond to production prices or to regulated prices, a redistribution is made automatically from the less-mechanized or less-protected branches to the more-mechanized or more-protected ones. These redistributions therefore involve *no actual payment* on the part of the capitalists suffering the redistributions and no actual payment in favour of the capitalists who benefit from it. They tend to take place completely without the knowledge of the capitalists concerned.

It is a different matter for the redistributions *outside* the production sector. The latter are revealed very clearly to the capitalists concerned, for they involve various *actual payments* levied on the surplus revenue or profit: payment of interest and dividends to money lenders, payment of taxes to finance the administration sector, payment of *rent* to landowners.[22]

The source of capitalist profit

Differences of mechanization or of protection do not *create* a new profit: they merely bring about *redistributions* of a given total amount of surplus revenue, which corresponds to the surplus value created solely by the productive workers.

The higher rate of profit of a *protected branch* (like branch I) should not mislead us. Protection does not *create* profit: it makes possible a redistribution, to the benefit of the protected branch, of a part of the total surplus revenue created by all workers.

In the same way, within any branch, the higher rate of profit of an *enterprise* which is *more advanced on the technological side* should not mislead us either. A machine embodying the most advanced technology cannot ever produce any value or surplus value: its value is simply transferred, without any addition, to the commodities produced. The higher profit of the most efficient enterprise (enterprise 1) in each branch (I, II and III) always corresponds to the surplus revenue created by wage-earners, but not necessarily (or not entirely) by the wage-earners of the enterprise in question. In reality, *the utilization of an advanced technology by a particular capitalist* always puts him in a favourable situation *to seize, at the expense of his competitors, some part of the aggregate surplus revenue created by all workers and created solely by them.*

NOTES

1. A part of this surplus revenue, as we shall see, is also transformed into revenue for the land-owners.
2. We must not lose sight of the fact that values and prices constitute different, non-commensurable orders of magnitude. One is liable to forget this when $E = 1$ and values and prices are in fact expressed by identical figures.
3. The concept of 'protection' will be clarified when we move on to the third case of transfer of surplus revenue within the production sector. Let us observe that the assumption of mechanization and of protection equal to the average is obviously complied with if we make the (stronger) assumption that *all* branches have *the same C/V ratio* and that they are in a situation of *generalized free competition* (complete absence of protection).
4. In the arguments in this chapter, we assume that the productive capacities are always fully employed: a doubling of capacity is reflected in a doubling of production (we therefore disregard the influences of underemployment of productive capacity on the unit costs of production and on the unit values).
5. The simple price is calculated by dividing the total value of a branch's production by the total quantity produced in that branch. In the example, the simple price calculated in this way ($12\,000 : 1000 = 12$)

corresponds exactly to the unit value in the 'average' enterprise (3600 : 300 = 12).

6. From a *dynamic* point of view, it would, however, be in enterprise 1's interest to sell slightly below 12 in order to capture some of enterprise 2's customers.

7. We will return to this subject in chapter 8 pp. 163–4.

8. This case of transfer of surplus revenue is the only one (within the production sector) which is closely examined in Marxist as well as in non-Marxist writings. Authors generally refer to it as the 'transformation problem'. We devote the final part of the theoretical appendix to this case (dispensing with a simplifying assumption made in the text below, see n. 11 (2)) in order to clarify some common misunderstandings on this issue.

9. The quantities produced are different from one branch to the other but they are not comparable (nor addable): the nature of the products being different (tons of steel, metres of cloth or gallons of beer etc.), there is no point in comparing the quantities produced (Q) from one branch to the other nor the unit values (c + v + s). Comparisons can only relate to the total magnitudes K, C, V, S, P and the relations between them.

10. The 'rate of valorisation' (S/K) relates the *surplus revenue created* to the total capital laid out. The rate of profit (P/K) relates the *profit obtained* to the total capital laid out (the profit obtained being equal to the surplus revenue created, increased or diminished by the surplus revenue transferred).

11. 1. The fact that profit is equal in each industry (P = 2000) is secondary: it is because the volume of K is assumed to be the same in each branch (K = 10 000). (This assumption is intended to make the diagram more evocative).

    2. The fact that total profit is equal to total surplus revenue (S = P = 6000) is due to a simplfied presentation, which will be abandoned in the theoretical appendix. The presentation of the problem of prices of production is simplifed here as it only shows the changes in the price of the commodity produced by each branch, but not the accompanying changes in the variables C and V in each branch (thus, for instance, if branch III uses machines produced by branch I, the change of price of the commodity I affects the magnitude of constant capital in branch III). The theoretical appendix will show that the accompanying changes in C and V actually bring about a change in total profit (which ceases to be equal to total surplus revenue) but only in money terms (the purchasing power of this modified profit does *not* change).

12. This redistribution of surplus revenue in favour of the more mechanized branches enables us to explain the profit of an entirely automated branch of production (L = 0, C/V = infinity), where no surplus revenue is created (S = 0).

13. Thus differences in the degree of mechanization (C/V) bring about

transfers of surplus revenue between enterprises as well as between branches. In both cases, the direction of the redistribution is the same: it is made at the expense of the less mechanized enterprises or branches and to the advantage of the more mechanized ones. However, the effect of the redistribution on the rate of profit is not the same in both cases: in relations between *enterprises*, the effect is a *differentiation* of the (particular) rates of profit; in relations between *branches*, the effect is an *equalization* of (average) rates of profit.

14. In the quantified example, we have assumed that branch I combines with the advantages both of a composition of capital *and* of a degree of protection higher than the average (the situation being exactly the opposite in branch III). The transfer of surplus revenue of 2000 from which branch I benefits at the expense of branch III is therefore explained half by the difference in C/V and half by the difference in the degree of protection.

15. Where the land has been *worked* (improved by the use of fertilizers, for instance), the price obtained corresponds partly to the value created and transferred by the labour in question and partly to the fact of private ownership as such. In the sequel, we assume, for the sake of simplicity, that the land embodies no labour.

16. In practice, let us remember, the production sector is bound to include circulation and administration activities, just as the circulation sector (at least the trade in commodities) includes production and administration activities.

17. In practice, productive workers' wages partly finance unproductive workers' wages (this is typically the case of trade union officials, financed by the contributions of all trade union members) as well as ground-rents (when wage-earners lease a plot of land).

18. When there is no unproductive labour and no landed property, the aggregate surplus value is equal to the aggregate profit ($S = P$). When there is unproductive labour and landed property, the surplus value provides not only the profits of various capitalist groups (industrialists, merchants, financiers) but also the wages of the unproductive workers and the ground-rent.

We must therefore write: $S = P + V' + R$.

19. The only changes in data concern the relation beween enterprises (1, 2, 3) within each branch (I, II, III). To accommodate the scale of the diagram, we have assumed that within branch II (average) the surplus revenue transferred from enterprise 3 (the least efficient) to enterprise 1 (the most efficient) was less than in Table 6.1. On the other hand, the table does introduce, within branches I and II, some differences between enterprises, which were omitted in Tables 6.2 and 6.3.

20. Since the total capital is assumed to be identical in the three branches I, II and III ($K = 10\,000$ cf. Table 6.2), the areas corresponding to the profit of each *branch* (P = profit = surplus revenue created, increased or

diminished by the surplus revenue transferred) provide an indirect comparison of the average rates of profit (P/K). If we assume in addition that, within each branch, the three enterprises have invested the same amount of capital (K = 3333) (they therefore only differ in the K/L ratio), the areas corresponding to the profit of each *enterprise* (P = surplus revenue created +/− surplus revenue transferred) provide the same indirect comparison of the individual rates of profit.

21. The areas cross-hatched with *slanting* lines represent (unproductive) surplus labour for which there is no corresponding profit: we are speaking of the surplus labour in the administration sector and of a part of the surplus labour in the circulation sector.

22. It is less clear in the case of the commercial margins financing the sector of commodity circulation: strictly speaking, there is no *payment* of a commercial margin by the production capitalists to the commercial capitalists: we could rather say that the former (consciously) accept a 'loss of earnings', in the sense that the prices at which they sell to commercial firms are less than the prices they could obtain by selling directly to the end-users (subject to some additional investment).

PART II

The Application of Marxist Economic Concepts to the Analysis of Capitalism

Up to this point we have been examining the essential concepts of Marxist economic theory. From now on we will attempt to apply these concepts to the analysis of capitalism.

This will be done in two distinct ways. First we will pay attention to a variety of *well-known 'real world' phenomena* (such as capitalist competition, mechanization, monopolies, state intervention, crises, inflation, etc.) and try to *interpret them in a coherent manner* with the help of the Marxist economic concepts developed in Part One: in this way we will provide a *factual* proof of the Marxist central thesis (according to which capitalist profit is based on the wage-earners' surplus labour). Secondly we will concentrate on *some basic ratios* of Marxist economic theory (that is the monetary expression of values and the rate of surplus labour) and try to *provide a statistical estimation* of their magnitude and evolution in recent years: in this way, we will provide a statistical proof of the Marxist central thesis. (The reader is referred back to chapter 1, pp. 13–16, where the three types of proof are introduced and located within the general framework of the book.)

The interpretation of 'real world' phenomena will, in its turn, be carried out from two distinct points of view. We will begin by a *'static' approach* (essentially based on the surplus revenue transfer schemes just examined), which is intended to analyse various *contradictions* prevailing in a capitalist society with regard to the appropriation of surplus revenue. We will then develop a more *'dynamic' approach*, which is aimed at revealing some essential *tendencies* of the capitalist system taken as a whole, and in particular the occurrence of crises and price movements (problems which will be examined in two specific chapters).

The structure of Part II can thus be summarized as follows.

1. An interpretation of 'real-world' phenomena.

    (1)   A 'static' approach. Chapter 7: Capitalist competition for the appropriation of surplus revenue.

    (2)   A 'dynamic' approach. Chapter 8: Some essential tendencies of capitalist growth; chapter 9: Accumulation and crises; chapter 10: Accumulation, money and prices.

2. A statistical estimation of some basic ratios. Chapter 11: An empirical analysis of the rate of surplus labour in five European countries. (1966–78)

7

Capitalist Competition for the Appropriation of Surplus Revenue

Capitalists do not constitute an homogeneous whole, but may rather be divided into various 'fractions': some specialize in production activities, other in circulation (trade or finance); some produce for export, others for the home market; some run large and efficient firms, others small and marginal ones and so on. How can we analyse the relations between these distinct capitalist fractions?

On the other hand, capitalists as a group are faced, not only with the wage-earners, but also with independent producers, with land-owners, and with a 'public sector'. How can we analyse the relations between capitalists and these other 'sectors'?

This chapter aims at throwing some light on these questions. Using essentially the surplus revenue transfer schemes examined in the preceding chapter, it will try and show to what extent these relations are – or are not – of a conflicting nature, and for what reasons.

We will examine successively the relations prevailing between the following fractions, groups or sectors:

(1) industrialists (producing either for export or for the home market), merchants, bankers and landowners
(2) large and small capitalist enterprises
(3) capitalist enterprises and independent producers
(4) capitalist enterprises and the public sector
(5) capitalists in various countries.

CONFLICTING AND CONVERGING INTERESTS WITHIN THE
DOMINANT CLASS

*The Relations Between Industrial, Commercial and Banking
Capital*

1.   The profit of capitalists investing in the sector of the circulation
of commodities (commercial capital) or of money (banking capital)
comes from a redistribution of the surplus revenue created in the
production sector ('industrial' capital in the wide sense).[1] The result
is that, from a certain point of view, there is a clash of interests
between industrial capital, commercial capital and banking capital,
since they all compete for a share in the same mass of surplus
revenue. In practice, these clashes of interest revolve around
commercial and financial margins: it is in the interest of industrial
capital that credit should be cheap (to reduce the amount of interest
payable to the banks) and that commercial margins should be kept as
low as possible.

2.   However, from another point of view, it is basically in the
interest of *all* capitalists that surplus revenue should be as large as
possible and that exploitation of the workers should continue and
increase. It is in their interest to maximize the exploitation of both
productive and of unproductive wage-earners. In increasing the
exploitation of the productive wage-earners, they reduce the variable
capital and increase the mass of surplus revenue created (in Table 6.4,
if the rate of surplus revenue was 300 per cent instead of 100 per cent,
we should have V = *3000* and S = *9000*). In increasing the
exploitation of the unproductive workers (both in the circulation and
in the administration sector), they reduce the sum total of wages
payable to them and reduce the drain of surplus revenue required for
the payment of unproductive wage-earners (in Table 6.4, if the rate
of surplus labour of the unproductive workers was 300 per cent
instead of 100 per cent, we should have V' = *800* instead of 1600). In
both cases, the total profit (P) available for capitalist consumption
and accumulation is increased.
The (secondary) clashes between industrial, commercial and banking
capital may even vanish for certain capitalists. This would be the case
for a capitalist group which at the same time controls industrial and
commercial firms as well as networks of banks and insurance
companies. If the commercial and financial network supports the
activities within the group exclusively, then the group avoids all loss

of surplus revenue. If it supports external activities as well, the group obtains as profit a share of the surplus revenue produced elsewhere.

The Relations Between Capitalists and Landowners

Similar considerations prevail regarding landed property:

(1) As rent for land is levied on the surplus revenue, landowners are in conflict with capitalists for the share-out of the surplus revenue.

(2) But they have the same basic interest in seeing that the total surplus revenue available is as large as possible, and therefore that the rate of surplus labour (of productive and unproductive wage-earners) should be as high as possible.

There is, however, an important difference between the case of commercial or banking capital and that of landed property. Commercial and banking activities render indispensable services to industrial capital (attracting savings on a large scale for investment, facilitating sale and purchase transactions), as do also administration activities. But landed property is parasitic: it appropriates a part of the surplus revenue without providing any labour at all in return. It is therefore in the interest of all capitalists to weaken the landowner class politically, to reduce the burden of rents, to seize landed property for themselves, or even to suppress all private ownership of land. Only political considerations hold capitalists back from such a demand: if they question the private ownership of land themselves, they fear that others may question the private ownership of the means of production.

Differentiations in Rates of Surplus Revenue according to Branches and Enterprises

We have seen that all capitalists share the same basic interest, namely, that the rate of surplus revenue should be the highest possible, so as to maximize the sum total of surplus revenue available.

This pressure to maximize the rate of surplus revenue does not, however, weigh on every branch and every enterprise in an equally compelling way. Let us look again at the example in Figure 6.4: two extreme cases can be considered.

In branch III, enterprise 3 loses the whole of the surplus revenue created by its wage-earners. If this enterprise does not wish to go under, it must, sooner or later, reduce its efficiency gap (reduce the disparity between its individual unit value and that of its competitors). In the immediate future, it can recover a minimal margin of profit only by lengthening the labour-time of its workers or by cutting the latters' wages; in both cases, the rate of hourly wage is reduced and the rate of surplus value is increased.[2]

The situation of the three enterprises of branch I is quite different: to the surplus revenue created by their own wage-earners, there has been added a surplus revenue obtained by transfer, thanks to the higher than average degree of mechanization and protection; their rate of profit is higher than the average rate of profit. These enterprises can therefore make concessions over the level of wages and over labour-time, without seriously impairing their profitability; it is even in their interest to make these concessions, so as to be in a better position to recruit and retain their staff.

We can therefore expect that the *rate of surplus value in a branch or an enterprise should be all the higher if the branch is relatively less protected* (as compared to the other branches) *and if the enterprise is relatively less efficient* (as compared to rival enterprises in the same branch).

In other words, the wages paid and the labour-time will vary according to the degree of protection and of efficiency of the branches and enterprises: the rates of hourly wages will be lower in the less protected branches and in the less efficient enterprises.[3] Empirical data on hourly wages in different branches or enterprises confirm this conclusion very clearly.

The Relations between Capitalists Producing for Export and those Producing for the Home Market

We have said that all capitalists have a common interest in maximizing the rate of surplus value (that is in minimizing the workers' rate of hourly wage). This statement, however, must be qualified. For workers' wages have to be considered from two distinct points of view.

(1) Wages are production *costs* that capitalists have a definite interest in *reducing* (thus *raising* the rate of surplus value).

(2) Wages create a *market* (a demand) for the commodities produced by the enterprises: from this viewpoint, capitalists, in order to sell their products (a necessary condition in a commodity society), have an interest in *raising* wages (thus *reducing* the rate of surplus value).

Capitalists therefore face a real contradiction to which we shall return in the next chapter.[4] We shall then see that the contradiction can be solved in a dynamic perspective thanks to increases in productivity, which enable capitalists to enjoy both an increase in the rate of surplus value and an increase in the demand stemming from the workers (through higher real wages or purchasing power).

In the meanwhile, we must see that all capitalists do not face this contradiction in the same manner. An important distinction must be drawn between those capitalists producing (essentially or exclusively) for *export* and those producing (essentially or exclusively) for the *home market*.

Those oriented towards export markets somehow escape from the contradiction. For them, the level of the hourly wage rate *within the country* only affects their production costs, and not their markets (which are located abroad). Not surprisingly, they will advocate restrictive wage policies within the country – while secretly hoping for less restrictive wage policies abroad. Actually, for those capitalists, the contradiction between wages as costs and wages as market outlets tends to weaken as it is shifted to the international level.

On the other hand, capitalists oriented towards the home market face the contradiction, head on. Being aware that the level of the hourly wage rate within the country directly affects their market, they will not be keen on unduly restrictive wage policies and will thus come into conflict with the export-oriented capitalists.

THE RELATIONS BETWEEN 'LARGE' AND 'SMALL' CAPITALIST ENTERPRISES

For the sake of clarity, two cases must be distinguished: either the large and small enterprises produce the *same commodity* (they compete with each other within the same branch), or they produce *different commodities* (they enter in relation with each other but belong, strictly speaking, to different branches).

Contradictions between Enterprises Competing within the same Branch

The relations between large (efficient) enterprises and small (marginal) enterprises are necessarily ambiguous. First, it is in the interest of large enterprises to *eliminate* their less well-placed competitors: in this way, they enlarge the scale of their production and increase the amount of surplus revenue created within themselves. Secondly large enterprises profit indirectly from the existence and *survival* of marginal enterprises: for the latter are under pressure to maximize the exploitation of their wage-earners[5] – to the benefit of the most efficient capitalists in the branch, who enjoy transfers of surplus revenue.

We know that, in the long term, the real tendency is that large efficient enterprises progressively *eliminate* most of their small-scale competitors and concentrate an increasing share of total production and employment within each branch: this general tendency of capitalist development will be considered in the next chapter.[6] The problem here is rather to examine why, in the short term, large efficient enterprises may be interested in what is called 'the *protection* of small enterprises'. This is a point where the ambiguity of relations between 'large' and 'small' enterprises is particularly obvious. We will see that, in each branch of production, *it is in the interest of large and efficient enterprises to ensure the survival and to increase the profit of the*

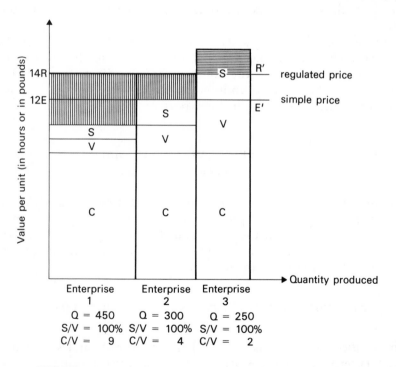

FIGURE 7.1   *Effects of the 'protection of the small enterprise'*

small inefficient enterprises, provided the measures applied to this effect are *measures of a general order, which benefit all enterprises* in the branch.

To understand this point, let us replace Figure 6.1 where branch II is considered to be '*average*' in all respects (and where consequently the surplus revenue gained by the most efficient enterprise offsets exactly the surplus revenue lost by the least efficient enterprise),[7] by Figure 7.1, where we assume that this same branch II enjoys higher than average protection. Let us assume that this protection enables branch II to sell its commodities at a regulated price of 14 (the simple price being equal to 12).

This price rise has a threefold effect.

(1)   The branch as a whole obtains an extra profit of £2 per unit: it now makes an overall profit higher than the surplus revenue created (P = 4000 > S = 2000).[8]

(2)   The marginal enterprise 3 achieves a profit of 500 and a rate of profit of 17 per cent (when, with the price at 12, its profit was nil): its survival as a capitalist enterprise is therefore assured (at least as long as the branch can continue to sell at 14).

(3)   The distribution of the additional profit from which the branch benefits is made in proportion to the quantities produced by each enterprise, and therefore essentially to the advantage of enterprise 1: the latter benefits by an extra profit of 900 (2 × 450), while enterprise 3 gains only 500 (2 × 250).[9]

In other words, the price rise (justified by the necessity of 'defending the small enterprise') results mainly in enhancing the profit and the accumulation potential of the *large* enterprises: they can still widen the gap which separates them from the small enterprises both as regards the size and cost of production.[10]

A general measure of protection therefore reinforces, in a cumulative way, the twofold advantage which the efficient large enterprise enjoys as regards transfers of surplus revenue: the advantage of size (of the higher volume of production) and of efficiency (of the lower individual unit value).[11]

Obviously, the protection enjoyed by a branch has its limits, imposed by the competition of other branches, in the share-out of the total surplus revenue. The extra profit obtained by branch II as a whole (in the last example P = 4000 > S = 2000) involves a loss of surplus revenue and a reduction in the average rate of profit in the other branches. The latter will fight back with the aim of destroying the protection enjoyed by branch II (that is, of bringing down the regulated price) or of obtaining compensatory forms of protection (price increases for their own products or other protective measures). This competition around measures of protection will be considered from a dynamic viewpoint in the next chapter.[12]

Subcontracting and Unequal Relations between Enterprises Operating in Different Branches

The relations between large and small enterprises often take the form of *sub-contracting*: large enterprises, rather than carry out all the operations normally involved in their branch of activity, delegate certain specialized activities to small enterprises, generally laying down strict norms of production.

The activities delegated may concern the production of specific intermediary products (A, B, C etc.) necessary to the making of the final commodity (X) that the large enterprise produces (for instance, a big car company may delegate the production of motors or spare parts to one or several small enterprises). The·norms of production dictated by the large enterprise may involve such conditions as inputs to use, delivery terms, quality to conform to etc. What changes does this kind of subcontracting involve in the status of the intermediary products and of the workers producing them? The intermediary products (A, B, C etc.), which were simple use-values moving from one department to another within the large enterprise, now *become commodities*: they are produced and sold by the specialized subcontracting enterprise. But this does not change the status of the workers in question, who *remain productive* workers: they were part of a large collective of workers contributing to the production of the final commodity (X), they now form a smaller collective of workers producing a narrower commodity (A, B, C etc.); they produced and continue to produce value and surplus value.

The phenomenon of subcontracting may also involve certain 'peripheral' activities which are not directly related to the production of the commodity X (cleaning services, for instance, are increasingly handed over to specialist subcontractors). Here also the use-value produced for internal use within the large enterprise is *transformed into a commodity* produced for sale by the subcontracting enterprise. And here this *does* change the status of the workers in question, who *become productive*: they now take part in the process of production of a commodity, they now produce value and surplus value.

Subcontracting (either of productive or unproductive activities) brings together a large enterprise and a small enterprise which produce different commodities and therefore belong to different branches of production (defined in a strict sense). It is advantageous to the large enterprise in so far as the latter can buy commodities at a price $(c + v + p)$ lower than the cost $(c + v)$ it would have incurred producing the products itself. The price $(c + v + p)$ of the sub-contracted commodity can be kept very low through the unequal relation prevailing between the two enterprises: the large enterprise is in a position to impose not only the norms of production, but also the price; the small enterprise is obliged to accept these conditions, all the more since subcontracting is generally a matter of its elimination or survival.

But the small enterprise, in order to survive as a capitalist enterprise, must enjoy a minimal rate of profit. Because of the low prices imposed by the large enterprise, it will be under pressure to reduce its variable capital per unit (v) through imposing lower hourly wage-rates on its workers or, in other words, through imposing a higher rate of exploitation on them. Both lower wages and longer labour-time are indeed usual in small-scale subcontracting enterprises, which means a higher rate of exploitation of the workers.

Subcontracting has thus a two-fold effect.

(1) It increases the average rate of surplus value (through a higher rate of exploitation of the workers in the small enterprise).

(2) It gives rise to a transfer of surplus revenue from the surviving small enterprise to the large enterprise (through the low regulated price imposed by the latter on the former).

THE RELATIONS BETWEEN CAPITALIST AND NON-CAPITALIST ENTERPRISES

Relations between (large) capitalist enterprises and (small) non-capitalist producers can be considered as a special case of the relations between 'large' and 'small' (capitalist) enterprises, a special case which does, however, exhibit a number of specific features.

As in the previous sector, two situations can be distinguished. Either the capitalist and non-capitalist producers compete within the *same branch*: this is the case, for instance, of large agricultural estates producing a given commodity – wheat – alongside peasant families. Or the capitalist and non-capitalist producers belong to *different branches* and are linked by subcontracting: this is the case, for instance, of peasant families producing agricultural raw materials (milk, vegetables etc.) on behalf of agro-business enterprises to which they sell their commodities.

Contradictions between Capitalist and Non-capitalist Enterprises Competing within the same Branch

To illustrate the similarities together with the specific features of the situation we are considering (compared with the relations between capitalist enterprises analysed in the previous section), we have constructed Figure 7.2. This uses the same basic data as Figure 7.1,

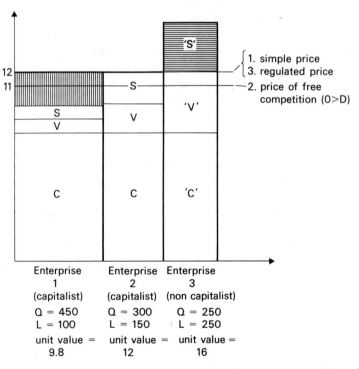

FIGURE 7.2   Relations between (large) capitalist enterprises and (small) non-capitalist enterprises

but marginal enterprise 3 is no longer a capitalist enterprise: it is replaced by a series of small independent producers or by various workers' collectives (for example co-operatives, self-managed firms) and we assume that together these are in a position to deliver the same production as the original capitalist enterprise (Q = 250) with the same number of workers (L = 250) and the same quantity of labour per unit produced (individual unit value = 16).

Specific features of the non-capitalist enterprise
In contrast to a capitalist enterprise, a non-capitalist production enterprise exhibits the following specific features.

1. The workers are the owners of the means of production. They do not sell their labour-power to anyone else and do not buy anyone else's labour-power, but work for their own account, whether as *individual commodity producers* (in the case of single producers) or as *collective commodity producers* (in the case of workers' collectives).

2. The labour of these commodity producers is *productive of value and revenue*. In the example (where L = 250 and where the working-day is 8 hours), the value created is 2000 hours, the revenue created is £2000 (we are still assuming that the monetary expression of value is £1 per hour). But this value and this revenue do not break down into corresponding value and surplus value, into variable capital and surplus revenue. Such a breakdown is in fact not possible: as the labour-power of the producers is not sold, the various distinctions appropriate to waged labour do not apply. (It is in order to emphasize this difference that the diagram puts the symbols V and S relating to enterprise 3 in inverted commas.)

3. The purpose of non-capitalist commodity production is not to build up capital and to obtain a rate of profit. For the commodity producer, the sums laid out for the purchase of means of production constitute expenditure to be recovered, and not constant capital in search of a profit. (This is why Figure 7.2 also puts the symbol C in inverted commas.) As we saw in chapter 3, the purpose of non-capitalist commodity production is to obtain a revenue intended for the purchase of *actual use-values* (means of production and means of consumption).

4. A commodity producer is in *equilibrium when the revenue obtained is equal to the revenue created*. Thus in the example: as enterprise 3 creates a value of 2000 hours and a revenue of £2000, it will theoretically be in equilibrium if it obtains a revenue which is also equal to £2000.

The relations between capitalist and non-capitalist enterprises
What happens when a non-capitalist enterprise finds itself facing the competition of more efficient capitalist enterprises? We shall first see that this non-capitalist enterprise gives up to its competitors a part of the revenue created by its own workers, and that this transfer of revenue (this additional profit for the more efficient capitalists) is even higher than it is in the case where the marginal enterprise is also a capitalist one. We shall thus understand the contradiction prevailing between capitalist enterprises and non-capitalist competitors, contradictions that are similar to those prevailing between large and small capitalist enterprises.

A higher transfer of revenue.   We explained that a less efficient *capitalist* enterprise loses a part of the *surplus revenue created* by its workers: this lost surplus revenue goes to swell the profit of the more efficient capitalist enterprises. In a similar way, a less efficient *non-capitalist* enterprise (like enterprise 3 in the example) loses a part of the *revenue created* by its workers: this lost revenue goes to swell the profit of the more efficient capitalist enterprises. The transfer mechanism is the same in both cases: it is the existence of a uniform market price (12 in the example) which penalizes the least efficient and benefits the more efficient enterprises.

Up to what point can a marginal enterprise afford to lose a part of the revenue created by its workers? In the case of a *capitalist* enterprise, the limit is the maintenance of a minimum rate of profit ensuring the enterprise's survival: in this sense, the price of 12 (in Figure 6.1) dooms the marginal capitalist enterprise to extinction, for it leaves it no profit (all the surplus revenue is transferred). In the case of a *non-capitalist* enterprise, the limit cannot be the obtaining of a minimum rate of profit, but the obtaining of a minimum revenue: the sale price must assure the independent producer or the members of the workers' collective of a revenue roughly equal to that of wage-earners in similar enterprises.[13] In the example in figure 7.2 (which deals with an 'average' branch of production as regards protection and mechanization), the simple price (= 12) does in fact assure the non-capitalist producers of a revenue equal to the wage paid in the rival capitalist enterprises. As a result of this, the *non-capitalist* marginal enterprise will continue to produce at this price, while the *capitalist* enterprise, under the same conditions, was bound to fail for lack of profit. The transformation of a capitalist marginal enterprise into a non-capitalist marginal enterprise (into a workers' collective) therefore appears as a means of maintaining employment, at least in the short term.[14]

Similar contradictions. What has been said of the contradictions between large and small *capitalist* enterprises competing within the same branch can be repeated here in an analogous manner, concerning the relations between large capitalist enterprises and small *independent* producers.

It is in the interest of large capitalist enterprises to *eliminate* less well-placed independent producers: in this way, they enlarge their scale of operation and the amount of surplus revenue their own workers create. However, large capitalist enterprises benefit indirectly from the existence and *survival* of marginal independent producers: as we have just seen, they benefit from a transfer of revenue which is even higher than where the marginal enterprise is also a capitalist one.[15]

In the long term, capitalist enterprises tend to progressively *eliminate* most of the independent producers. In the short term, however, they may be interested in '*protecting* the independent producers', through general measures which actually benefit the whole branch (but which are subject to retaliation on the part of other branches).

To understand this interest in protecting independent producers, let us look again at Figure 7.2. Let us assume that, as the result of an excess of supply (seasonal, cyclical or structural), the price of free competition falls to 11. At this price, the non-capitalist producers will only obtain a revenue *lower* than the wages paid by the capitalist enterprises: they will therefore bring pressure to bear in order to obtain, from the public authorities, a regulated price *higher* than the price of free competition (the regulated price of 12 in the example). The large capitalist enterprises will join them in this general demand which will be essentially to their own benefit: producing more, they will make an even larger additional profit. But the capitalists of other branches, being indirectly victims of the protection granted to the first group, will endeavour to have it reversed.[16]

Two theoretical questions reconsidered

We have seen that a part of the revenue created by non-capitalist enterprises is transformed, through the market mechanism, into an additional profit for capitalist enterprises. This fact leads us to reconsider two questions: the source of capitalist profit and the commodity producers' possible 'surplus labour'.

Capitalism's sources of profit.   Capitalism's typical source of profit is obviously the surplus *revenue* created by the wage-earners employed in the production of commodities. It is a profit which arises from *capitalist production* itself (even if a part of the surplus revenue produced is redistributed in various ways among capitalists).

To this primary source of profit there is added another, that is, a part of the revenue lost by the non-capitalist producers, who have to face more efficient capitalist enterprises on the market. This second source of profit is not linked to the exploitation of wage-earners and is therefore not typical of capitalism: this profit arises in reality from *circulation* (that is, from the market, from the exchange) and not from capitalist exploitation as such.[17]

The independent producers' 'surplus labour'.   As indicated in chapter 3, the concepts of surplus labour, surplus value and surplus revenue are *typical* of *waged* labour only. All wage-earners provide surplus labour, and those involved in commodity production create surplus value and surplus revenue. By contrast, *non-waged* labour *in principle* does not provide surplus labour, surplus value or surplus revenue. (This principle applies perfectly in the case of an average producer within the framework of a generalized simple commodity production: this producer creates as much labour and value as he consumes, as much revenue as he gets and spends).

But independent producers competing with more efficient capitalist enterprises have to give up a part of the revenue they create. For that reason they actually find themselves in an *analogous* situation to the wage-earners: they 'produce more labour (more value, more revenue) than they consume' and this 'surplus labour' (or 'surplus value', 'surplus revenue') can be equal to that of the wage-earners (this is the case if the labour-time is the same and if the revenue retained by the independent producers is comparable to the wages received by the wage-earners). It is to emphasize this analogy that we will speak of the independent producers' possible 'surplus labour' (or 'surplus value', 'surplus revenue') (in inverted commas and represented by 'S' in Figure 7.2) and also of a rate of 'surplus labour' (or 'surplus value') (still in inverted commas), to which they may possibly be liable.

Subcontracting and Unequal Relations between Capitalist and Non-Capitalist Enterprises

Similar principles apply here as in the case of relations between two capitalist enterprises.

The large (capitalist) enterprise is in a position to impose a very low price on the independent producers from whom it buys 'subcontracted' commodities. This low price means that these independent producers have to content themselves with a very low income: their hourly income is much lower than the hourly wage the capitalist enterprise would have to pay if it did not have recourse to subcontractors; it is normally even lower than the hourly wage which would be paid in a *capitalist* small subcontracting enterprise.

Subcontracting to independent producers has thus a two-fold effect.

(1) It increases the average rate of surplus value (through a higher rate of 'surplus value' imposed on the independent producers).

(2) It gives rise to a transfer of 'surplus revenue' from the independent producers to the capitalist enterprise (through the low regulated price fixed by the latter).

THE RELATIONS BETWEEN 'PRIVATE SECTOR' AND 'PUBLIC SECTOR'

This section will consider how capitalist enterprises stand with regard to various measures of state intervention in the economy. We shall first consider the case of *nationalization* (of enterprises or of branches of production), then the case of *other measures of public intervention* (public subsidies to enterprises, public sector contracts, directly social labour within the administration sector).

State Ownership of Enterprises or of Branches of Production

General principles

In a capitalist society, public enterprises are on the same footing as capitalist enterprises as regards the creation of *surplus revenue* and as non-capitalist enterprises as regards the demand for *profitability*.

Wage-earners of public enterprises create surplus revenue under the same conditions as wage-earners of private enterprises: for this, it is necessary – and sufficient – that they are employed in the production of commodities, in contrast to circulation and administration activities. Thus the wage-earners of British Gas are productive of surplus revenue but those of the Bank of England are not.

But public enterprises, in the same way as non-capitalist produc-ers, can produce without making a profit. Referring to Figure 7.2, let us assume that enterprise 3 is a public enterprise: while the marginal capitalist enterprise is doomed to elimination with a price of 12, the public enterprise, just like the non-capitalist enterprise, can perfectly well survive: its returns enable it to meet its production costs (C + V).[18] The capacity for survival of the public enterprise is even greater than that of the non-capitalist enterprise: if the sale price falls too low (to the level of 11, for example) the public enterprise can count on government subsidies to meet its production costs.

Transfers of surplus revenue from a public enterprise
Public enterprises take part, jointly with private enterprises, in the mechanisms of transfers of surplus revenue. A public enterprise which is more efficient than its competitors takes surplus revenue created in other enterprises. A less efficient public enterprise (a marginal public enterprise, for instance) loses surplus revenue to the benefit of its better-placed competitors.

In the case of a marginal public enterprise, one must consider whether it *covers its costs* or keeps going with the help of *subsidies*. If the public enterprise *covers its costs* (without making a loss or a profit), the surplus revenue produced by its wage-earners is in fact appropriated by the better placed rival enterprises (this is the classic situation described in Figure 7.2). If the public enterprise is *in deficit*, and keeps going with the help of subsidies, the situation is less clear. On the one hand, the subsidies can be considered as a drain on the surplus revenue created in the whole of the system: this is the way things look. On the other hand, keeping this unprofitable public enterprise in operation ensures, as we have just seen, a transfer of surplus revenue to the benefit of its better-placed competitors: this aspect of the matter is not obvious but is no less essential.

Transfers of surplus revenue from a public branch of production
The foregoing concerns marginal public *enterprises* within any branch of production. What about placing under public control (nationaliza-tion) of a whole *branch of production* (iron and steel, electricity or all forms of energy, rail transport or all forms of transport etc.)? The principles are fundamentally the same.

Nationalized branches of production take part, jointly with private branches, in the mechanisms of transfers of surplus revenue. A nationalized branch, which sells its commodities at a price of production (or at a regulated price) higher than the simple price,

TABLE 7.1   Transfers of surplus revenue from the public sector to the private sector

Branches of production			Value and revenue created (in hours or in pounds)				Incomes distributed (in pounds)					Transfers of surplus revenue (in pounds)
	K	L	V	S	V + S	V	P	V + P	S/K	P/K	P − S
1. Branches											
private	30000	1500	6000	6000	12000	6000	6000	12000	20%	20%	0
public	—	—	—	—	—	—	—	—	—	—	—
Total	30000	1500	6000	6000	12000	6000	6000	12000	20%	20%	0
2. Branches											
private	20000	1000	4000	4000	8000	4000	6000	10000	20%	30	+ 2000
public	10000	500	2000	2000	4000	2000	0	2000	20%	0%	− 2000
Total	30000	1500	6000	6000	12000	6000	6000	12000	20%	20%	0

takes surplus revenue created in other branches. A nationalized branch, which sells its commodities at a price lower than the simple price, loses surplus revenue to the benefit of other branches.

In the case of a nationalized branch which does not make a profit, one must again distinguish as above. If the nationalized branch sells its commodities at a price which allows it just to *cover its costs* (without loss or profit), it does without the surplus revenue created by its wage-earners and enables other (private) branches which use its commodities to benefit from it. If the nationalized branch sells *at a loss* and calls on subsidies, these partially reduce the profits which the private sector gains from the favourable public sector prices.

Table 7.1 illustrates the transfer of surplus revenue from the public to the private sector on the assumption that the nationalized branches (the public sector) sell at cost price and therefore make no call on subsidies.[19] The first part of the table assumes that all the branches of production belong to the private sector: we see that the average rate of profit is 20 per cent (corresponding to the rate of valorization). The second part of the table assumes that the public sector controls one-third of the production (it produces one-third of the total surplus revenue) but that it sells at cost price (so P=0): as a result, there is, in the private sector, a rise in the average rate of profit which goes up by 30 per cent.

The actual mechanism of this transfer of surplus revenue to the benefit of the private sector is well-known. The public sector can sell its commodities (steel, electricity, transport services etc.) *at cost price* or even *at a loss*, and therefore at a lower price than if the same commodities were produced by capitalists. The production costs of the private sector are that much reduced, and the average rate of profit is that much increased.

Conclusion
The result of all the foregoing is that the placing under public control of a marginal *enterprise* – or of a *branch of production* which it is difficult to make profitable – makes it possible for production and employment to continue, while giving the private sector the benefit of various transfers of surplus revenue which raise the average rate of profit. The advantage of nationalization for private capitalists does not stop at these transfers of surplus revenue: in so far as nationalization is carried out by *buying in* private capital (rather than by expropriation without compensation), the capitalists recover money capital which they can re-invest in more profitable enterprises or sectors.[20]

Similar advantages arise in the case of state participation in the capital of private enterprises (transformed into *'mixed enterprises'*).[21] This state participation can be considered as partial nationalization. What was said above about public enterprises applies here to the part of the capital which comes under public control.

The development of public enterprises (or mixed enterprises) is surrounded by great ideological confusion: people go so far as to present these measures as 'seeds of socialism', when their object (and anyway their effect) can only be, as we have seen, a strengthening of capitalism.

A final comparison can be made between nationalization of landed property and nationalization of enterprises. Like the takeover of landed property, the development of an 'auxiliary' public (or mixed) sector does not harm the interests of the capitalist class, very much the opposite. What capitalists are afraid of, here as in the question of land, is 'setting the ball rolling': there is the fear that if they come out themselves in favour of some limitation in the private ownership of the means of production, others may challenge *all* private ownership of the means of production.

Other Measures of State Intervention

Through *public enterprises* (limited to individual firms or extended to whole branches), the state takes part in commodity production, generally transferring surplus revenue to the private sector. The state also intervenes in the economy in various other ways: through *public sector contracts*, it acts as a purchaser of commodities, providing the capitalist enterprises with an additional market for their products; through *public subsidies*, it ensures the survival of public or capitalist enterprises, enabling them to cover their costs or to restore a minimal margin of profit; through the *administration sector*, it acts as a producer of collective goods and services, ensuring the reproduction of the capitalist system as a whole.

There is, however, an important difference between public enterprises and the other three types of intervention. Public enterprises produce commodities, their workers are productive of value and revenue, of surplus value and surplus revenue; part of this surplus revenue is transferred to the private sector. The picture is quite different in the case of the other measures of intervention: no commodities are produced, no value or revenue is created; on the contrary, financing these unproductive activities involves a levy on the surplus revenue created in the private sector.[22]

Capitalists thus face a new contradiction regarding these unproductive state activities. These activities provide capitalist enterprises with a series of economic advantages, especially in the form of enlarged markets, lower costs and higher profitability: from this viewpoint, capitalists have an interest in an *extension* of state activities. However, these same activities involve a levy on their surplus revenue, which tends to affect profitability: from this viewpoint, capitalists have an interest in a *limitation* of state activities.

This contradiction is analogous to the contradiction concerning wages mentioned earlier in this chapter:[23] for capitalists, wages are both a cost (which they have an interest in reducing) and a market (which they have an interest in expanding). As we shall see in the following chapter, both contradictions can only be solved through productivity increases in commodity production.

In the same way as the contradiction concerning wages does not affect all capitalists equally (we have seen that it affects more directly those capitalists producing for the home market), the contradiction concerning state activities also divides the capitalist class in various possible 'fractions': for instance, it will oppose those capitalists who benefit from important public subsidies and/or public sector contracts to those who do not.

INTERNATIONAL CAPITALIST COMPETITION

The synthetic Figure 6.4 can also be used, with some adjustments, to illustrate the different types of surplus revenue transfers on the *international* level. Branch I (high C/V, high protection) could, for example, represent the world-wide oil industry or machine-tool industry; branch II would correspond to industries such as textiles or car assembly; branch III (low C/V, low protection) would include especially the production of primary foodstuffs, such as cocoa and ground-nuts.

Unlike what we have assumed implicitly so far, enterprises 1, 2 and 3 within each branch are not necessarily located in the same country: enterprise I.1 could represent a typical oil enterprise in the Middle East, enterprise I.3, a marginal oil enterprise somewhere else in the world. These differences in geographical location suggest that there is another cause of differentiation in the rates of surplus value: the rates of surplus value of the different enterprises and branches will depend, in the first place, on the overall balance of power between capitalists and wage-earners in each *country* and, in the second place, on the degree of efficiency and of protection of each *enterprise or branch* in relation to other enterprises and branches. In practice: the rate of surplus value will be *on average* higher in the less developed countries than in the developed countries, but it will be much higher in small marginal enterprises producing cocoa or ground-nuts than in the oil companies which are the most favourably placed in international competition.[24]

Besides this, Figure 6.4 enables us to draw the same basic conclusions on the international as on the national level. The total amount of profits (of private or public enterprises), the incomes of ownership (rents, royalties), as well as the wages of the unproductive workers, correspond to the amount of surplus revenue created by all productive workers and to the amount of 'surplus revenue' provided by commodity producers in the capitalist society world-wide. Productive wage-earners (whether farm workers in Ecuador or chemical technicians in Germany) create a surplus revenue (S) in the strict sense; to this is added a part ('S') of the revenue created by the multitude of small independent producers spread around the world and facing the competition of more efficient capitalist enterprises. This twofold amount of surplus revenue (S + 'S') is the object of multiple redistributions among capitalists (and landowners). In this struggle for redistribution, the capitalists of the most efficient enterprises, of the most protected branches and of the dominant countries, always enjoy an advantage in relation to the capitalists of inefficient enterprises, of unprotected branches, of dominated countries. All of them, however, have the same basic interest to maximize the degree of exploitation of all workers, both productive and unproductive, both in Togo and in the United Kingdom: the heavier the collective exploitation of the workers, the greater the amount of surplus revenue available for the dominant classes as a whole, and the more smoothly the problems of redistribution among them will be resolved.

What happens if the aggregate of surplus revenue is insufficient in relation to the capital invested (if, in other words, the average rate of profit for the capitalist system as a whole is too low)? The clashes over its redistribution will be all the more bitter, and the urge to increase the rate of surplus value all the fiercer. The various means of raising the rate of surplus value will be examined in the following chapter, but we must mention here the role of wars in the solution of the conflicts over the redistribution of surplus revenue on the international scale: wars make it possible, on one hand, to destroy a part of rival capital; they can, on the other hand, cause a drastic reduction in the peoples' standard of life and at the same time push up the rate of surplus value.

NOTES

1. 'Industrial' capital is understood here in the broader sense: it also includes capital invested in agricultural production and in the production of commodity services – the term 'production capital' would perhaps be more appropriate.
2. On the relations between rate of hourly wage and rate of surplus value, see chapter 4, pp. 93–4.
3. The same conclusion applies equally to the circulation sector: the rate of surplus labour will tend to depend on the profitability of the sector as a whole and of each particular enterprise (commercial or financial).
4. See chapter 8, pp. 169–70.
5. See above, pp. 137–8.
6. See chapter 8, pp. 173–4.
7. For the sake of simplicity, we overlook the differentiations in the rates of surplus value between large and small enterprises and assume (as in chapter 6) that the ratio S/V is equal in all enterprises.
8. In Figure 7.1, this additional overall profit is represented by the rectangle ERR'E'.
9. Enterprise 3 continues to produce more surplus revenue than it realises as profit (S $=$ 1000 $>$ $=$ 500). But the raising of the price reduces this transfer of surplus revenue and ensures a rate of profit (P/K $=$ 17%) which can be considered as 'normal' (the average rate of profit is 20 per cent in the examples in Figures 6.1 and 6.3).
10. Figure 7.1 describes perfectly the situation of a *cartelized industry*. The cartel agreement divides the market between the enterprises taking part (the quota system) and fixes a sale price enabling the least efficient to make a 'normal' profit and indirectly assuring the most efficient enterprises of an even higher rate of profit.
11. The raising of prices is a typical example of a general measure: other examples would be the reduction of the rates of taxation, the obtaining of cheaper credit, the guaranteed sale of products etc. As long as these measures are general (applying to all producers), they mainly favour the big producers. Only selective measures (applicable only to small producers) do not suit the immediate interests of the big producers: hence the opposition to the policy of subsidies to ailing enterprises and branches. We will return to this later in the chapter.
12. See chapter 8, pp. 177–8.
13. We should note that the will to continue working on their own account may induce the workers to be satisfied with an income often well below the wage level taken as a reference.

14. In the long term, the question is always whether the marginal enterprise (capitalist or not) will be able to keep up with the rate of technological progress prevailing with its better-placed competitors (if it can lower its *individual* unit value at the same rate as the *social* unit value). This necessity of adapting to the technological methods of competitors (as well as to their methods of management, financing and publicity etc.) explains why workers' collectives fitted into a capitalist society are inevitably bound to disappear or to be transformed into disguised capitalist enterprises (we may recall here the history of 'workers' co-operatives').

15. The relations between large capitalist enterprises and small enterprises (capitalist or non-capitalist) are considered in this chapter from a strictly economic point of view, in terms of profit for the large enterprises. It is obvious that these relations are just as much determined by political considerations: a too brutal elimination of the small enterprises (whether capitalist or not) would deprive the whole of the capitalist class of a good deal of political support.

16. The problem of agricultural prices in the EEC gives a good illustration of this analysis. Agricultural prices are fixed at levels intended to assure the marginal small farmers of a 'decent' income: it is well known that these prices have mainly served to increase the profits of the biggest capitalist farms. But the growing burden of financing the Common Agricultural Policy (a question particularly of stockpiling and ensuring the disposal of excess production) and the high prices of food products (with their incidence on the level of wages payable to all the workers) were bound to provoke a reaction on the part of non-agricultural capitalists: this reaction was reflected in the 'Mansholt plan', intended to 're-establish the truth of prices' in the agricultural sector.

17. Without non-capitalist producers, overall surplus revenue is equal to overall profit (S = P). With non-capitalist producers, this overall profit is equal to the aggregate of surplus revenue created (S), increased by the revenue created – but lost – by non-capitalist producers ('S').
We therefore have: S + 'S' = P.
If we take account of the necessary deductions to pay the wages of the unproductive workers (V') and the ground-rent (R), the equation becomes: S + 'S' = P + V' + R.

18. As the producers in public enterprises are wage-earners, they provide surplus value and surplus revenue in the proper sense of the term: in this sense, the symbol S would be more correct than the symbol 'S'. But as public enterprises are not bound by the need for profit, the expenditure on labour-power and means of production do not constitute 'capital' in the strict sense: in this sense the symbols 'C' and 'V' are justified.

19. This table is constructed on the model of Table 6.4 but leaving out the unproductive sectors (circulation, administration, landed property).

20. As long as an enterprise or a branch is profitable, capitalists recover

automatically the money capital they have laid out, increased by a profit (according to the cycle $M - C_0 \ldots P \ldots C_1{}^+ - M^+$). When the enterprise or the branch ceases to be profitable, the capitalists hand it over to the public sector, once again recovering some money capital.

21. *Translator's note.* In the UK, the quasi-public corporation, for example the British National Oil Corporation, where the government proposes to hold 51 per cent of the share capital.

22. Alternatively, the unproductive state activities may be financed through money creation. This problem will be considered in chapter 10.

23. See chapter 7, pp. 138–9.

24. The rate of surplus value in the less-developed countries is also influenced in a decisive way by the relative importance of the *domestic production* of the means of subsistence. The greater the domestic production, the smaller the number of necessaries of life which the wage-earners have to *buy*: the value of labour-power is that much reduced, which raises the rate of surplus value. (This aspect of the matter will be considered in chapter 9, pp. 205–6.)

8

Some Fundamental Tendencies of Capitalist Growth

The object of this chapter is not to sketch out a history of capitalism and divide it up into different phases. It is rather to show some logical consequences arising from three general principles explained in previous chapters, namely:

(1) capitalist production is production aiming at profit;
(2) this profit is essentially the result of the exploitation of labour-power (of the creation of surplus value by the wage-earners);
(3) capitalists are in competition with each other to maximize their rates of profit.

These logical consequences appear in the form of *basic tendencies* in the evolution of capitalism: the tendency to develop mechanization (as a weapon in the competition among capitalists and as a means of asserting their control over the workers), the tendency to expand the sources of surplus value and the markets for production, the tendency to increase the rate of surplus value, the tendency to develop monopolistic practices and to modify the forms of competition, and so on.

The basic tendencies thus set out only hold good as *general* and *long-term* tendencies. They do not exclude the possibility that different developments may appear at *particular levels* (country, branch of industry, particular category of wage-earners etc.); it is also possible that the basic tendencies do *not* appear *immediately* and that they may *lie dormant* for fairly long intervals.

This chapter will leave aside two important tendencies of the capitalist system, namely the occurrence of periodic crises of overproduction and the occurrence of price movements (deflation or inflation). Given their special importance in today's world, these problems will be analysed more thoroughly in the two following chapters (9 and 10).

(9 and 10)

THE DEVELOPMENT OF MECHANIZATION AND THE STRENGTHEN-ING OF CAPITALIST DOMINATION

One of the most obvious tendencies of capitalist production lies in the growing mechanization of the production processes. After briefly recalling the role played by mechanization in relations *between capitalists*, we would emphasize here the role it plays in relations *between capitalists and wage-earners*, the way in which it contributes to the strengthening of the capitalists' domination over the workers.

Mechanization and Capitalist Competition

The incentive to mechanize
At the most obvious level, the development of mechanization results from the competition between capitalists. As we have seen, the utilization of an advanced technology by a particular capitalist always puts him in a favourable situation to seize a sizeable share of the aggregate surplus revenue at the expense of his competitors.

In actual fact, the capitalists who are innovators on the technological side are in a position at one and the same time to produce *more* and *at less cost* (the individual unit value of their commodities is lower than the social unit value). They thus increase their rate of profit and their potential for accumulation, at the expense of less well placed rival capitalists. The latter are obliged in their turn to introduce the techniques introduced by the innovating capitalists: if they do not (if they continue to produce commodities whose individual unit value is too great in relation to its social unit value), they will inevitably be eliminated.

Two consequences of mechanization
Imposed through competition, the introduction and the spread of technological progress (and also the elimination of backward competitors) have the effect of increasing the average productivity in all branches of production and conversely of *lowering the social unit value of all commodities.*

This drive towards mechanization also has the effect of stimulating technological progress in the production of the machines themselves: it takes less and less time for a machine to be overtaken by an improved type, for it to become out-of-date technologically before being worn out physically. This technological ageing of machines (in contrast to their physical wearing out) is known by the name of *obsolescence*. We shall see in chapter 9 that the obsolescence of machines can be considered an important factor of inflation after the Second World War. Let us mention here that obsolescence explains the interest of enterprises in operating their means of production round the clock (the system of continuous production or of the three 8-hour shifts). In fact, these enterprises see a number of advantages in this system: in utilizing their productive capacity more fully, they reduce the costs of production per unit; in having three shifts working a day, they treble the daily flow of surplus value; and in wearing out the machines three times faster, they can replace them all the more quickly by improved machines which will improve their competitive position on the market.

Mechanization and Capitalist Domination

An essential weapon in *capitalist competition*, mechanization plays just as basic a role in the *collective struggle between capitalists and workers*: as we shall see, the development of mechanization facilitates the actual imposition of capitalist domination over waged labour through the technical transformations it involves.

The capitalist transformation of production techniques
Capitalism did not change the techniques of production overnight (and it does not necessarily change them overnight when it enters sectors of pre-capitalist production). Schematically, starting from a typical small-scale production by craftsmen, we can distinguish the three following stages in the capitalist transformation of production techniques (see Table 8.1).

1. *Manufacture with simple cooperation.* The first stage is the replacement of independent workers by a *workers' collective*: the craftsmen, working at home, are brought together in one place (the workshop) and under one command (the capitalist's).

This first stage is not accompanied by any particular change in the nature of the means of production or of the labour process: the workers brought together in the manufacture each continue to carry out the same craft with the same tools. There is still no differentiation in the tasks within the workers' collective, no technical division of labour: each worker carries out as before the complete series of operations required to arrive at the finished product. Each makes use of a variety of different skills which make him a proper qualified worker. Each controls the different means of labour he uses to carry out the different operations of his craft.

This first stage is that of *simple cooperation*. Cooperation, for the individual independent workers give way to a workers' collective brought together in the manufacture. Simple cooperation, for the different elements of this workers' collective do not yet carry out specialized technically differentiated tasks.

2. *Manufacture with complex cooperation.* The second stage is that of *complex cooperation*: within the workers' collective, we observe a *differentiation of tasks*, a technical division of labour. Each worker no longer carries out, as before, the complete series of operations required to arrive at the finished product: the different operations are now split up and each handed over to a specialized group of individuals. Each worker becomes a *'fragmented' worker*, employed in a specialized category of operations: he only develops a particular category of skills and only masters a particular range of tools (a 'fragmented' tool).

This second stage, while modifying the labour process, does not basically modify the means of labour: the difference from the first stage is that each worker, in order to fulfil the specialized function in which he is employed, only uses a specialized category of tools (and a specialized category of skills).

3. *Large-scale industry.* The third stage is the replacement of 'fragmented' tools by a system of machine tools (in combination and functioning at the same time). From here, the worker becomes an appendage of the machine, subject to the machine. In Marx's words:

> In the manufacture (first and second stages), the worker uses the tool; in the factory (third stage), he serves the machine. In the first case, it is he who sets the means of labour in motion; in the second, he has only to conform to its motion. In the manufacture, the workers are members of a living mechanism; in the factory, they are only the living complements of a lifeless mechanism which exists independently of them.[1]

This situation deprives the worker of all control over the functioning of the means of production and over the product of his labour. While in the manufacture, the quantity and quality of production depend basically on the efficiency of each worker (on his skill, on his *savoir-faire*); in the factory, they depend basically on the efficiency of the machines (on the scientific progress embodied in them). Compared with the efficiency of the machines, the particular skill of the workers counts for little: subordinated to the machine, they are also increasingly unskilled and interchangeable.

The strengthening of capitalist domination
The three stages in the transition from the craftsman's workshop to large-scale industry are synthetized in Table 8.1. This however only

TABLE 8.1   *Capitalist transformation of the techniques of production*

| | TYPE OF ENTERPRISE | | | |
| | Craftsmen's workshop | Capitalist enterprise *(workers' collective working for a capitalist)* | | |
	(independent individual workers)	*Manufacture with simple cooperation*	*Manufacture with complex cooperation*	*Large-scale industry*
Technical division of labour	No	No	Yes	Yes
Means of labour used	Simple tools	Simple tools	Simple tools	Machine-tools
Type of labour and 'technical relations of production'	Skilled labour controlling all tools	Skilled labour controlling all tools	'Fragmented' labour controlling one tool	'Fragmented' labour subordinated to the machine

brings out the transformations in the *technical relations of production* and more or less passes over the basic change that the development of machinery introduces into the 'quality' of the *social relations of production*, in the 'quality' of capitalist domination.[2]

Before the introduction of mechanization, we can speak of the capitalists' *'formal* domination'. By this we understand the domination they exercise from the simple fact that they – and not the workers – have control of the *ownership* of the means of production: this enables them to purchase the wage-earners' labour-power and to extract the surplus revenue from it, even though the wage-earners still have control of the functioning of the means of production.

With the development of mechanization, capitalist domination becomes *real*. By this we mean the domination exercized by the capitalists controlling not only the *ownership* but also the *functioning* of the means of production. Now the workers are doubly subordinated to the capitalists: obliged to work for the benefit of the owners of the means of production, they also become instruments of the machine controlled by the capitalists.

The control of the functioning of the means of production is ensured, in the capitalists' name, by a minority of workers specialized in the tasks of technical and social supervision: researchers working on the perfection of new techniques, engineers, ensuring the control and adjustments of the production processes, technicians and foremen responsible for overseeing the workers' discipline and their submission to the rhythm of the machines etc. In other words, the *capitalists' real domination* (by way of the development of mechanization) *is necessarily accompanied by a dissociation between manual labour and intellectual labour*: a growing majority of workers find themselves reduced to purely routine tasks, to unskilled and mindless jobs; at the other extreme, a minority of workers monopolize the control tasks, which call for a skilled intellectual type of labour.[3]

INCREASING THE RATE OF SURPLUS VALUE

The development of mechanization not only has the effect of *establishing capitalist domination* over the workers: it also makes it possible to raise the rate of surplus value, that is, *to increase the degree of exploitation* to which the workers are subjected. This is what we shall see as we study the two main ways in which the rate of surplus value can be increased: on one hand, the prolongation of labour-time, on the other, the reduction of the value of labour-power.[4] These two methods of increasing the rate of surplus value are generally called (a) *'production of absolute surplus value'*, and (b) *'production of relative surplus value'*.[5]

The Lengthening of Labour-time (the 'Production of Absolute Surplus Value')

The lengthening of labour-time is the most direct means of increasing the rate of surplus value.

Let us assume that the daily value of labour-power is 3 hours (and that the monetary expression of values is £3 per hour, hence a daily wage of £9). If the daily labour-time at t_0 is 8 hours, the surplus labour is 5 hours (hence a surplus revenue of £15 per worker) and the rate of surplus value is 166 per cent. If the daily labour-time goes up to 10 hours at t_1, the surplus labour is 7 hours (hence a surplus revenue of £21) and the rate of surplus value = 233 per cent. The situation is illustrated in this diagram:

This first method of increasing the rate of surplus value was normally used at the beginning of capitalism: the labour-time was systematically increased, going from 12 to 14, even to 16 hours a day! But this method came up against physical barriers (a minimum of time required to ensure the workers' rest and recovery) and social barriers (the resistance of the working-class and its struggle for the statutory limitation of the working-day).

With the development of capitalism, the significance of this first method has become comparatively minor. We should note, however, that it still applies in many less-developed countries. It also enables us to understand the resistance of the employers, today as in the past, to the reduction of labour-time: to reduce labour-time (while paying the same wage), is to reduce surplus labour, and is consequently to lower the rate of surplus value and the rate of profit. This resistance on the part of the employers therefore confirms indirectly the Marxist analysis, according to which capitalist profit is based on the surplus labour of the wage-earners.[6]

The Reduction of the Value of Labour-power (the 'Production of Relative Surplus Value')

The second method of increasing the rate of surplus value works through the reduction of the value of labour-power. Let us assume that the daily labour-time is 8 hours. If the value of labour-power at t_0 is 3 hours, the surplus labour is 5 hours, and the rate of surplus value = 166 per cent. If the value of labour-power falls to 2 hours at t_1, the surplus labour is 6 hours and the rate of surplus value = 300 per cent. The situation is illustrated in the following diagram (in hypothesis A, we assume that the monetary expression of value is still £3 per hour; in hypothesis B – a period of inflation – we assume that E increases to £10 per hour).

	3 hours	5 hours
t_0	£9	£15

	2 hours	6 hours
t_1 (Hyp. A)	£6	£18

	2 hours	6 hours
t_1 (Hyp. B)	£20	£60

The conditions for an increase in the rate of surplus value

The problem is to know the conditions in which the value of labour-power can fall. Let us recall that the value of labour-power is equal to the value of the means of subsistence purchased: it depends therefore on the *number* of means of subsistence purchased and on their *average value*.[7]

Now the introduction and the development of mechanization (which are explained by competition between capitalists and by the necessity of strengthening their common domination over the workers) have the effect of increasing the productivity of labour and of reducing the value of commodities. *The development of mechanization has the particular effect of reducing the average value of the means of subsistence purchased by the workers.* It is so from the moment there is an increase in productivity, (a) in the industries producing the means of subsistence (bakeries, household appliances etc.), and/or (b) in the industries producing the means of production (wheat, metal etc.)

used by the 'means of subsistence' sector (which has the result of reducing the *past* value of the means of subsistence).

The conditions for the value of labour-power to fall (and for the rate of surplus value to increase) then appear as follows: it is necessary (and sufficient) that the *number* of necessaries of life consumed should increase less than the fall in their *average value*. In other words, it is necessary (and sufficient) that *the workers' level of consumption should increase less rapidly than productivity* in the (direct and indirect) production of their means of subsistence.

Now the development of mechanization does in fact make it possible – not only to increase productivity – but also to limit the rise of the workers' level of consumption. This is so because the development of mechanization modifies the overall balance of power between capitalists and workers in different but complementary ways.

(1) The continual transformations of labour processes, bound up with the development of mechanization, are constantly putting a proportion of the active workers out of employment (in this respect, see the role of 'industrial restructuring' today).

(2) The development of mechanization makes workers all the more interchangeable: as we saw, machine labour requires much fewer special skills and less specific training.

(3) It facilitates the introduction of *new* categories of workers, in particular women and immigrants. These new categories of workers exert a twofold pressure on the average level of wages and of consumption: on one hand, because they swell the total volume of the labour supply, and on the other, because they are in a particularly unfavourable bargaining position *vis à vis* the capitalists.

The compatibility between a rise in real wages and an increase in the rate of surplus value

The fact that the development of mechanization makes it possible to limit the level of consumption does not in any way mean that this level of consumption must *fall* in order for the rate of surplus value to increase. The conditions mentioned above show on the contrary that *there can be simultaneously a rise in real wages and an increase in the rate of surplus value:*[8] in other words, the increase of the workers' consumption can very well be accompanied by an intensification of the exploitation to which these same workers are subjected.

TABLE 8.2   Real wage, value of labour-power and rate of surplus value:
a theoretical example

	t_0	t_1 (Hyp. A)	t_1 (Hyp. B)
Monetary expression of values (E)	£3 per hour	£3 per hour	£10 per hour
Number of means of subsistence consumed per day (= daily wage) (x)	6	8	8
Average value if a 'means of subsistence' (px)	½ hour	¼ hour	¼ hour
Average price of a 'means of subsistence' $(px = px.E)$	£1.50	£0.75	£2.50
Value of labour-power per day (= total value of means of subsistence per day) $(w = x.px)$	3 hours	2 hours	2 hours
Price of labour-power, daily money wage (= total price of means of subsistence per day) $(w = w.E = x.px)$	£9	£6	£20
Surplus labour or surplus value per day	5 hours	6 hours	6 hours
Surplus revenue per day	£15	£18	£60
Rate of surplus value	166%	300%	300%

The numerical example in Table 8.2 is intended to explain this important point. In it we assume that the number of means of subsistence consumed daily (x) has gone up from 6 to 8 between t_0 and t_1 (which represents an increase of 33 per cent of the real wage, of the standard of living), but that simultaneously, the labour-time necessary to produce each of these necessaries of life (px) has gone down from ½ to ¼ hour (which represents a rise in productivity of 100 per cent). The joint effect of these two factors is to bring down the value of labour-power $(w = x.px)$ from 3 to 2 hours a day; for an 8-hour working-day, the surplus labour goes up from 5 to 6 hours and the rate of surplus value from 166 per cent to 300 per cent. As for the daily money wage (w = w.E), it is reduced in hypothesis A (somewhat unrealistic today, as it assumes that the monetary expression of values remains stable) and increases in hypothesis B (where E increases, which is realistic in a period of inflation). But the change in the money wage is not decisive: what is important, in order to evaluate the change in the workers' living standards, is the change in the *real wage*; and what is important in order to determine the change in the rate of surplus value, is the comparison of the changes in the *real wage* and in *productivity* in the production of the means of subsistence (which determines the *value of the various means of subsistence*).

We will find, in chapter 11, an empirical analysis of the changes in these different magnitudes in five European countries for the period from 1966 to 1978: we will see then the confirmation that the rise in real wages is perfectly compatible with stability (or even a rise) in the rate of surplus-value. Let us content ourselves here with a brief examination, in the light of the preceding theoretical analysis, of the strategies of the employers regarding wages and productivity. The 'defensive' strategy consists in linking the increase in the (average) real wage to the increase in average productivity: for a given labour-time, this objective amounts to *keeping the rate of surplus value constant*. The strategies aiming to limit the rises in money wages to the index of consumer prices have, contrary to appearances, a clearly 'offensive' significance from the employers' point of view: this objective amounts in effect to *keeping the real wage constant*; therefore, and taking account of the continued increase in productivity, it amounts to *guaranteeing an increase in the rate of surplus value*. The same applies, *a fortiori*, to present-day strategies aiming to suppress or to slow down the linking of money wages to the index of consumer prices and thus to *reduce* the real wage.[9]

Between the maintenance of the rate of surplus value (with an assured increase in the real wage) and the stabilization of the real wage (with an assured increase of the rate of surplus value), there is room, let us repeat, for a 'pacific' development, combining a rise in the standard of consumption *and* in the degree of exploitation.

This third type of development is not only important in order to ensure some degree of 'social peace' for capitalism. It is all the more important as the progress of mechanization confronts the capitalists, as we shall see later in this chapter, with a problem of markets: the increase in *productive* capacity due to mechanization, requires in the long-term a parallel increase in markets, that is to say in the *consumption* capacity of the masses. The development of mechanization thus confronts the capitalists with two contradictory requirements: to increase the rate of surplus value (and thus to *produce* more surplus value), it is in their interest to *limit* the masses' consumption: to ensure markets for the commodities produced (and therefore to *realize* the surplus value produced), it is in their interest to *increase* the masses' consumption. This contradiction between the two requirements is resolved by an increase in consumption lower than the increase in productivity: thus it is possible to increase, at the same time, the rate of surplus value and the size of the markets.[10]

THE CONTRADICTORY EFFECTS OF MECHANIZATION ON THE AVERAGE RATE OF PROFIT

The 'law of the falling rate of profit' is often presented as a cornerstone in Marx's thought. Is there any such law in Marx's thought?

Let us note first that this 'law' was put forward by Marx's predecessors, by Ricardo in particular. He declared that the rate of profit was *bound* to fall, because of circumstances *external* to the functioning of capitalism (decreases in agricultural yields, hence increase in the price of subsistence goods and rise in wages). Marx's position can be set out under three headings.

1.   A (possible) fall in the rate of profit should be explained by the very functioning of capitalism, in this case by the growth of mechanization. The latter is inherent in capitalism, as we saw earlier. But *the growth of mechanization results in less and less workers being employed in proportion to an increased mass of means of production*; since labour-power is the exclusive source of profit, a falling tendency in the average rate of profit follows logically.

This first relation between the growth of mechanization and the rate of profit can be illustrated with the help of Table 8.3, where we assume that the price of the means of production (pm), as well as all the factors influencing the rate of surplus value (x, px, d) remain constant. Here we see that the mass of the means of production used (M) doubles between t_0 and t_2, while the number of wage-earners (L) remains constant: the M/L ratio itself therefore doubles as well. If the value and price of each of the instruments of production used remain constant (pm = 8), as well as the value and the price of labour-power (x.px = 4), the C/V ratio similarly doubles. Now, an increase of the C/V ratio for a given rate of surplus value, is bound to be reflected in a fall in the rate of profit (cf. chapter, p. 98): in the example, the rate of profit falls from 33 per cent to 20 per cent.

2.   But the very growth of mechanization equally brings into play other forces which operate in a contrary direction. More precisely, the *growth of mechanization brings about rises in productivity which hold*

back the rise in C/V and make possible an increase in S/V. We already saw how the increases in productivity in the sectors (directly or indirectly) producing the workers' means of consumption involve a reduction in the value of each of them (px), a reduction which tends to offset the increase in the number of necessaries of life consumed (x): the result may very well be a reduction in the value of labour-power (x.px) and a rise in the rate of surplus value. In the same way, the increases in productivity in the sectors producing the means of production (tools, materials etc.) involve a reduction in the value of each of them (pm), a reduction which tends to offset the increase in the number of instruments of production used (M): the result will be a less rapid increase of C than of M.

The contradictory effects of the growth of mechanization on the evolution of the average rate of profit are illustrated in Table 8.4. We assume here that the increases in productivity cause the value of each of the instruments of production (pm) to fall (from 8 to 6); they cause the value of each of the means of subsistence (px) to fall as well (from 1 to 0.5) and make possible a rise in the level of consumption (the number of necessaries of life consumed (x) goes up from 4 to 6). The result of these different developments is that the rise in the composition of capital (C/V) is offset by the rise in the rate of surplus value (S/V), so that, in the example, the rate of profit is virtually stable.

The figures in the example are purely illustrative and do not justify any conclusion regarding the actual changes in the average rate of profit: they are intended solely to explain the contradictory influences which the growth of mechanization exercises on the rate of profit.[11] But the growth of mechanization, as we shall see, is not the only variable affecting its evolution.

3.   Independently of the contradictory influences of mechanization, other factors can influence the evolution of the average rate of profit.

(1)   International trade makes it possible to obtain raw materials and consumption goods, which are produced in more favourable natural conditions and are therefore less expensive (hence reduction of C and of V).

(2)   Capitalist investments in new branches where the volume of means of production is less significant (such as the tertiary of commodity production) have the effect of lowering the overall composition of capital.

(3)   Capitalist investments in less-developed countries, where

*TABLE 8.3   Growth of mechanization and tendency of the average
rate of profit to fall*

	M	L	x	pm	px	C	V	S	M/L	C/V	S/V	S/K
	(number)			*(hours or £)*								
t_0	100	100	4	8	1	800	400	400	1	2	100%	33%
t_1	150	100	4	8	1	1200	400	400	1.5	3	100%	25%
t_2	200	100	4	8	1	1600	400	400	2	4	100%	20%

*TABLE 8.4   The contradictory effects of mechanization on the evolution of
the average rate of profit*

	M	L	x	pm	px	C	V	S	M/L	C/V	S/V	S/K
	(number)			*(hours or £)*								
t_0	100	100	4	8	1	800	400	400	1	2	100%	33%
t_1	150	100	5	7	0.7	1050	350	450	1.5	3	129%	32%
t_2	200	100	6	6	0.5	1200	,300	500	2	4	167%	33%

Notes to tables 8.3 and 8.4:
(1) For the meaning of the symbols, see text here or chapter 4, p. 92.
(2) The monetary expression of values (E) is assumed to be £1 per hour.
     Hence pm, px, C, V, S may equally represent values or prices.
(3) Principal relations. C = M.pm and V = L.x.px (see chapter 4, p. 92);
     V + S = 8L (labour-time assumed equal to 8).

wages are much lower, have the effect of raising the average
rate of surplus value worldwide.[12]
(4)   Finally, we must remember that the evolution of the rate of
       surplus value, in advanced as in less-developed countries, is
       never determined automatically by the growth of mechaniza-
       tion and the increases in productivity which accompany it.
       The rate of surplus value depends just as much on the overall
       balance of power between capitalists and workers: within the

limits set out by the advances in productivity, it is this
balance of power which determines the masses' level of
consumption and the rate of surplus value.

In conclusion, it appears difficult to defend the existence of a 'law of
the falling rate of profit'. We should rather consider the falling rate of
profit as the *danger to be avoided* by capitalism and see in the rate of
profit the general indicator of capitalism's 'state of health'. In this
perspective, rather than seeking to verify a hypothetical law through
figures, it is better to analyse the different tendencies and counter-
tendencies which can effect the rate of profit. Among these, the
evolution of the balance of power between capitalists and workers
throughout the world seems just as decisive as the growth of
mechanization.

CHANGING FORMS OF CAPITALIST COMPETITION

Relations between capitalists (or capitalist groups) have always been
competitive: each enterprise or group seeks to maximize its *particular*
rate of profit, at the expense of other enterprises or groups. But the
actual forms of this competition have become more complex with
the growth of capitalism. Schematically, we can distinguish the two
following stages. In the first stage, capital can move freely from one
branch to another and within each branch and competition takes
place essentially by means of the reduction of costs and of prices. In
the second stage, obstacles are put in the way of capital movements
and new forms of competition are superimposed on 'classical'
competition.

Price Competition

The essential weapon in capitalist competition consists in producing
goods and services more cheaply than one's competitors: the
capitalist who produces at lower cost is in a postion to sell at a lower
price than his competitors and so to increase his scale of production
and his profit at their expense.

The very best means of producing more cheaply, as we have
already noted, lie in technological innovation, in mechanization: the
innovating capitalist introduces new techniques in order to produce
in greater quantity and at lower unit cost.

The results of this competition through prices are well known:
progressive elimination of the marginal enterprises (who are unable to

keep up with technical innovation) and *progressive concentration of production in large enterprises* (in each branch, increasingly large enterprises, limited in number, monopolize a growing proportion of capital, production and employment).

The increase of these large enterprises was obviously bound to create a financing problem for individual capitalists: with the growing importance of mechanization, the funds necessary for the launching and development of a (large) enterprise increasingly exceeded the capitalist's personal means. The formula of *limited companies* and the activity of the banks (acting as *financial intermediaries*) made it possible to find a way round this obstacle: they made possible the assembly of a multitude of small amounts of capital and so ensured that the capital funds required were available to capitalist entrepreneurs.[13]

Another way of ensuring the availability of capital funds to capitalist entrepreneurs was found in the development of credit money created by the banks (acting here as *money creators*): as we shall see in chapter 10, banks are in fact in a position to lend the entrepreneurs capital funds which have not been previously assembled from other outside sources, but which constitute fresh money, created from nothing by the banks themselves.

Obstacles to Free Competition and New Forms of Competition

Monopoly agreements

The concentration of production and the intervention of the banks in financing were favourable to the conclusion of *agreements between enterprises*, agreements aiming to limit competition through prices. The reduced number of competitors remaining in a branch (following the elimination of the marginal producers) brings about a clearer conception of the common interest: better to agree on a common price profitable to all than to carry on an anarchic competition, costly and dangerous to all. On the other hand, the important role played by the banks in the financing of limited companies gives them a certain control over industry:[14] having interests vested in competing enterprises, they would naturally tend to favour the conclusion of agreements between them on prices profitable to all of them.

These agreements between producers are called *monopoly agreements*. They are intended to *fix prices (regulated prices) at a level higher than would result from free competition*, and thus to raise the rate of profit of the various participants.[15]

Restrictive practices of monopolistic enterprises

In order to keep the benefit of a higher rate of profit, monopolistic enterprises have to exercise strict control over any increase in production and therefore over any new investment in the sector. For an excessive increase of investment and of production would lead to a reduction of prices and of the rate of profit in the branch. So monopolistic enterprises have to be restrictive in two respects.

First, they have to avoid reinvesting all their profits in their own branch.[16] The part of the profits, which it is not in the monopolistic enterprises' interest to reinvest in the original branch, constitutes *surplus capital* for that branch. It is in the interest of the enterprises concerned to invest their surplus capital *in other branches*, even if the latter have no relation to the original one. This is the phenomenon of *conglomerates*, or unified groups of enterprises producing ranges of different commodities; if these conglomerates distribute their investments in several countries, they can also be described as *multinational companies.*[17]

Second, it is in the interest of monopolistic enterprises that there should be *barriers to the entry of new competitors* (logically attracted by the high rates of profit in the monopolized sector). These barriers are of two types: natural and artificial.

The *natural (or technological) barriers* are created by the size of the investments which, as a result of the growth of mechanization, are required, in numerous branches of production, to establish a new enterprise. Such investments consitute a double obstacle to the entry of rival enterprises. On the one hand, the greater the size of the investment, the harder it is to assemble the money-capital required in the launching of such enterprises. On the other hand, the larger the investment, the bigger the share of the market which must be taken over in order to be able to compete with the enterprises which are already established (and which are sufficiently developed to benefit from the 'economies of scale' linked to the investments they have carried out).[18]

Technological barriers are not equally significant in every branch. In branches where mechanization is less advanced, the money-capital required to set up a new enterprise is less and 'economies of scale' are not great. In these conditions, the check on the introduction of new capital involves the setting up of *artificial barriers*.

The first consists in embarking on expenditure in *advertising*, which plays a role similar to that of investing in machines: the greater the necessary investment in advertising, the harder it will be to stake out a share of the market large enough to be able to minimize the unit charge of this outlay and to compete with enterprises which are already established.

A second artificial barrier involves products (for example cigarettes, soap) whose consumers frequently change their choice of brand. The floating population which is disposed to brand changing constitutes a potential clientèle for a new enterprise. But the greater the *number of brands* sold by the existing enterprises, the more changes will take place between existing brands: which reduces accordingly the percentage of potential customers for the brand – or brands – which a new competitor might introduce.

New forms of competition between monopolistic enterprises within a protected branch[19]
Agreements to regulate prices and to raise the rates of profit *do not put an end to competition between the enterprises concerned.* Such agreements put an end to price competition but not to competition itself. Each enterprise seeks as always to maximize its particular rate of profit, and with this aim in view, seeks both to win over the customers of rival enterprises and to reduce its own production costs.

The means adopted to win over the customers of rival enterprises are different, however. Instead of going back to the price war, each enterprise intensifies the *advertising* of its own products and multiplies its own *brands*. These steps therefore constitute both an obstacle to the entry of new competitors *and* a new form of competition between firms which are already established.

To reduce production costs appears profitable both in the short term and in the long term. In the short term, the monopolistic enterprises take advantage of the regulated price they have agreed on. Given the level of this price, it is clear that a lower cost will result in a higher profit for the enterprise concerned. In the long term, the enterprises taking part in the agreement may very well lose the protection they enjoy: whether through 'outsiders' succeeding in getting round the entry restrictions or through other capitalist groups succeeding in having this protection destroyed.[20] Foreseeing this possibility, monopolistic enterprises continue to invest in plant capable of producing still more and at lower cost: they prepare themselves for the ever possible reopening of the price war.

The monopolistic enterprises thus continue to increase their productive capacity. On the other hand, as we saw earlier,[21] they have to control and limit the growth of their production in order to maintain their high rates of profit. The result of this is a *continuous underemployment of the (increased) productive capacity*

In an attempt to remedy the underemployment of their productive capacity, the monopolistic enterprises seek to swell demand artificially by *deliberately limiting the use-life of their commodities*. The *physical* use-life of commodities is limited by downgrading the quality and strength of the materials and assemblies turned out (it is well known that, for example, cars, shoes and electric household appliances could be designed and made to last much longer) or in limiting the availability of spare parts. The *social* use-life of commodities is limited by imposing cóntinual changes of fashion, both in clothes and in other consumer goods (new models from car manufacturers, launching new varieties of the same food product etc.).

As the use-life of commodities can be planned by enterprises, it becomes an extra weapon in competition: it is in the interest of a producer who wishes to launch a new variety of commodity to guarantee initially a superior quality to that of rival products and a longer use-life: as soon as his product is established on the market, it is in his interest (like other rival firms) to limit its use-life in order to bring about an artificial renewal of demand.[22]

Competition between branches over protection
The new forms of competition mentioned so far involve relations between (monopolistic) enterprises *within each (protected) branch*. But with the increasing number of monopoly agreements, competition also extends to the relations *between branches* of production.

In fact, as long as protection lasts – the protection enjoyed by monopolistic enterprises within particular branches of production – the branches in question benefit from a higher than average rate of profit. But, as we saw in the analysis of the transfers of surplus revenue, the high rates of profit of the protected branches involve a reduction in the rate of profit of the unprotected (or less protected) branches.

Faced with the reduction of their rate of profit, the rival branches are compelled in their turn to carry out defensive measures of reorganization and of regrouping: the setting up of trade associations or cartels, regulation of the access to various professions (degrees, *numerus clausus*), official price control, all measures intended to establish *compensatory forms of protection*. The branches whose rate of profit is threatened can equally seek to *do away with the forms of protection* enjoyed by other branches: this is the explanation for example of the proposals for anti-trust policies or of the plans aiming to reduce agricultural prices in the EEC. Competition is therefore no longer limited to economic relations between enterprises within each branch: it extends to political relations between different branches, who compete for the ear of the authorities to obtain some specific forms of protection or to have others forms of protection abolished.

As we can see, the divergences from free (price) competition are unavoidable and cumulative; whether to increase their rate of profit or to defend it, all branches feel compelled to surround themselves with various forms of protection and to compete with each other over them. Consequently, differences in the average rates of profit reflect primarily the differences in the degree of power – political as much as economic – enjoyed by each branch.

THE GROWTH OF PRODUCTION, OF THE MARKET AND OF MONEY UNDER CAPITALISM

As we explained in chapter 3, the purpose of capitalist production is profit sought for its own sake. The result of this is that the profits obtained are mainly *accumulated* rather than consumed by the capitalists: the capitalists reinvest them in additional means of production and labour-power, in order to obtain subsequently even larger profits. So the reproduction of capitalism is an *expanded reproduction*: the successive cycles of capital, represented by the formula

$$M - C_0 \begin{cases} M.P \\ L.P \end{cases} \ldots P \ldots C_1{}^+ - M^+$$

are repeated on an ever increasing scale.

The expansion of the scale of reproduction affects the different forms in which capital appears in each cycle. The *money-capital* (M at the beginning, M^+ at the end) grows continuously. It is the same for *productive capital*, that is, for the mass of means of production and of labour-power brought together under capitalist control in a growing proliferation of interdependent production processes. The resulting *commodity capital* continues to swell; this increase in the number of commodities produced is all the more rapid as the mechanization of the production processes increases: the characteristic of mechanized labour is that it can produce more (and at a lower unit value) than simple manual labour, that it can expand the production of commodities more than the labour (past and present) required to produce them.

The expanded reproduction of capitalism obviously involves more than the simple increasing of capital in the three forms we have set out. In addition, the conditions of interdependence between the different branches must be fulfilled, the supply of the various commodities must correspond to the demand for them, the rate of profit must be sufficient to induce the capitalists to accumulate etc. As capitalist reproduction is based on the initiative of thousands of competing entrepreneurs, these conditions are never more than roughly fulfilled; they appear rather as a (theoretical) norm to ensure the balanced growth of capitalism. It follows that the expanded reproduction of capitalism is characterized in practice by a succession of imbalances, of breakdowns and of 'crises'.

The following chapter will deal with this problem of *periodic crises*, inherent in the growth of capitalism. In this section, attention is centred on *three long-term problems* facing the expanded reproduction of capital.

The first problem is that of *increasing the amount of labour-power available for purchase* by the capitalists. The expansion of productive capital is the increase in the number of instruments of production *and in the amount of labour-power* brought together under capitalist control. In theory, capitalists control the production of the means of production and can increase it according to the requirements of the expanded reproduction of capital (similarly they can, in theory, ensure the desired increase in the production of the means of consumption). But this capacity for increasing the capitalist production of commodities itself assumes a continuous increase in the supply of waged labour-power: it is on this that the whole of capitalist production of commodities is ultimately based. But the waged labour-power, unlike the means of production or consumption, cannot be turned out at will in the factory. Hence the problem: how to ensure the expanded reproduction of this particular and indispensable commodity – waged labour-power?

A second problem is that of *expanding the markets* for capitalist production. The growth of productive capital and increasing mechanization have the effect of vastly multiplying the productive capacity of enterprises, their supply of goods and services. But it is still necessary for these infinitely multipliable goods and services to be sold: failing which, the commodity capital cannot be converted into money-capital and there will be no profit.

The third problem is that of *adjusting the quantity of money* to the needs of the expanded reproduction of capital. The expanded reproduction of capital involves a proliferation of market transactions:

increased purchases of means of production and labour-power, increased sales of commodities. As market transactions involve the utilization of money, it is necessary that the quantity of money should match this increased volume of transactions.

The Expansion of the Supply of Waged Labour

The breaking up of non-commodity communities
The breaking up of non-commodity communities has always been an essential means of expanding the supply of waged labour.

One basic feature of a typical non-commodity community (whether it be an African clan, a Polynesian tribe or an Indian settlement) is essentially its self-sufficiency. The means of production and of consumption necessary to the community are produced within it: its own agricultural and artisanal activities ensure the production of tools, food, clothing, housing etc. consumed by its members. In such a system, neither the products of labour nor labour-power are commodities.

It is in the interest of capitalism to break up this type of community, to induce its members to sell their labour-power (in capitalist enterprises) and to purchase commodities (produced in capitalist enterprises).

The most radical means of achieving this is by force. The lands of the community are seized or a number of its members are conscripted for various kinds of forced labour (road and railway construction, work in the mines or the plantations). Without land or sufficient working hands, the community is no longer able to ensure by itself the subsistence of its members. They are compelled, in order to subsist, to sell their labour-power or at least to produce and sell commodities. In the first case, they directly swell the supply of waged labour. In the second, they subsist in the capacity of simple commodity producers facing capitalist competition: as soon as this competition has eliminated them, they too will come in to increase the supply of waged labour.

The other way of breaking up non-commodity communities, is *to introduce a minimum of commodity relations* which are intended to 'snowball'. It is possible for example to compel the communities to pay a *monetary tax*. This forces them to earn money, either by the sale of labour-power or by the sale of commodities. According to the amount of tax to be paid and according to the sale price of labour-power and of commodities sold, a varying quantity of social labour available in the non-commodity community will be diverted in this way from its traditional functions. The community's *patterns of consumption* can also be modified, more or less peaceably: they can be persuaded to consume or use certain non-traditional products (for example transistors or feeding-bottles). As these products have to be purchased, they must, in this case too, sell commodities or labour-power to earn the money required for the purchases.

Whichever way is taken, the break-up of non-commodity communities has the result of separating the producers from their means of production: this separation is immediate for some producers (those who sell their labour-power) and merely deferred for others (those who become commodity producers and so find themselves facing capitalist competition).

This separation of producers from their means of production is not a simple phenomenon of the past. We find it obviously in the beginnings of capitalism, but it continues throughout the *whole* history of capitalism, which is constantly driven to call on additional labour-power in order to be able to reproduce itself on an increased scale. The phenomenon continues at the present time and all over the world. In the less developed countries, the traditional communities continue to break up and to release manpower. This manpower swells the ranks of the proletariat in search of employment, whether in the big cities of the third world (more precisely in the 'poverty belts' surrounding these big cities) or in the developed countries (where immigrant workers find themselves herded together in 'deprived areas'). In the developed countries, the independent producers (whose historical origins goes back to the break-up of the feudal system) continually lose ground to capitalist competition and become wage-earners.

The increase of female labour

The foregoing concerned *traditional* non-commodity communities living in self-sufficiency, sheltered from commodity relations. Capitalism has available another potential reserve of waged labour in the *modern family*, more precisely in female labour.

The family itself also constitutes a non-commodity community, but a community in direct relation with commodity production. A non-commodity community, for a variety of goods and services required by its members are produced within the family: these domestic productions cover cooking, housework, sewing, education, gardening, odd jobs, repairs etc. A community in direct relation with commodity production, both by the sale of products or of labour-power (on the part of at least one person per household) and by the purchase of a range of consumer goods and of equipment intended for domestic production.

Capitalism can increase the supply of waged labour by encouraging women's labour outside the home (and if necessary child-labour, as was the case at the beginning of capitalism). In so far as it is women who actually carry out most domestic productions, the increase in their labour away from home obviously involves a reduction of the working time they devote to them. This reduction of work in the home is achieved in two complementary ways: on one hand, by *reducing the extent* of domestic production (through entrusting the care of children to crèches, making use of tinned foods instead of cultivating a bit of garden), on the other by *increasing efficiency* in housekeeping (through the use of various electric household appliances).

The Expansion of Capitalist Markets

As we have already said, the growth of productive capital and increasing mechanization have the effect of multiplying the productive capacity of enterprises and their supply of goods and services on a vast scale. This continuously increasing supply has to be matched by a demand which also continuously increases. There are three main ways to this end:

(1)   The penetration of commodity relations into non-commodity communities and the consequent increase in the number of wage-earners.
(2)   The growth of the wage-earners' purchasing power.
(3)   The increase of public sector contracts.

Let us briefly consider them.[23]

The expansion of market relations and of the wage-earning labour force

The progressive break-up of traditional communities and the release of female labour offer capitalism a twofold benefit. Not only does the supply of labour-power increase but the markets for capitalist production expand with the fall in communal and domestic productions. Transformed (immediately or in the long-term) into sellers of labour-power, the members of traditional communities in the process of dissolution are forced to acquire a growing proportion of their means of subsistence *on the market*. Cutting down her work in the household, the woman working away from home is forced to *purchase* a whole range of goods and services which she used to provide herself.

The increase of the wage-earners' purchasing power

The penetration of non-commodity communities and the correlated expansion of waged labour are not sufficient to provide the markets required by the growth of capitalist production. For the growth of mechanization is accompanied by an accelerated expansion of the supply of goods and services: capitalist production becomes mass production. *For this mass production, typical of large-scale capitalist industry, there must be corresponding mass consumption.* The growing flow of commodities can only be sold off if the purchasing power of the mass of wage-earners increases. The relatively recent phenomenon of the 'consumer society' is thus a necessary product of capitalism and today constitutes a necessary condition of its reproduction.

We must make it clear that, like all the tendencies described in this chapter, mass-consumption and the increase of the wage-earners' purchasing power only constitute *general* and *long-term* phenomena: it is not impossible that purchasing-power may stagnate or diminish in certain circumstances or for certain categories of the population.

We must also make it clear that the majority of commodities, taken individually, do not enter overnight into mass consumption. For every new commodity (cars, electric household appliances, television sets, travel abroad), the classic scenario is rather as follows. In the first stage, the product is manufactured in a relatively limited quantity and on a 'trial' basis; its value and price are relatively high and its consumption is reserved for a minority with high incomes. The second stage is where the product, perfected technologically, is then mass-produced; its value and price have come down and its consumption spreads to larger and larger sections of the population.

This spread of the new product, made possible by the fall in value and price, is fostered in various ways. It is particularly fostered by *advertising*, together with the growth of *personal credit* (the hire-purchase system). Advertising thus plays a threefold role in capitalism: it is a means of competition between monopolistic enterprises within each branch of production, it is a means of limiting the entry of outside competitors into the branch and it is at the same time a means of stimulating the mass-consumption which is necessary for the growth of capitalism. Mass-consumption is equally stimulated by the 'gatekeeper effect' ('keeping up with the Joneses').

We mean by this that the consumption of the higher income group of the population appears spontaneously (and is so presented by advertising) as a 'consumption model' for the masses. Because of this 'gatekeeper effect', the maintenance of a *pyramid of unequal incomes* plays an entirely functional role in the reproduction of capitalism: the privileges of consumption enjoyed by the minorities at the top of the pyramid have the effect of fuelling the desire and the demand of increasingly wider layers, lower and lower down the pyramid.[24]

The growth of public sector contracts

This phenomenon must be considered in relation to the long-term growth of monopolistic practices which we spoke of earlier. We saw that it was in the interest of monopolistic enterprises to invest their 'surplus capital' in branches of production other than their own. We also saw that monopolistic practices tend to be progressively widespread among all branches. As a result, the problem of profitably investing surplus capital becomes increasingly difficult: the profits made by the conglomerates in new branches of production have themselves to be reinvested and the field of profitable investments is reduced by the prevalence of monopolistic practices.

The growth of public sector expenditure helps to resolve this problem. Government contracts for armaments, for road construction and for space exploration (and before long for the anti-pollution campaign or for urban renewal) facilitate the profitable investment of the capital of the large monopolistic enterprises which obtain the contracts. These enterprises can produce, while enjoying both a secure *market* and a guaranteed *rate of profit*: in fact, government and enterprises come to agreements on prices which guarantee to the latter a rate of profit equal to or higher than the average.

But the profits thus obtained have now to be accumulated (that is, reinvested in order to obtain further profits): hence the pressure for government contracts to be kept up, at least to existing levels. Moreover, surplus capital tends to mount up with the growth of monopolistic practices: hence the pressure for government contracts not only to be kept up but to be renewed on an ever expanding scale.

This explains the continual increase in the number of public sector contracts, designed to provide a market which is increasingly essential to capitalist production. This also explains the shift in liberal ideology regarding government intervention: for long supporters of a broad *laissez-faire* policy, capitalists have been brought round to defend the benefits of measures of state intervention, presented as 'regulators of economic activity'. These 'regulators' do not incidentally only suit the long-term demands of capitalist growth: as we shall see, they may be particularly welcome in times of crisis.

The Growth of the Quantity of Money

As we have already said, the expanded reproduction of capital involves a proliferation of market transactions: increased purchases of means of production and of labour-power, increased sales of commodities. As market transactions involve the utilization of money, this increased volume of transactions has to be matched by a corresponding increase in the quantity of money.

We will consider first the factors which determine the quantity of money necessary for market transactions. We will then outline the essential transformations which made it possible for the money supply to meet these particular needs.

The quantity of money required for market transactions

The basic principle involved can be stated in the following way: in so far as money is used to exchange commodities, *the quantity of money required depends primarily on the sum total of the prices of the commodities which are exchanged.*

We can illustrate this principle by a simple example. Let us assume that in the course of a given period (one day), ten commodities are offered for sale and are actually purchased for a total price of £1000: the quantity of money required to carry out these transactions is £1000. Let us now assume that twenty commodities are offered and purchased at a total price of £2000: the quantity of money required is £2000.[25]

Now the sum total of the prices of the commodities is equal to the sum total of the values of these commodities expressed in monetary terms:

Sum total of prices = sum total of values × E.

The possible variations of the monetary expression of values (E) will be examined in chapter 10 (pp. 228–33). We will see that, in the long-term, the normal tendency is for E to *rise*. This makes for an increase in the sum total of prices, and therefore in the quantity of money required.

Disregarding the variations of E, how does the sum total of the value of commodities evolve along with the growth of capitalism? This total value consists of past value transferred (C) and new value created $(V + S)$. Now the expanded reproduction of capital causes both to increase. As we saw, it involves first of all an expansion of the waged labour employed in the production of commodities and therefore an increase in the new value created.[26] It also involves increased mechanization, which increases the quantity of means of production used per wage-earner (the M/L ratio) and tends to increase the $C/(V + S)$ ratio: as a result of this, the mass of past value transferred normally grows and may even grow more than the mass of new value created.[27]

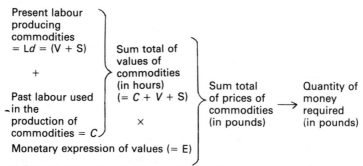

FIGURE 8.1   *Essential factors determining the quantity of money required for market transactions.*

Figure 8.1 synthetizes the essential factors which determine the quantity of money required for market transactions. Since L, C and E tend all three to increase in the long-term, the sum total of prices of commodities must necessarily increase, and hence also the quantity of money required.[28]

The adjustment of the money supply to the needs of market transactions
Faced with the continuous increase of the sum total of values and of the sum total of prices of commodities, the corresponding growth of the money supply has been made easier by the progressive 'dematerialization' of money: *metallic money*, originating in metal production, has been gradually replaced by *credit money*, originating in banking activity.

In the dawn of capitalism, the prevailing form of money was metallic: the quantity of money available was thus linked to the hazards of metal production and was strictly limited by the size of the exploitable deposits.

With the growth of capitalism, metallic money progressively lost ground, faced with the expansion of 'credit money'. The distinctive feature of this new money (which takes the form of bank-notes and then of entries in bank accounts) is that it is created by the banks *when credits are granted to economic agents*. It is created especially to assist industrialists who want to expand their business. The banks create monetary means (bank-notes or advances) which enable these industrialists to purchase the means of production and labour required to increase production. In so far as the new products find purchasers, the sum total of values increases. And this *increase in the sum total of values* is accompanied (and even preceded) by an *increase in the quantity of money* (in the form of credit money).

Chapter 10 will analyse more closely the evolution of the different types of money and the specific problems connected with credit money. The few indications provided here should be enough to suggest how the growth of credit money has facilitated the adjustment of the quantity of money to the needs of the expanded reproduction of capital and of market transactions.

NOTES

1. Marx, *Capital*, Volume II, Book 1.
2. The *technical relations of production* can be defined as the relations of domination/subordination which bind the workers to the means of labour. The *social relations of production* can be defined as the relations of domination/ subordination which bind the workers to the owners of the means of production. The analysis of the capitalist transformation of the techniques of production suggests the following conclusion: in *capitalism, social relations influence the evolution of the technical relations of production in a direction which strengthens capitalist domination.*
3. The 'fragmentation' of tasks and the complete subordination of the mass of workers, characteristic of large-scale capitalist industry, are today increasingly called in question. They now constitute obstacles to the development of capitalism, as much from the economic point of view (they are a cause of low productivity) as from the ideological point of view (they tarnish the democratic facade of capitalism). Hence the present experiments in *job development* (a worker carries out a relatively complex cycle of operations rather than a 'fragmented' and repetitive job) and *job enrichment* (which consists in giving the worker responsibility for jobs of adjustment, inspection etc. hitherto reserved to the supervising staff). Such experiments can only remain marginal within the framework of capitalism; their very significance is entirely different according to whether the initiative comes from the workers or the capitalists.

4. In a more general way, the lengthening of labour-time and the reduction of the value of labour-power constitute two ways of increasing the rate of *surplus labour*, both of productive and of unproductive wage-earners. The analyses of the increase of the rate of surplus value therefore apply equally to the increase of the rate of surplus labour of unproductive wage-earners.

5. These expressions are ambiguous, for they suggest that there may be two kinds of surplus value (absolute and relative). In fact, the two expressions should be understood in the sense of '*absolute method of increasing* the production of surplus value per worker' and '*relative method of increasing* the production of surplus value per worker'.

6. Can the increase in the *intensity* of labour be put on the same footing as the increase of labour-*time*? Opinions on this subject are divided. We consider that the increase in the intensity of labour constitutes rather one of the means of increasing the productivity of labour, thus making possible the increase of the 'production of relative surplus value'. (The question of intensity will be discussed again in chapter 11, pp. 244–5).

7. Using the symbols defined in chapter 4, the value of labour-power (w) depends on the number of necessaries of life (x) and on their average value (px): $w = x.px$.

8. Let us recall that the *real wage* is merely the level of consumption, the number of commodities which can be purchased for a given *money wage*. The rise in the real wage can be statistically determined by dividing the rise of the money wage by the appropriate figure in the index of consumer prices.

9. If we can thus 'translate' the employers' strategies into Marxist terms, we must also bring out the theoretical differences which underlie the employers' and the Marxists' conceptions.

   The employers base their 'defensive' strategies on the prevailing economic theory. According to this, the wage is the remuneration of the *labour* 'factor' and this remuneration is linked to the productivity of labour (whatever the enterprise, branch or the economy as a whole). In this sense, an increase in productivity would justify a rise in the real wage (the employers obviously 'forget' this theoretical link when they take up an 'offensive' position).

   According to Marxist theory, the wage is the remuneration of *labour-power* and this remuneration is linked, on one hand to the wage-earners' consumption needs (to the recharging of their labour-power) and on the other, to average productivity *in the* (direct and indirect) *production of their means of consumption*. For Marxist theory, an increase of this productivity makes it possible to lower the value of labour-power and thus to increase the rate of surplus value, in so far as the increase in productivity is not offset by a proportionate increase in the real wage.

10. The preceding arguments are sufficient to discredit a current

preconception, according to which Marxist theory would imply a stability of the masses' level of consumption (near the subsistence level, they usually add).

11. The contradictory effects of the growth of mechanization on the average rate of profit can also be analysed starting from the general formula of the rate of profit (P′), the rate of surplus value (S′) and the composition of capital (C′) established in chapter 4:

$$P' = \frac{S'}{C' + 1}, \ S' = \frac{d}{x.px} - 1, \ C' = \frac{M}{L} \cdot \frac{pm}{px} \cdot \frac{1}{x}$$

Mechanization has contradictory effects on S′ since it tends to lower px (increasing productivity) and calls for a rising x (increased consumption to match the increased production). It has also contradictory effects on C′ since it raises the technical composition of capital (M/L) and calls for a rising x (thus reducing 1/x), while the evolution of the ratio pm/px cannot be determined *a priori* (increasing productivity reduces both pm and px). The overall effect of mechanization on S′ and C′ is thus indeterminate, and so is its overall effect on P′.

12. See on this subject chapter 9, pp. 205–6.

13. Money-capital obtained through the founding of limited companies and through bank loans did not become the *juridical property* of the capitalist entrepreneurs: but for them, the important point was to have the effective disposal, *the real ownership* of the capital.

14. This marks the advent of *finance capital* (a merger of banking capital and industrial capital) with a tendency, at the time, to a preponderance of banking capital.

15. These agreements can be *explicit* or *implicit*. An example of an *implicit* agreement is that of '*price leadership*', by virtue of which the prices fixed by a dominant enterprise are spontaneously adopted by its immediate competitors. The typical case of *explicit* agreement is the cartel agreement which fixes market quotas as well as a sale price, enabling the least efficient participant to realize a 'normal' profit (this situation was described in chapter 7, Figure 7.1).

16. A part of the profits will obviously be reinvested in the branch: whether to meet an increase in demand, or to introduce improved techniques lowering the costs of production (this aspect is dealt with below).

17. The existence of surplus capital can often modify the relations between industrial capital and banking capital. Thanks to their surplus capital, large-scale industrial enterprises can finance their own expansion by means of *ploughing back profits*. They are no longer so directly dependent on the banks; on the contrary, they can buy shares which ensure their control of them: the situation is therefore characterized rather by the *interpenetration of industrial and banking capital* (and no longer by the tendency to the control of industrial capital by banking capital).

18. By 'economies of scale', we mean the fact that the unit cost of

production is reduced with the increase of the production. The higher the fixed costs represented by machinery, the greater must be the volume of production to be achieved, in order to minimize the charge of this cost per unit produced.

19. The new forms of competition examined here assume the existence of monopoly agreements between producers. 'Classical' price competition does not, however, disappear: it continues, in so far as monopoly agreements are neither universal nor permanent; it even assumes a worldwide significance with the internationalization of production and the rise of new capitalist strongholds (Japan, Taiwan, Brazil etc.).

20. See pp. 177–8.

21. See p. 175.

22. This deliberate shortening of the use-life of commodities is bound to involve a *waste of raw materials and of energy*, a waste which people have recently become aware of. It involves equally a *waste of labour-power*, and artificially maintains employment in the branches in question: but the latter amounts to a maintenance of the flow of surplus revenue for the capitalists concerned.

23. We shall see in the next chapter that the growth of the wage-earners' purchasing power and the increase of public sector contracts are two essential features of capitalist development after the Second World War.

24. This downward spread of a consumption model is a continually repeated process: yesterday's privilege (the private car for example) is today enjoyed by (nearly) everyone, but higher income groups always have access to new privileges (the second house or the second car, the yacht or safari) which a growing number of consumers are anxious to copy. Let us also make it clear that if differences in incomes have the *effect* of stimulating consumer demand, *this does not explain them*: differences in incomes arise essentially from differences in the balance of power among the different social groups.

25. While not questioning the basic principle we have stated, we should explicate various elements which are implicit in the example given (and which should be integrated into a more precise theoretical construct). The example is actually based, for simplicity's sake, on several hypotheses.

    (1) It assumes that the money requirements result solely from transactions involving *commodities*. In fact, money is also necessary for *other* transactions, for example those which involve securities (shares, bonds etc.) or natural resources.

    (2) It assumes that the money requirements arise solely from *present* transactions. In fact, money is also necessary to settle *previous* forward transactions when they fall due.

    (3) It assumes that the same sum of money is used for only a single transaction per day (the '*velocity of circulation*' of money = 1 transaction per day). In fact, if the same sum of money can be used

for several transactions, the total quantity of money required for them is reduced accordingly.

(4) It assumes that there is no 'clearing' (mutual cancelling out) in the payments to be made. In fact, if there is such 'clearing', only the outstanding *balances* have to be paid in money and the total quantity of money is reduced accordingly.

26. More precisely, the new value created depends on the number of productive workers (L) and on the labour-time per productive worker (*d*); we can write: $(V + S) = L.d$. If the labour-time per worker (*d*) remains constant, $(V + S)$ increases in the same proportion as the number of productive workers (L). If the labour-time varies, $(V + S)$ grows more or less rapidly than L.

27. Using the symbols, introduced earlier, we can write:

$$C = L.\frac{C}{L} = L(\frac{M}{L}.pm)$$

It appears that C will rise provided the decline of *pm* (due to productivity increases in the sectors producing the means of production) does not offset the rise of *both* L and M/L; and C will *rise more* than L (or more than $V + S$ for a given labour-time) if C/L increases, that is, if the decline of *pm* does not offset the rise of M/L.

28. Two important observations must be made to clarify the meaning and the scope of the preceding argument.

1. The *sum total of prices* of commodities should not be confused with the *general level of prices* (or the average unit price of commodities): algebraically, the sum total of prices is equal to the quantity of commodities exchanged, multiplied by the general level of prices. The evolutions of the general level of prices (in the long and the short term) are examined in chapter 10.

2. The preceding argument passes over several important questions which will also be examined in chapter 10. It actually ignores:

(1) the existence of *non-commodity production*: we assume here that all the workers are employed in commodity production.

(2) the possibility of '*losses of value*' in commodity production: we assume here (a) that all the commodities produced are sold (all the present labour therefore creates value), and (b) that the past labour or the value of the means of production is normally transferred to the finished products (there are no losses due to the obsolescence of machinery).

(3) the possibility of an *excess of money*: we assume here that the quantity of money is perfectly adjusted to the requirements arising from market transactions.

9

Accumulation and Crises

As we observed earlier, the expanded reproduction of capital cannot be a balanced process, since it is based not on a conscious and coordinated organization of economic activities, but on the initiative of thousands of entrepreneurs taking independent and thus not necessarily compatible decisions.

This chapter deals with the problem of the imbalances inherent in the expanded reproduction of capital and more specifically with the problem of crises. With this aim in view, we will begin schematically by making a twofold distinction.

First we will distinguish two main stages in the expanded reproduction of capital: a stage of *'classical' accumulation* up to the Second World War and, subsequently, a stage of *'contemporary' accumulation*.[1] As we shall see, the context in which accumulation takes place differs markedly from stage to stage with regard to the wage-earners' situation (in terms of employment, remuneration and consumption) and to state intervention in the economy. As a result, production and markets (or aggregate supply and demand) tend to grow in a *non-parallel* way before the Second World War, but in a *parallel* way after the Second World War.

Secondly, we will distinguish two types of crisis: *'conjunctural' crisis* and *'structural' crisis*. A *conjunctural crisis* is a situation of *temporary overproduction* (supply exceeds demand) within a trade cycle: it is followed by a recession (decline of production) which makes it possible for an equilibrium between aggregate supply and demand to be restored. A *structural crisis* is a situation in which *fundamental problems* impede the normal functioning of the prevailing type of accumulation (whether classical or contemporary): it tends to call for a change in the context (with regard to the wage-earners' situation and to state intervention) and for a new type of accumulation. As we shall see, a conjunctural crisis may in some cases reveal the presence of a structural crisis.

'CLASSICAL' ACCUMULATION BEFORE THE SECOND WORLD WAR

The Tendency to a Non-Parallel Growth of Production and Markets

One essential feature of the whole period covering the nineteenth century and continuing up to the Second World War is the permanent tendency towards a disequilibrium between the growth of aggregate supply and demand: while technical progress and growth of the wage-earning labour force make a continuous increase possible in the capitalist production of commodities, *there is nothing to ensure a parallel growth of markets* for this production. This insufficient growth of markets can be explained by the prevailing context with regard to the wage-earners' situation and to state intervention.

1. There is no guarantee that wage-earners will increase their *consumption of capitalist commodities* or that they will do so on a regular basis. This is so for several reasons.

(1) Wage-earners ensure the reproduction of their labour-power with relatively small recourse to the purchase of capitalist commodities. They mainly consume traditional goods or services, purchased from small-scale *independent* producers or produced in the circle of *domestic* activities.

(2) The majority of labour contracts are individual contracts, linking *one* capitalist to *one* wage-earner. Each capitalist only considers the wage as a cost to be minimized, neglecting its complementary 'market' aspect; and this cost of minimization is all the easier to ensure as the capitalist negotiates with individuals rather than with a trade union. In these conditions, the consumption capacity of wage-earners always tends to increase less rapidly than the productive capacity of enterprises (in other words, the real wage per worker tends to increase less rapidly than the physical productivity per worker).

(3) *Jobs and incomes are precarious* (that is, not stable) and liable to *great variations*. The labour contracts concluded between capitalists and wage-earners only cover limited periods: wage-earners can therefore easily be deprived of their jobs. It is true that the state provides steady jobs for officials (in the sector of administration or of non-commodity production) but the latter only constitute a small proportion of the

working population. Wage-earners who lose their jobs (because of unemployment but also because of illness, accident, or age) also lose thir wages and this loss of wages is not made up by a 'social wage' (unemployment benefit, allowances etc.).

2.   On the other hand, the state intervenes relatively little to support aggregate demand:

(1)   As we have indicated, employment in the non-commodity production sector is still extremely low.
(2)   Similarly, state contracts for the private sector and other measures of state intervention in the economy are still very limited.[2]

The Cyclical Character of Production

In the context of accumulation described above, the growth of capitalism takes place through an alternation of phases of expansion (increase in production) and of recession (decline of production). A phase of expansion tends to proceed cumulatively but reaches a limit which necessitates a reversal (this is the conjunctural crisis). In the same way, the recession which follows proceeds cumulatively but it also reaches a limit which permits a recovery and a new expansion.

Let us briefly describe the successive phases of this 'trade cycle' before making some comments on crises and recessions.

The 'trade cycle'[3]

1.   *Expansion.* The expansion of production proceeds cumulatively: an increase in production brings about an increase in employment and wages, and therefore an increase in demand; increased demand in its turn stimulates a rise in prices, in profits, in investment, in production; and so on.

2.   *Crisis.* Expansion takes place in a competitive and disorganized way. Competition compels each *individual* capitalist to increase his capacity and level of production without the *total* increase in production being planned with a view to possible markets. Now, as we saw, the markets tend to develop in a relatively limited way. The result is that, sooner or later, *supply exceeds demand*: this is the *crisis of overproduction*. The excess of supply results in the accumulation of unsold stocks and in the increase of unused productive capacity.

3.   *Recession.* The excess supply brings about a fall in market prices and a *reduction in rates of profit.*[4] This situation affects particularly the marginal enterprises in each branch: already working with the highest unit costs and the most slender profit margins, they are faced with *bankruptcy*. As for the surviving enterprises, they cut back their production and try to lower their costs by carrying out measures of *rationalization.*

Following the bankruptcies, cut-backs in production and measures of rationalization, *unemployment* spreads. As the workers who are discharged lose their wages and the lost wages are not replaced by unemployment benefit, *aggregate purchasing power contracts.*

The process described is that of *recession*. This tends to have a *cumulative* character. In fact, the contraction of the masses' purchasing power amounts to a reduction of demand: as a result, prices and profits fall and bankruptcies become widespread.

4.   *Upturn and recovery.* The process of recession does not, however, continue indefinitely. After a certain time, it stops and gives way to a *recovery*. Recession, in fact, exercises a 'curative' influence on the rate of profit of the (surviving) enterprises. First, the elimination of the marginal enterprises amounts to a rise in productivity, which tends to increase the rate of surplus value (through a reduction of the value of the means of subsistence); the rise in unemployment depresses the masses' living standards, which also tends to increase the rate of surplus value. As regards markets, the elimination of the marginal enterprises increases the potential clientèle of the surviving enterprises and the fall in market prices stimulates a recovery of demand.

The surviving enterprises dispose of their stocks, market prices go up, as do the rates of profit. The recovery then becomes a new cumulative expansion: investment picks up, production increases and with it, employment, wages and demand.

Absurdity and functional character of crises and recessions
On the one hand, the process of crisis and recession seems *absurd*. The recession brings about a reduction of popular purchasing power and consumption. But this reduction in consumption is not due to a shortage of production or to any scarcity (as in the case of pre-capitalist crises, where the reduction in consumption was due for instance to a shortfall of harvest). In capitalism, *the reduction of consumption is due to an excess of production* in relation to popular consumption capacity: it is this excess of production which brings about bankruptcies and rationalizations, loss of jobs and of wages

and a reduction of purchasing power and consumption. The process seems absurd from yet another point of view: the closed-down enterprises and the unemployed workers constitute so many *unused resources* in relation to the masses' consumption needs.

The process is nevertheless *functional*. Crisis and recession are not 'routine hazards', regrettable but fortuitous events in the progress of capitalism. On the contrary, they constitute the very mechanism through which the rate of profit is periodically restored and a certain equilibrium re-established in a society based on the producers' free initiative and competition. Certainly new structural conditions can mitigate considerably the 'trade cycle' and the cumulative process of recession: this will appear when we examine the post-war developments. But these new conditions do not completely suppress the conjunctural fluctuations and the crises: experience of recent years is sufficient proof of this.

The conjunctural crisis of 1929–30: the expression of a structural crisis of 'classical' accumulation

The crisis of 1929–30 constitutes a classic *conjunctural* crisis resulting from the type of accumulation prevailing before the Second World War. It marks the limit of a phase of cumulative expansion and the starting point of an equally cumulative recession.

However, the trade cycle culminating in 1929 differs from the majority of previous cycles in its duration and in the intensity of the phases of expansion and recession. The expansion begins around 1920 and continues for nearly ten years (instead of the usual three or four); it is characterized by much greater advances in productivity than ever before. The recession results in a catastrophic fall in production and employment which takes a very long time to put right: in most countries, the production and employment levels reached in 1929 are not to be achieved again until the forties.

The extent of this recession enables us to designate the crisis of 1929–30 not only as a conjunctural crisis but also as a *structural* crisis of 'classical' accumulation. While the previous conjunctural crises constituted 'normal' incidents of growth, the crisis of 1929–30 by contrast shows that capitalist accumulation encounters a fundamental problem, the solution of which is politically unacceptable. The problem lies in the increasing imbalance between the rapid growth of productive capacity (supply) and the relatively limited growth of consumer capacity (demand). The solution, in the context of 'classical' accumulation, is recession (the downturn of production), and this is bound to be severe in view of the seriousness of the previous imbalance. But a severe recession, on the thirties' scale, involves such an economic wastage and such a high social cost that it is no longer politically acceptable. Another type of growth is called for.

'CONTEMPORARY' ACCUMULATION AFTER THE SECOND WORLD WAR

The tendency to a parallel growth of production and markets

One essential feature of the new type of growth progressively adopted after the Second World War is that *aggregate demand tends to grow in parallel to the growth of capitalist production.*[5] This parallel growth can be explained by the new context prevailing with regard to the wage-earners' situation and to state intervention.

1.   The wage-earners' *consumer demand* now looks quite different.

   (1)   The wage-earners ensure the reproduction of their labour-power primarily through recourse to the purchase of *capitalist commodities*. Their pattern of consumption shows a considerable reduction of the proportion of domestic products (partly as a result of the growth of female labour) as well as of the proportion of commodities produced by craftsmen (the independent producers being progressively eliminated by capitalist enterprises).

   (2)   Wages and labour conditions are regulated in essentials by *collective agreements* reached at branch or national level. Implicitly or explicitly, these collective agreements tend to link the evolution of wages to productivity. In these conditions, the consumer capacity of the wage-earners tends to develop more or less at the same pace as the productive capacity of industry (or again, the real wage per worker tends to grow in parallel to the physical productivity per worker).

   (3)   *Employment and incomes tend to stabilize.* Greater job stability is ensured, on the national level, by the growth of the state sector (an increased number of officials in the sector of administration or non-commodity production). Further, the 'social wage' develops in different forms (unemployment benefit, pensions, health insurance etc.) and constitutes a growing proportion of household income. Job stability and

the expansion of the 'social wage' help to stabilize aggregate purchasing power and therefore the wage-earners' consumer demand.

(4) Besides this, consumer credit develops, which stimulates and regularizes domestic demand (especially for durable goods).

2. The *state* for its part exercises an increasingly strong influence on aggregate demand.

(1) It provides a growing number of stable jobs in the non-commodity production sector; it regulates the growth of the social wage.

(2) It influences the level of economic activity by means of public sector contracts as well as by other forms of intervention (nationalization, assistance to industry etc.).

The new features of capitalist development

New conditions affecting wage-earners' consumer demand as well as the public sector demand enabled capitalism to take on an entirely new growth after 1945. This new growth is characterized by a considerable mitigation of conjunctural crises and cycles and by a sustained increase in production over a period of some 30 years.

The mitigation of conjunctural crises and trade cycles

The cumulative processes of recession, typical of 'classical' accumulation (downturns in production spread over 2–3 years), have disappeared since 1945: they have been replaced by mere *slowdowns* in the growth of production, sometimes by very *short* downturns followed by rapid recovery. To what is this change due?

As capitalist crises are crises of overproduction (excess of supply in relation to demand), it is possible, with 'contemporary' accumulation, to reduce their extent by various measures of *demand support*. These measures help to stop the cumulative process of the recession, the process where falls in production bring about falls in purchasing power, which, in their turn, limit the scope for production. The appropriate measures to support demand in a period of recession can be grouped in two main categories: those which have the direct effect of relatively stabilizing the masses' purchasing power, and those which have the direct effect of relatively stabilizing the level of economic activity.

1. *The relative stabilization of the masses' purchasing power.* The growth of *stable jobs* (in the administration sector) and of *replacement income* (particularly unemployment benefit) has the effect· of maintaining permanently a relatively high level of demand for consumer goods. Officials with secure jobs and incomes maintain their level of consumption; the wage-earners who are laid off have to reduce their consumption but this reduction will be less severe, the higher the unemployment benefit available.

Besides this, consumer credit enables households to maintain a certain stability in their purchases. If credit conditions are made easier in periods of recession, this helps to ensure the stability of private consumer demand.

2. *'Anti-cyclical' measures of state intervention. Public sector contracts* constitute a typical measure for mitigating conjunctural fluctuations. Thus a programme of motorway construction in a period of recession has the effect of immediately increasing demand for consumer goods (through the incomes paid out to the workers) and demand for production goods (with the need for new machinery).

Other measures of government intervention can help to mitigate the trade cycles: for example, the *placing* of marginal enterprises (or branches) *under public control.* As we saw in chapter 7, these measures of intervention have the effect of putting off the elimination of these enterprises or branches (while ensuring a transfer of surplus revenue to benefit the private sector): they therefore mitigate the cumulative process of bankruptcies and lay-offs typical of periods of recession.

The sustained growth of production and consumption

The mitigation of the trade cycles does not in itself signify a sustained growth of production and of consumption in the long term: we could envisage slight conjunctural fluctuations around a slightly rising long-term trend. In reality, the capitalist economies have experienced, over a long period of 30 years (1945–75), a growth in production and in consumption which is without precedent in history. To what can we attribute this remarkable growth? Two facts appear fundamental: on the one hand, the coincidence of a rapid increase in productivity and in wage-earner consumption; on the other the growth of public expenditure.

1. *The rapid advances in productivity and in wage-earner consumption.* The period which follows the Second World War is characterized by rapid increases both in industrial productivity and in worker

consumption, which enable capitalists to maintain a high rate of surplus value while also expanding their markets.

Productivity and consumption stimulate each other. The increases in productivity reduce the unit value of consumer goods and so make them more accessible to the mass of wage-earners. Conversely, the growth of consumer demand stimulates mass-production and therefore increases in productivity (mass-production of standardized goods of reduced unit value).

	Quantities	Unit values	Proportion of total consumer expenditure
Food and clothing	+	− −	− −
Durable goods	+ +	− −	+
Services	+ +	=	+ +
Taken together	+ +	− −	

Key: +: increase; + +: large increase; −: reduction;
− −: large reduction; =: (quasi) stability.

TABLE 9.1   Principal changes in the structure of consumption after the Second World War

This mutual stimulation of productivity and consumption has been more significant for some products than for others, so that the *structure* of consumption has undergone far-reaching changes. The principal changes, schematized in Table 9.1, can be summed up in the following way. The consumption of *food and clothing* has certainly increased in quantity; it has changed mainly in the direction of greater standardization, which has made possible a reduction of unit values; in total, the proportion of expenditure on food and clothing in the household budget has declined steadily. *Durable goods* (cars, electric appliances, televisions etc.) have been subject to the most marked changes, both in the direction of a fall in unit values and of a rise in quantities (the two trends supporting each other, as we have seen). *Services* (leisure, accommodation, education, health etc.) have presented a different picture: slight gains in productivity have resulted in a relative stability of unit *values* (and therefore in a relative rise in the cost and in the price of services); despite this, the *quantities* consumed have grown steadily (due to the growth of purchasing power); as a result of these two tendencies, the proportion of services has shown the most marked increase in the household consumption budget.

The simultaneous and rapid increases in worker consumption and in industrial productivity have enabled capitalists to expand their markets while maintaining a high rate of surplus value. The increased consumption by the wage-earners helps to resolve one of the fundamental problems of capitalist growth, namely the expansion of markets. As we have already indicated, the growth of mechanization and of productivity continuously expands the productive capacity of industry. For this expanded production there has to be an equally expanded consumption, if the cumulative recessions, typical of 'classical' accumulation, are to be avoided. All the same, from the capitalist point of view, the increase in the worker consumption must not jeopardize the rate of surplus value. On this point, we saw that the increase in productivity, by reducing the unit value of consumer goods, makes it possible to reconcile the increase of worker consumption and the maintenance (even the increase) of the rate of surplus value. And the greater the growth of productivity, the greater the growth of consumption compatible with the maintenance of the rate of surplus value. The is precisely what took place during the period 1945–1970.[6]

2. *The growth of public expenditure.* The unprecedented increases in production and in consumption which capitalist economies have experienced since 1945 are also due to the growth of public expenditure. We are speaking here of the increase in state expenditure in the long term, independently of its possible adjustment according to the stage of the trade cycle. Let us recall briefly some of the elements we have already referred to.

(1) The state has taken on an increasing number of officials in the non-commodity production (or administrative) sector. The number of officials has grown not only in absolute terms, but also in relative terms (in relation to the working population as a whole).

(2) The state has also intervened increasingly as a consumer of capitalist commodities, both through the purchase of consumer goods (office equipment, uniforms) or of investment goods (motorways). As we saw earlier, the growth of public sector contracts with the private sector answers a fundamental

need of capitalism, faced with the problem of the proliferation of 'surplus capital'.

(3) In certain cases, the state has itself intervened as a commodity producer (nationalized enterprises or branches of industry), particularly in the case of unprofitable products.

State intervention (public sector contracts or other forms of intervention) is obviously limited by the amount of financial resources at the state's disposal. These resources come either from recourse to borrowing or from taxation. Unable to resort indefinitely to borrowing, the state must rely on an increase in fiscal revenue. If these resources increase the scope for public intervention in order to sustain aggregate demand, the increase in taxation bearing on wages and profits tends on the other hand to reduce the private consumer demand and the potential for accumulation in every enterprise.

We find again here a contradiction analogous to that brought out earlier regarding wages and consumption. We saw that the growth of mechanization presents capitalists with two contradictory requirements: in order to maintain or increase the rate of surplus value, it is in their interest to limit wages and consumption; but to assure themselves of markets, it is in their interest to increase wages and popular consumption. This contradiction can be resolved by means of increases in productivity: these make it possible to ensure, at the same time, both the stability (and even the growth) of the rate of surplus value and the growth of the level of consumption (and therefore of markets).

Similarly, measures of state intervention present contradictory features from the capitalists' point of view: on the one hand, they assure them of markets and of the other advantages we have mentioned (survival of enterprises, transfers of surplus revenue); on the other hand, they involve the levying of taxes which reduce the households' demand and the aggregate surplus revenue available for accumulation. Once again, increases in productivity have made it possible to resolve the contradiction: in tending to raise the rate of surplus value, they have increased the mass of surplus revenue which can provide financial resources required for measures of state intervention in economic life.

The Conjunctural Crisis of 1974–5: the Beginning of a Structural Crisis of 'Contemporary' Accumulation

The specific character of the crisis

In all capitalist countries, the year 1974–5 is characterized by a net downturn in production, lasting for several months.

In certain respects, this recession is a *conjunctural* recession, typical of the stage of contemporary accumulation. As we have said, under contemporary accumulation, sustained demand from the wage-earners and from the state has the effect of mitigating considerably the cumulative processes of recession (which give way to mere slowdowns of growth or to downturns of short duration). The recession of 1974–5 is indeed very different from the long and severe recessions under 'classical' accumulation (and in particular from the recession of the thirties): the cumulative process of declining production is halted after only a few months, giving way to a recovery from the end of 1975.[7]

But equally the year 1974–5 signifies a radical change in the long-term tendencies of the capitalist system. While production and consumption grew at an unprecedented rate from 1945 to 1975, subsequently they only grew at a very moderate rate, with a succession of downturns and slow uncertain recoveries and with a rising level of unemployment. This interruption of sustained growth can be classified as a *structural crisis* of contemporary accumulation.

Reasons for the structural crisis

To what must we attribute this interruption of sustained growth at the contemporary accumulation stage? An important explanatory factor seems to reside in the *braking effect that productivity and consumption have on each other.*

On the one hand, the slowing down of consumer demand in certain sectors (due to a relative 'saturation') tends to act as a brake on the progress of productivity. This is so in the case of the *consumption of food products and clothing*. Cheap and standardized food and clothes enjoyed rapidly expanding markets during the whole period of the spread of new patterns of consumption in these fields. Once these patterns became widespread, the consumption of the standardized products increases but at a much slower rate. It is the same for the *consumption of durable goods* (cars, television sets, household equipment). The demand for these goods increased most rapidly after the war but gradually slowed down later on: as households became better equipped, their demand became limited primarily to replacement needs.[8] Just as a rapid growth of demand tends to stimulate increases of productivity in production, a slowed-down growth of demand tends to act as a brake on them. This slowing-down of increases in productivity can actually be observed in most branches of industry from around 1970.[9]

On the other hand, the low productivity of the *services* sector slows down increases in consumption, not only of the services themselves but of all means of consumption. We have already mentioned that from 1945, services accounted for a growing proportion of household consumption; this tendency has been accentuated with the relative 'saturation' observed with regard to food products, clothes and durable goods. But the services sector has remained traditionally closed to mass-production: hence the increases in productivity in this sector are very much lower than in the branches of industrial production.

In order to examine the effects of this low productivity, it is useful to distinguish between commodity services, and non-commodity services. The former are sold (by independent producers or by capitalists) at a price which tends to fluctuate around the social value: this is, for example, the case of the commercialized leisure services, accommodation, catering etc. The latter are not sold but provided free or practically free by the public authorities: this is, for example, the case of education and health services in so far as they are nationalized.[10]

If the *commodity* services are characterized by low productivity, their social value and therefore their price remains high. The consumption of these services can only continue to grow at the price of increasingly high expenditure: this increased expenditure on high-cost services must necessarily limit the growth of other forms of consumption.

As regards *non-commodity* services, the low productivity, coupled with the expansion of demand and supply of these services, results in a rapid increase in the social cost to be borne. In its response, the state may waver between two solutions. Either it can *reduce its expenditure* on non-commodity services: discontinuance of certain services (closure of schools, reduction of the number of teachers etc.), pressure on officials' salaries, reduction of national insurance benefits (unemployment benefit, refunds on health services).[11] This first type of solution acts as a brake on the growth of aggregate consumption. On the one hand, because the measures tend to shift the cost of certain socialized services (for example the expenditure on health services) back onto the private sector and this limits the growth of other forms of consumption. On the other hand, and more directly, because the reductions in employment, in salaries and in national insurance benefits reduce the volume of income available for the households' consumption of commodity goods and services. Or the state can maintain a growing supply of non-commodity services, by *increasing its levies*on the community (taxes and National Insurance contributions paid by enterprises and by individuals). But these increased levies reduce proportionately the income available for the households' commodity consumption (and also the surplus revenue available for capitalist accumulation). The second type of solution therefore also results in a brake on the consumer demand for commodity goods and services.[12]

Attempts to find a way out of the structural crisis
If the foregoing analysis has pointed to the essential factors in the structural crisis of contemporary capitalism, we can now make a rapid appraisal of some of the policies, suggested or adopted, for a way out of this crisis.

1. In the first place, the severity of the crisis of the seventies accentuated a tendency (starting around 1960) towards a *world-wide restructuring of capitalist production*. Numerous industrial products consumed in the metropolitan capitalist countries are produced today in growing proportions in less-developed countries under the aegis of multinational companies: this is true for products as diverse as steel, tinned goods, textiles, clothes, car and engine parts, etc.[13]

The primary object of this worldwide restructuring is to raise the average rate of surplus value. This object is achieved simultaneously in two ways. Industrial firms set up in less-developed countries benefit from a higher rate of surplus value than in the home country, while industrial firms which remain in the home country may benefit from a rise in their rate of surplus value as an indirect consequence of this industrial migration.

The rate of surplus value in the less-developed countries is higher than in the more-developed countries for two basic reasons. First, the role of domestic labour in the production of the wage-earners' means of subsistence remains very significant for most of them (especially in the country or on the outskirts of cities, where the wage-earners and their families cultivate a patch of ground, build their makeshift dwellings, produce their own clothes etc): as we know, this tends to reduce the value of labour-power and the wages to be paid. Secondly, the overall balance of power between capitalists and wage-earners is clearly in favour of the former: this too makes it possible to ensure a high rate of surplus value by exerting pressure on the level of consumption of the masses and on labour-time (working hours).[14]

Industries which remain located in the more-developed countries are faced with a rate of surplus value lower than that in the less-developed countries, but the transfer of industries tends indirectly to raise this rate of surplus value: the transfer of industries creates a significant degree of unemployment in the more-developed countries, adding to the unemployment typical of the present structural crisis; the extent of unemployment modifies the balance of power in favour of the capitalist class, which brings pressure to bear to stabilize or reduce real wages and thus to increase its rate of surplus value.

But while the world-wide restructuring of capitalist production makes it possible to increase the average rate of surplus value, it does not bring about a significant expansion of markets: it does indeed expand the markets in the less-developed countries, if it contributes to a greater penetration of market relations; but it tends to limit their expansion in the more-developed countries through pressure on the real wage. Consequently, it does not basically resolve the problem of giving a new impetus to production and to consumption on a world-wide scale.

2. The same criticism can be made regarding all the national policies which aim to *raise the rate of surplus value by putting pressure on the workers' wages*. This pressure can be in response to external motives (to improve the competitive position of enterprises) and/or to internal motives (to improve the profitability of enterprises and therefore the potential for investment). Such policies can help to modify the share-out of markets between different countries: with equal productivity, the countries who best 'manage' their wages tend to increase their exports. But globally, for the capitalist economies as a whole, the forcing down of wages is equivalent to forcing down consumer demand: the latter, in its turn, limits the opportunities for profitable investment.

3. Alternative policies aim to restore a parallel growth of production and consumption by means of a *revival of demand*. The idea here is, to stimulate *private consumption* demand by means of a rise in household purchasing-power (increase of wages), and/or to increase

demand coming from the *public sector*. By themselves, these measures cannot revive the economy: while it is true that they tend to increase the market outlets for capitalist production, they also tend to reduce the rate of surplus value and the surplus revenue available for accumulation. Here again, we see the contradictory aspects both of wage increases and of increased state intervention in the economy.

4. These contradictions, we know, can be surmounted by capitalism, but on one condition: the gains in productivity must be sufficient to maintain the rate of surplus value and the surplus revenue available for accumulation. The capitalist solution to the crisis therefore implies a *parallel revival of productivity and of consumption*, with the cumulative effects that they have on each other. This applies both to the more-developed and to the less-developed countries. For the *less-developed countries*, it means giving up a type of growth centred on the consumption of the dominant classes and on exports (of raw materials or of industrial products), for another type of growth directed to a type of mass consumption comparable to that of the advanced countries. Obviously, there is nothing automatic about such a transformation: it presupposes a class struggle and an overthrow of the allied interests in power at the time. In the *more-developed countries*, it involves integrating into mass-consumption a new range of goods and services produced in conditions of increased productivity (through automation, computerization etc.). This restructuring of production and of consumption comes about through growth of unemployment, increased mobility of labour, large-scale reorganization of work, etc.: here too, the class struggle will determine to what extent capitalism will be able to solve the crisis.

NOTES

1. The terms 'expanded reproduction' and 'accumulation' can both be taken as synonyms of 'growth'. The growth of capitalist production is the reproduction *on an expanded scale* of the cycle $M — C \ldots P \ldots C^+ — M^+$ and this expanded reproduction involves the *accumulation* of the surplus revenue created, that is, the purchase of additional means of production and labour-power (rather than the complete consumption of the surplus revenue).

2. Some measures of state intervention have the effect of *limiting* aggregate demand. Such is the case when the state prohibits workers' association:

this reduces the workers' bargaining power and therefore their wages and purchasing power.

3. The description which follows concentrates on the *production* aspect. The conjunctural fluctuations of prices are merely mentioned: they will be considered again in chapter 10.

4. A strongly protected branch can maintain its prices and its rates of profit for a fairly long time. This only aggravates the difficulties of the less protected branches, difficulties which eventually affect our first branch. The course of the crisis described here disregards the differences in the degree of protection enjoyed by different branches; we are considering the crisis on a global, macro-economic, level.

5. The parallel growth of aggregate supply and demand does not alter the basic fact that a capitalist economy is a *market* economy, and hence subject to the uncertainties any such economy necessarily involves: each capitalist has to find purchasers for his own commodities if he wants his private labour to be recognized as social labour, and each of them may very well fail in this venture.

6. The stimulating effect that productivity and consumption have on each other also affects indirectly the branches producing the means of production. The increase in consumer demand brings about an increase in the demand for industrial equipment, which stimulates increases in productivity in the branches engaged in its production. However, the continual pursuit of productivity increases in the production of consumer goods (linked to inter-capitalist competition and to the necessity of maintaining the rate of surplus value) stimulates a demand for increasingly improved plant, and so a more rapid diffusion of technical progress in the production of the machines themselves. As a result, the demand and supply of machines are constantly renewed, which speeds up their obsolescence: less and less time is required for a machine to become technologically out-of-date without being physically worn-out. This phenomenon increases the markets for the branches of the machine-tool industry and so contributes to the growth of capitalist production. We shall see in chapter 10, from another point of view, how it also contributes to the inflation which is typical of contemporary accumulation.

7. Compared to the very slight recessions of the fifties and sixties, the recession of 1974–5 results in a real and very marked falling-off in production: the *extent* of the recession is unmistakably greater, but it is still a recession typical of contemporary accumulation.

8. Replacement demand can of course be speeded up by the deliberate limitation of the use-life of durable goods. This practice cannot, however, offset the fact that most households have gradually reached a degree of saturation in consumer durables (cars, fridges etc.).

9. The slowing-down of productivity increases in industry can also be explained in part by the workers' resistance to 'technical progress' and

its consequences (loss of jobs, higher intensity of labour).

10. In several countries, health services – which constitute one of the most dynamic forms of consumption in recent years – belong both to commodity and non-commodity production. In so far as they are provided by private individuals and not by 'officials', they count as commodities. But in so far as payments are refunded by the public authorities, these commodities become practically free: their cost is socialized, like the cost of state education (Translator's note. In the United Kingdom, treatment under the National Health Service is free, apart from fixed charges for certain specialized services and for medical prescriptions).

11. Translator's note: see comment on note 10.

12. The braking effect that productivity and consumption have on each other and which we have just described, affects directly the branches producing the means of consumption. But it also affects indirectly the branches producing the means of production: the slowing-down of consumer demand brings about a slow-down of the demand for industrial equipment, which tends to act as a brake on the increases in productivity in the branches engaged in its production.

13. This world-wide restructuring of capitalist production constitutes the beginning of a *new* international division of labour. In the *traditional* international division of labour, the less-developed countries mainly produced raw materials (mineral and agricultural) which were exported to the more-developed countries: the latter produced almost all the industrial products and exported the proportion of them intended for consumption in the less-developed countries. In the *new* international division of labour which is gradually becoming established, the less-developed countries become providers not only of traditional raw materials but also of industrial products, mainly incorporating unskilled labour; the more-developed countries reserve to themselves the production of more sophisticated goods and services (machine tools, technology etc.) which call on highly skilled manpower.

14. The maintenance of this favourable balance of power assumes the existence of strong governments supporting the multinational companies who move their industrial production to the less-developed countries. The recent proliferation of military dictatorships and other strong régimes (in Latin America, Africa and Asia) does not arise from historical accident: the phenomenon is linked with the new international division of labour and is intended to make it as profitable as possible.

We must add that the pressure on the value of labour-power and on wages is of direct interest only to capitalists working for the export market: for them, wages constitute only production costs and not market outlets. The capitalists working for the local market are in a situation comparable to the more-developed capitalists: for them, wages figure as costs but also as market outlets; it is therefore in their interests that market relations should penetrate domestic production to the maximum, so that the wage-earners consume the maximum of the commodities (the capitalists will then increase the rate of surplus value by increasing productivity in the production of these commodities).

10

Accumulation, Money and Prices

The last chapter distinguished two stages in the expanded reproduction of capital (the stages of 'classical' and of 'contemporary' accumulation) and offered an analysis of the lines along which each stage developed. This analysis did not cover the problems relative to the evolution of money and prices. The object of chapter 10 is precisely to move on to the study of these problems, returning again to the distinction between the two types of accumulation.

The first section concerns *money*. It brings out the twofold transformation which money has undergone with the growth of capitalism: on the one hand, in the 'classical' accumulation stage, the gradual increase of the importance of *credit money* in relation to metallic money; on the other, moving on to the 'contemporary' accumulation stage, the definitive replacement of convertible credit money by *inconvertible* credit money.

The second section concerns '*excess money*', that is, a growth of credit money exceeding the growth of the sum total of values. It shows that such an imbalance may have two quite distinct origins: one inherent in the functioning of capitalism (the 'losses of value' in commodity production), the other contingent (the budgetary deficits of the state). It also shows that the reaction of the banking system, with regard to these imbalances, varies according to the type of money involved: if credit money is *convertible*, the banking system will help to get rid of the excess by creating less money; if credit money is *inconvertible*, the banking system will on the contrary be able to continue to create money with no parallel growth of the sum total of values.

The third section deals with the problem of the *evolution of prices* in the two stages we have distinguished (before and after the Second World War). Building on the arguments of the two previous sections, it seeks to explain the evident contrasts presented by these two stages: the *alternation of rises and falls* in prices before the Second

World War (both in the long and short term) and the *continuous rise* subsequently, accelerated with the structural crisis of contemporary accumulation.

THE EVOLUTION OF TYPES AND FORMS OF MONEY

Before the Second World War: Metallic Money and Convertible Credit Money

Metallic money

1. *Its evolution.* Money exists from the moment commodities are exchanged: it has therefore existed for several thousands of years. Originally various material goods constituted money but, as time went by, *precious metals* (especially gold and silver) were adopted by virtue of their intrinsic qualities (solidity, homogeneity and divisibility).

Metallic money first appeared in the form of ingots of no settled weight or form: these ingots had to be weighed and their actual metallic content summarily verified. It then appeared in the form of coins bearing the official mark of the person (money-changer, merchant) 'coining money': this mark attested the weight and the purity of the metal in the coin. From this time, money could be counted out instead of being weighed.

The rulers quickly took over the monopoly of minting money: a mint takes in the metal from private owners and gives back authenticated coins bearing a name. At the same time, the rulers make their coins 'legal tender': everyone is legally obliged to accept them as means of payment (while previously the acceptance of coins issued by such and such a person was based solely on trust and not on legal constraint).

2. *The definition of (the metallic content of) the monetary unit.* We know from chapter 2 that the value of commodities is expressed as a certain price, that is, as a certain quantity of money. In the case of metallic money, how do we obtain, from a form of price expressed as a certain quantity of *metal* (which we assume to be gold), another form of price expressed as a certain quantity of *monetary units* (*pounds* for example)?

Without trying to stick to historical facts, let us briefly explain – by way of a purely hypothetical example – the transition from one form of price to the other. In practice, the authority which mints money chooses a certain weight of metal as *standard* or *unit of measure* (for example a weight of 10 g of gold), gives this unit a *name* (for example the 'pound') and inscribes, on the gold bars or coins it turns out, the number of units (expressed in pounds) they contain: thus a gold piece of 10 g will carry the inscription '1 pound', another of 50 g will be called '5 pounds', and so on.[1]

As we can see, the standardization carried out to express and measure values is analogous to the standardization carried out to express and measure lengths. In order to express and measure the length of objects, a fixed 'quantity' of length is chosen by the competent authority as unit of measure and this unit is given a fixed name, for example, the 'metre': thanks to this double choice (of the unit of measure and of its name) all lengths can be expressed in metres. In order to express and measure values, a quantity of metal is chosen by the monetary authority as a unit of measure (for example 10 g of gold) and this unit is given a fixed name, for example, the pound: thanks to this double choice, all values can be expressed in pounds. In both cases, the unit of measure and its name are chosen in a purely conventional (arbitrary) way; but at the same time, these need to have a universal character (at least within given frontiers): they must therefore be fixed by law.[2]

In deciding on the monetary standard (that is, the weight of metal serving as a unit of measure) and also on its name, the monetary authority determines the *definition of the metallic content of the monetary unit* or again (in shorter but less precise terms) the 'definition of the currency'. This may be seen as the weight of metal officially contained in the monetary unit expressed in pounds (in the example, 1 pound = 10 g of gold, or 10 g of gold per pound), or, conversely, as the number of pounds represented officially by a unit of metal expressed by weight (in the example, 1 g of gold = 0.10 pounds or 0.10 pound per g of gold).[3]

Convertible credit money

The nature of the bank note. The seventeenth century saw the birth of a second form of money, the bank-note; as it developed, the use of the bank-note was superimposed on the use of metallic money. This note is an acknowledgement of debt, issued by a bank and exchangeable at any time for metallic money: the bearer of a note can always go to the bank which has issued it and obtain immediate repayment, in metallic money, of the sum written on the note; in other words, the note is completely 'convertible' (into metal).

The issue of such notes by the banks arises from two quite distinct types of operation.

(1)   The notes can be issued in exchange for a *deposit* of metallic money, made by individuals. Let us call these notes receipt notes.

(2)   They can also be issued in response to requests for credit on the part of the bank's clients. Rather than lend metallic money, the banks lend notes which can be exchanged for metal (brought in by depositors or belonging to the bank). Let us call these notes credit notes.

In so far as the public relies on the promise of conversion into metal written on the notes, these notes can play the same role as metallic money: they can be used *inter alia* as means of payment (as a medium of exchange) and circulate on the same footing as metal coins (over which incidentally they have obvious practical advantages: less weight, easier to carry).

And in so far as the notes effectively play this role of medium of exchange, their conversion into metal is not normally requested. This allows the banks, when credit is requested, to issue notes not backed by metal. The usual degree of acceptance of notes by the public gives the banks an empirical indication of the normal proportion to be kept between the amount of notes issued and the amount of metallic money held. Whatever this proportion may be, the notes which are not backed by metal constitute *additional* money and money of a different kind: they are added to the existing metallic money and constitute, specifically, credit money.[4]

From multiplicity to standardization of bank-notes. Within each of the capitalist countries, we can distinguish two stages in the history of the bank-note.

The first stage sees a *multiplicity* of bank-notes. Each bank issues its own notes, its own promises to pay in metallic money. In each country, the monetary mass therefore comprises (apart from metallic money which is legal tender) a mass of different private notes coming from different banks but whose common characteristic is that they are all convertible into metallic money (which enables notes to circulate between clients of different banks).

The second stage sees the *standardization* of bank-notes, following action by the public authorities. The monopoly of issuing notes was usually given to one bank, which was promoted to the status of central bank. Its notes were declared legal tender and everyone was now obliged to accept them without question as means of payment, on the same footing as metallic money.

The central bank's monopoly does not in any way prevent the other banks from carrying on their earlier operations: they continue to accept metallic money as deposits and to grant credits. But the notes they issue for this purpose are now the central bank's notes, and it is from the central bank that they have to obtain them. The central bank provides them with its notes in accordance with the two standard types of operation: either the banks *deposit* their metallic money at the central bank or they obtain *credit* from the central bank.[5] The situation can be summed up in the following way. The only notes in circulation are the notes of the central bank (while formerly different notes issued by each of the individual banks were in circulation). But the different banks retain the power of giving credit and of thus injecting additional money in the form of the central bank's notes.

Incidentally, the legal tender of notes does not in any way affect their convertibility. Legal tender means that the notes are recognized by law as valid means of payment: no seller or creditor can oblige his debtor or purchaser to pay in metallic money rather than in notes. But these notes are still convertible into metallic money: every holder of notes has the right to exchange them for metallic money at the central bank. So the central bank must ensure that it maintains a reasonable proportion (variable according to the degree of acceptance of notes by the public) between the mass of notes in circulation and the stock of metallic money held.[6]

Current account money[7]. Another form of credit money developed alongside the bank-note: current account money, created by the different banks. This new form of money developed mainly in the twentieth century and was to become the prevailing form of money after the Second World War.

Like the bank-note, current account money is an acknowledgement of indebtedness issued by a bank. Here the acknowledgement of indebtedness takes the form of sums entered by the banks in their clients' accounts: the holders of these accounts can always arrange with their banks for the sums entered to be changed into notes issued by the central bank. While notes circulate from hand to hand (like metallic coins in earlier times), current account money can circulate from one account to another and from one bank to another by a simple entry: the instructions relating to these transfers of money are given to the banks by means of cheques or transfer orders (such as standing orders).

As with the bank-notes, current account money can originate in two ways.

(1)   It can arise from *deposits* (in notes) made by the banks' clients: these deposits are recorded by entries in the depositors' accounts.

(2)   It can arise from *credits* granted by the banks to their clients. Rather than lend notes, the banks open a credit for a certain amount in favour of their clients: the latter are authorized to draw cheques or to make transfers up to the amount of their credit.

In so far as the amounts entered in the accounts can be freely converted into notes, current account money can play the same role as notes: it can *inter alia* be used as a means of payment (as a medium of exchange) and circulate on the same footing as notes (over which incidentally it offers obvious practical advantages: speed of settlements, no risk of loss or theft etc.).

In so far as the public effectively accepts the use of current account money (in so far as it does not ask for it to be changed into notes), the banks can, when credit is requested, open accounts for an amount larger than the amount of notes they hold. Here too, the usual degree of acceptance of current account money by the public indicates empirically to the banks the right proportion to be maintained between the total amount of credits in their books and the total amount of notes they hold.[8] Whatever this proportion may be, current account money not backed by notes constitutes *additional* money created by the banks (beyond the direct control of the central bank).[9]

Bank-notes and current account money therefore constitute two different forms of the same type of money, that is, credit money. Whatever its form, this money is *created* by the banks when credit is requested. And the money thus created is *destroyed*, ceases to exist as money, when the credit is repaid (when the client gives back to the bank the notes he has borrowed or when he repays the sum credited to his current account). If the total mass of credit money continues to grow, it is because new credits are constantly being granted before repayment of previous credits.

After the Second World War: Inconvertible Credit Money

The foregoing pages described in some detail both metallic money and the two forms of credit money which competed with it (bank-notes and current account money). Confining ourselves to essentials, we can sum up under two heads the evolution of money prior to the Second World War (the 'classical' accumulation stage). On the one hand, metallic money, while continuing to be effectively used in market transactions, is gradually superseded by the growth of *credit money* (especially in the form of notes) and the proportion of metallic money in the total quantity of money in circulation is gradually reduced. On the other hand, this expanding credit money is still *convertible* into metallic money.

It remains to indicate by contrast the major changes affecting money after the Second World War (the 'contemporary' accumulation stage).

On the one hand, metallic money ceases in practice to be used in the internal transactions of each country. Gold may still have a role as a means of payment at the international level but it is no longer used for the settlement of internal transactions. At this level, metallic money is entirely superseded by credit money (which develops more in the form of current account money than of bank-notes).

On · the other hand, credit money ceases definitively to be convertible into metallic money: the 'contemporary' accumulation stage is also the stage of inconvertibility. It is true that the previous stage saw certain periods of inconvertibility (especially in periods of war and political unrest): but these were only temporary exceptions to the well-established principle of convertibility. After the Second World War, on the contrary, the principle which has continued to prevail is the principle of the inconvertibility of credit money: current account money can of course be changed into notes but there is no further question of changing bank-notes into metallic money.[10] Therefore the central bank is no longer liable, as it was earlier, to the constraint of convertibility, which required it to maintain a reasonable ratio between the credit money in circulation and its own metallic holding.[11]

The move from convertibility to inconvertibility will have important consequences in at least two fields: it will affect the means of *absorbing an excess creation of money*; it will also affect the principles governing the *evolution of the general level of prices*. This is what will emerge from the following two sections.

GAPS BETWEEN THE QUANTITY OF MONEY AND THE QUANTITY OF VALUE

We saw at the end of chapter 8 that the quantity of money required for market transactions depends on the sum total of the prices of the commodities exchanged and therefore, for a given level of E, on the sum total of the values of the commodities (comprising past and new value).

We also saw that, in principle, credit money makes a flexible adjustment possible between the quantity of money and the sum total of values: in granting credit to the capitalists who wish to expand their business (and thus to increase the total value transferred or created), the banks increase correspondingly the total quantity of money put into circulation.

However, this principle raises two questions:

(1) If credit money is issued in this way by the banks in order to finance commodity production, which should normally result in a corresponding increase of value, what happens if *the anticipated increase of value is not fully realized*? This is typically the case when credit-financed products do not find a purchaser: it is also the case, as we shall see, when, due to technical progress, the machinery employed is made obsolete.

(2) What happens if credit money is issued by the banks in order to finance activities which do not produce commodities and are therefore *unproductive of value*? This is typically the case with unproductive activities carried out by the state, when they are financed by credit rather than by taxation.

In the first as in the second situation, we have to do with an excess creation of money, with a gap between the quantity of money created and the quantity of value. We will see that the solution to the problem of this gap differs according to whether the credit money issued is convertible or inconvertible. But we must first emphasize that the two situations we are considering do not have the same significance for our analysis of capitalism: the first is inherent in the very functioning of capitalism (we cannot imagine the expanded reproduction of capital without recourse to credit or without the risks of not selling or of obsolescence) while the second is relatively contingent (the expanded reproduction of capital in no way implies that state expenditure should be financed by credit). So we will devote the greater part of the analysis to the problems involved in the first situation.

Credit Money and 'Losses of Value' in Commodity Production

Let us consider the case of an 'average' industrial capitalist, taken as representative of the whole group of capitalist commodity producers, who borrows money from the banking system in order to expand his production.

Let us assume for example that this capitalist borrows £500 000. Our capitalist uses this money to purchase a machine, the value of which is 500 000 hours (and the price £500 000). This machine has a normal use life of 5 years and should ensure an annual production of 2 000 units of a commodity A: the past value to be transferred is therefore 50 hours per unit of A.[12] If we assume that the new value per unit is 10 hours, the unit value (past and present) is 50 hours + 10 hours = 60 hours. If these figures correspond to the average conditions of production, the unit price of A is £50 + £10 = £60.

The hypothesis of complete valorization

Let us assume that our capitalist is entirely successful in his aims: the machine acquired by means of the loan works effectively for 5 years (it is not made prematurely obsolete through the competition of improved machinery) and the commodities produced during these 5 years are sold in their entirety at a price of £60. What are the consequences, as regards value and revenue, of this twofold success of the capitalist's private initiative?

The *sale* of the commodities shows (after the event) that the production venture has been sound from the viewpoint of society. This sale has a twofold impact as regards value and revenue. The labour-power has been usefully employed: the labour carried out in the production has created value, the variable capital is recovered (increased by the profit); and the means of production have also been usefully employed: with no obsolescence, their value is transferred to the commodities produced, the constant capital spent in acquiring them is recovered.

That there was no obsolescence shows (after the event) that the choice of machinery has also been sound from the viewpoint of society. This favourable situation allows the capitalist who sells his commodities to transfer *in full* the value of the machinery employed and to recover *in full* the capital spent on acquiring it. In the example, the capitalist recovers £50 per unit, £100 000 per year, £500 000 after 5 years: the price of the machinery is thus fully recovered.

As he has now recovered the capital he has laid out, the industrial capitalist is in a position to repay the borrowed money (plus interest). This repayment confirms in its turn the soundness of the banker's private initiative: the money issued for the purpose of the credit has been created judiciously from the viewpoint of society since it has made possible the creation of new commodities and has then been repaid to the banker; the latter then obtains, in the form of interest, a part of the profit created in the production.

This example enables us to deduce the two following principles:

(1) The success of the industrial capitalist's private initiative (in the creation and transfer of *value*) entails the success of the banker's private intiative (in the creation of *money*): the sale of commodities makes possible the repayment of the loans and the industrialist's profits are shared with the banker (in the form of interest).

(2) On the other hand, the joint success of industrialist and banker entails a 'parallelism' between the variation of the quantity of *money* and the variation of the quantity of *value*. This applies both to rises and falls. The granting of credits entails the issue of notes (or of bank advances), and therefore the increase of the quantity of money in circulation; but it increases the production of commodities and therefore brings about the increase of the total quantity of value in circulation. Once the commodities are sold, the total mass of value in circulation is reduced; but the sale makes it possible to repay the credits (to liquidate the debts): the money advanced returns to the bank, and this reduces the quantity of money in circulation.[14]

The reality of 'losses of value'

Let us now assume that the industrial capitalist of the previous example does not completely succeed in his aims: either because he fails to sell his product or because his machinery becomes obsolete. Let us examine each of these two cases in turn.

The non-sale of products

1. *Loss of value and excess money.* Failure to sell is a risk in all commodity societies. It shows (after the event) that the capitalist's private initiative was not sound from the viewpoint of society. It has a

two-fold impact as regards value and revenue. The labour-power has not been employed usefully: the present labour put into the unsold productions has not created any value and the variable capital laid out has not been recovered. The means of production have not been usefully employed either: their value is lost (it is not transferred to the finished product, as this, being unsold, has no value) and the constant capital laid out to acquire them is not recovered. At the worst, the industrialist becomes bankrupt.

As he does not recover the capital laid out and may even become bankrupt, the industrial capitalist is not in a position to repay the money he has borrowed. The non-repayment shows in turn that the banker's private initiative was not socially sound either: it results in a loss for the banker (and in bankruptcy if he continues to grant credits which turn out badly).

The case of non-sale therefore allows us to draw the two following conclusions.

(1) The failure of the industrial capitalists' private initiatives (lack of value creation and of value transfer, losses of revenue, possibly leading to bankruptcy) entails failures and losses for the bankers in so far as they do not recover the money they have lent out.

(2) These joint failures result in a discrepancy between the variation of the quantity of *money* and the variation of the quantity of *value*: the mass of money in circulation increases without a corresponding increase in the mass of value in circulation. Credit money has been created and put into circulation (the industrialists have purchased their means of production and labour-power) but the mass of value has not increased in proportion (the industrialists have produced use-values which are socially useless, without value). In so far as the credit money cannot be repaid by the industrialists, the imbalance between the quantity of money in circulation and the mass of value is not spontaneously taken up: the excess of money is not automatically cancelled out.

2. *Reactions of the banking system.* What are the possible reactions of the banking system, when faced with these joint losses and this excess of money in circulation? They differ according to whether the credit money is convertible or inconvertible.

The case of convertible credit money. Let us consider the case of a 'non-unified banking system and of a unified banking system.

In a *non-unified* banking system, each private bank issues its own notes and must itself provide for their conversion into metal on the bearer's demand. Each bank is therefore obliged to maintain a reasonable proportion between the metallic money it holds and the amount of notes it issues. As we know, this 'reasonable' proportion takes account of the usual degree of acceptance of the notes by the public. But this degree of acceptance is dependent in turn on the soundness of the industrialists' and the bankers' private initiatives.

If these initiatives result in the effective creation of value (if the commodities produced are *sold*), the additional credit money circulates effectively and is not normally presented for conversion, the ratio (metallic holding/notes in circulation) is reduced, but the demands for conversion do not increase.

On the other hand, if the initiatives are unsound (if the bank has injudiciously granted too many credits) the ratio (metallic holding/notes in circulation) is reduced, while the demands for conversion tend to increase. The insufficiency of the metallic holding tends to bring about a general loss of confidence among the bearers of notes and a massive demand for conversion into metal. The bank loses all its metal (without being able to repay all the bearers of notes) and becomes bankrupt. The notes which have been repaid are replaced, in the monetary circulation, by the metal obtained in exchange for them. As for the notes which are not repaid, they disappear from monetary circulation: they are in fact demonetized (they cease to count as money), since the bank can no longer honour the promise of conversion. The total money in circulation is therefore reduced by the disappearance of the private banks which have injudiciously created too much credit money and by the subsequent demonetization of their credit money.

In the case of a *unified* banking system, the constraint of convertibility is less immediate and less powerful than it was previously: convertibility is no longer the responsibility of each private bank, but of the central bank, which has the monopoly of the issue of bank-notes; besides which, the fact that these notes are legal tender increases their degree of acceptance by the public. All the same, the central bank must ensure the aggregate convertibility of its notes and must maintain a reasonable proportion between the metallic money it holds and the amount of notes in circulation. If it appears that the private banks have injudiciously granted too many credits, setting off a dangerous reduction in the ratio (metallic holding/central bank's notes in circulation), the central bank must react by restricting its credit to the private banks, who will themselves have to restrict the credit granted to industrialists. This restriction of credit amounts to a *reduction of monetary creation* and therefore to a reduction of the total quantity of money in circulation.[15]

Consequently, when there is convertibility, the initial imbalance between the growth of the quantity of money and the growth of the sum total of values is bound to be taken up by a reduction of the money in circulation (through the demonetization of the private banks' notes or the reduction of the volume of the central bank's notes).[16]

The case of inconvertible credit money. In this case, the reaction of the banking system may be different. No longer having to maintain any metallic backing, the central bank is no longer obliged to restrict credit nor to take up the excess of money in this way. The banks may even continue to lend in order to enable industrial enterprises facing shortfalls of sales to make up their losses and to continue working.[17]

Consequently, when there is inconvertibility, the imbalance between the increase of the quantity of money and the increase of the sum total of values is not necessarily taken up and may even become more marked. Further on, we will see the consequences as regards the evolution of prices.

The obsolescence of equipment

1. *Loss of value and excess money.* Obsolescence has already been defined as the technological ageing of machines, in contrast to their physical wear and tear. It refers to the situation where equipment, which has been installed and is still capable of functioning, is overtaken by new equipment which is technologically more advanced and can be produced and/or used at lower cost. Obsolescence is inherent in capitalist society which is based on competition and technical progress and it also results in losses of value and of revenue (even if the whole production is sold). Let us illustrate these points, working from the previous example.

We assumed that a capitalist borrows money in order to purchase a machine, the value of which is 500 000 hours and the price £500 000. This machine has a normal use-life of 5 years and it should be capable of an annual production of 2000 units of a commodity A: so the past value to be transferred is 50 hours per unit of A. The unit value (past and present) is reckoned to be 50 hours + 10 hours = 60 hours, the market price, £50 + £10 = £60. Our capitalist recovers £50 of constant capital per unit, £100 000 per annum, £500 000 over 5 years:

the constant capital recovered therefore enables him to repay his loan (the interest on the loan is taken from the profit realized).

Let us now assume that after 3 years, rival producers adopt a new production technique which requires a machine of equal use-life (5 years) but of only half the value (250 000 hours) or capable of double the production (4000 units per annum): in both cases, the value transferred is only 25 hours per unit. If we assume that the new value per unit is still 10 hours, the social unit value falls to 25 hours + 10 hours = 35 hours, and the unit price on the market becomes £25 + £10 = £35. Our capitalist can in theory choose one of two solutions: either of immediately adopting the new technique introduced by his rivals (adjusting his individual unit value to the social unit value) or of using his obsolete equipment until it is physically worn out (while adjusting to the new market price). Whatever his choice, he finds himself faced with losses of value and of revenue. If he adopts the new technique, only three-fifths of the value of the old machine will have been transferred to the final commodities (300 000 hours instead of 500 000 hours), and equally only three-fifths of the constant capital will have been recovered (£300 000 instead of £500 000): to repay his loan, our capitalist will have to cut substantially into his profit. If he carries on for two more years with the old machine, he will have to conform to the new norms of value and of price: he will only be able to transfer 25 hours of past value per unit or £25 of amortization of the constant capital (instead of the previous 50 hours and £50), which will bring about in 2 years a loss of value (not transferred) of 100 000 hours and a loss of revenue (constant capital not recovered) of £100 000 (which in this case too, has to be recovered by cutting into the profit).

In so far as the purchase of machinery is financed by recourse to credit, the obsolescence of equipment and the resultant losses of value bring about a situation analogous to that described in the case of the 'non-sale': the quantity of credit money in circulation grows more than the sum total of values.

2.   *Reactions of the banking systems.* As in the case of 'non-sale', the reaction of the banking system, faced with this imbalance (between quantity of credit money in circulation and sum total of values), varies according to whether the credit money issued is convertible or inconvertible. With *convertibility*, the banking system will have to reduce the quantity of money in circulation: banks will refuse to grant new credits and thus to 'consolidate' the debt of enterprises faced with losses through obsolescence. With *inconvertibility*, the

banking system is not obliged to reduce the excess of money in circulation: banks can 'consolidate' the debt of an enterprise, thus increasing the initial imbalance.[18]

Credit Money and the Financing of Public Expenditure

The previous chapters showed that the state intervenes in economic activities in various capacities: as commodity producer (through public or quasi-public enterprises), as purchaser of commodities (through public sector contracts), as initiator of non-commodity production ('administration', including education, social security etc.), as provider of subsidies (for public or private enterprises). What is the position of these various public activities with regard to the relations between value creation and money creation?

Public enterprises can be considered in the same category as the whole body of private enterprises engaged in commodity production. Like them, they produce value and revenue (their activities are 'productive') and they can have recourse to credit in order to finance these productive activities; and in so far as they rely on credit but face the problems of obsolescence or non-sale, an imbalance develops between money creation and value creation.

Public sector contracts, non-commodity production and subsidies present quite a different problem, for the state no longer intervenes as a producer of value and of revenue: public sector contracts constitute *consumption of value*, non-commodity productions employ labour which by definition is *not intended to create value* (as it does not produce commodities), subsidies *make good losses of value* and of revenue in public or in private enterprises. So we have the problem of the financing of these 'unproductive' activities, which produce neither value nor revenue: where can the state find the money required for its purchases of commodities, for the payment of its officials, and for the granting of subsidies?

The financing of this unproductive expenditure can be carried out in two main ways: recourse to taxation (or to other obligatory charges, like National Insurance contributions) and recourse to credit.

Recourse to taxation does not affect the total quantity of money in circulation: a proportion of the revenue created in commodity activities is simply transferred to the state. The state therefore finances its expenditure without altering the overall balance between the quantity of money and the quantity of value.

If taxes are not sufficient to finance state expenditure, the budgetary deficit must be made up by recourse to credit. Here the situation is quite different. In so far as the granting of credit amounts to the creation of money (rather than to mere financial intermediation), the financing of unproductive state expenditure by means of credit results in the creation of an imbalance between the total quantity of money in circulation and the total quantity of value in circulation.

The reaction to this imbalance depends once again on the prevailing monetary system. With *convertibility*, the choice is the following. Either the principle of convertibility is maintained and the state is obliged to restrict its recourse to credit (either by reducing its unproductive expenditure, or by increasing its fiscal burdens). Or the state maintains the amount of its unproductive expenditure financed by credit and convertibility is temporarily suspended: this has typically been the case in time of war.[19] With *inconvertibility*, as we have already seen, the banking system is not obliged to absorb any excess of money in circulation: it can step up its credits to the state ('consolidate' the public debt), thus increasing the overall imbalance between the quantity of money and the quantity of value.[20]

THE EVOLUTION OF THE GENERAL LEVEL OF PRICES

The evolution of the general level of prices (that is, of the 'average' unit price of commodities) presents some marked contrasts according to which of the two main periods we'are considering.

Before the Second World War, the evolution could be characterized in the following way. First, we observe an alternation of long-term trends of rising and falling prices, schematically represented below:

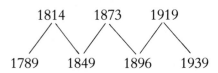

Second, superimposed on each of these long-term trends, there are *conjunctural fluctuations* of prices, parallel to the conjunctural fluctuations of production: the boom periods of production are also periods of rising prices (the conjunction of expansion and 'inflation'), the periods of downturn of production are also periods of falling prices (depression and 'deflation').

The evolution is very different *after* the Second World War.
First, during the period of rapid growth which prevailed up to
around 1970, we observe a slow but *continuous* rise in prices,
('creeping' inflation): 'contemporary' accumulation saw the disappearance both of conjunctural recessions and of the falling prices
associated with them. Second, the period of crisis and of slow
growth of the seventies presents an entirely unprecedented character:
the downturns or slowdowns of production are accompanied by an
acceleration of the rise in prices ('open', even 'galloping' inflation).

Such are the phenomena which we will try to explain in this third
section, building on the previous arguments concerning the evolution of types of money (pp. 212–17) and the gaps which may occur
between the growth of money and the growth of value (pp.
218–26).

Factors Affecting the Evolution of Prices

We know from chapter 2 that the unit price of commodities is equal
to their unit value, multiplied by the magnitude of the monetary
expressions of values:[21]

Unit price = unit value × E

Hence the evolution of the general level of prices depends on the
factors affecting the unit values of commodities on the one hand and
E on the other.

Factors affecting the unit values of commodities

We know that the unit values of commodities depend on labour
productivity. The latter is influenced by such factors as natural
conditions, work organization, skill and intensity of work, but
above all by the state of technology and the degree of mechanization.

Technical progress and increased mechanization continuously raise
productivity and bring down the unit value of commodities in the
different branches of production. In itself, this therefore tends
constantly to bring down the general level of prices.

If we observe periods where there is a rise (or even stability) in the
general level of prices, there must necessarily be a growth of E more
than proportionate (or at least proportionate) to the fall of unit
values. What, therefore, are the factors affecting E and capable of
counteracting the influence of technical progress and mechanization?

Factors affecting the monetary expression of values
Let us recall first, that the magnitude of E is obtained statistically by
dividing the sum total of prices or of revenues by the sum total of
values.[22]

$$E = \frac{\text{sum total of prices}}{\text{sum total of values}} = \frac{\text{sum total of revenues}}{\text{sum total of values}} = \ldots \text{ pounds per hour}$$

But a *method of calculating* E does not show us the *factors which affect*
E. Let us consider what these factors are, first in the case of *convertible*
credit money, then in the case of *inconvertible* credit money.

The case of convertible credit money.   In this case, the level of E may be
affected by two kinds of factors: an excess creation of money (that is,
an imbalance in the growth of the quantity of money and that of the
sum total of values); a change in the definition of the currency or in
the value of metal.

1.   *Excess creation of money.* We saw at the end of chapter 8 that the
quantity of money necessary for the circulation of commodities
depends on the sum total of prices: allowing for the restrictive
assumptions we have made (velocity of circulation = 1, absence of
'clearings', of non-commodity transactions and of deferred
payments),[23] the quantity of money *necessary* is equal to the sum total
of prices of the commodities. And if the quantity of money *effectively*
in circulation corresponds to the quantity necessary, we can write:

Sum total of prices = quantity of money in circulation

It then becomes possible to express the magnitude of E in a new
form:

$$E = \frac{\text{sum total of prices}}{\text{sum total of values}} = \frac{\text{money in circulation}}{\text{sum total of values}} = \ldots \text{ pounds per hour}$$

The foregoing equation enables us to advance the following
proposition: if the money in circulation increases in parallel to the
growth of the sum total of values, E remains constant; on the
contrary, if the monetary mass grows more than the sum total of
values, E increases (as does the relation, sum total of prices/sum total
of values).

2.   *Changes in the definition of the currency or in the value of metal.* The
foregoing equation is valid whatever the prevailing monetary
system. But in a system based on metallic money and convertible

credit money as before the Second World War, the magnitude of E can equally be expressed as a function of two other factors: the legal definition of the currency (expressed in pounds per unit of weight of metal) and the unit value of the metal (or more exactly the labour time socially necessary to produce a unit of weight of metal).

$$E = \frac{\text{definition of the currency}}{\text{unit value of the metal}} = \frac{\text{pounds/g of metal}}{\text{hours/g of metal}} = \ldots \text{pounds per hour}$$

Consequently, in a system based on metallic money and convertible credit money, E can increase for two reasons: a *devaluation* of the currency (the pound is defined by a smaller quantity of metal, which amounts to expressing the same weight of metal by a greater quantity of pounds) and/or *a fall in the unit value of the metal* (due to the discovery of deposits which are easier to exploit and/or to the introduction of technical progress in their exploitation).

In the framework of the assumptions we recalled above, and provided there is no excess creation of money, the two theoretical expressions of E should coincide.

The case of inconvertible credit money: excess creation of money. When credit money ceases to be convertible into metallic money, as is the case since the Second World War, the level of E no longer depends on the definition of the currency or on the value of the metal. Its evolution can be analysed only from the first equation given above:

$$E = \frac{\text{sum total of prices}}{\text{sum total of values}} = \frac{\text{money in circulation}}{\text{sum total of values}} = \ldots \text{pounds per hour}$$

As stated above, E increases if there is excess money creation, that is, if the quantity of money in circulation grows more than the sum total of values.

An Explanation of the Observed Evolution of Prices

Before the Second World War

The long-term trends of rising and falling prices. These long-term trends can be explained by comparing the evolution of productivity in the production of commodities on the one hand, and the evolution of productivity in the production of metals on the other.

During the whole of this period where the monetary system is based on metallic money (metallic coins are in circulation and credit money is convertible into metal), we can in fact express the unit prices of commodities in the following way (taking the second theoretical expression of E)

$$\text{unit prices} = \text{unit values of commodities} \times \frac{\text{definition of the currency}}{\text{unit value of the metal}}$$

or again:

$$\text{unit prices} = \frac{\text{unit values of commodities}}{\text{unit value of the metal}} \times \text{definition of the currency}$$

For a given definition of the currency, the evolution of the general level of prices consequently depends on the evolution of the unit value of commodities and of the metal, respectively, and therefore on the evolution of productivity in the production of commodities and in the production of the metal, respectively.

Thus rises in prices from 1849 to 1873 and from 1896 to 1920 may be explained by the more rapid fall of the value of gold (compared to commodities as a whole), following the discovery and exploitation of more productive gold mines (California and Australia around 1850, Alaska and South Africa around 1890). The falls in price from 1814 to 1849 and from 1873 to 1896 may be explained by the fall in productivity in the principal mines in operation: the value of the metal levels off or tends to increase, while the general advances in productivity bring down the value of commodities.

We should observe that the recorded price *rises* (in the long term) cannot be explained by the phenomenon of devaluation or by a possible excess in the creation of money. A *devaluation* can certainly explain a sudden increase in prices at a given moment, but not a long-term rising trend. As for *excesses in the creation of credit money* (as a result of losses of value or of the financing of budgetary deficits), the banking system must absorb them rapidly in order to maintain the convertibility of the currency;[24] their influence can therefore only be exercised in the short-term, as we shall see in examining the conjunctural fluctuations of prices.

The conjunctural fluctuations of prices.   Conjunctural fluctuations of prices are to be explained primarily by the variations of the relations between commodity supply and demand, on which are superimposed the effects of an excessive issue of credit money in the final stage of the expansion.

The recovery is characterized by an upsurge of demand coinciding with productive capacity considerably reduced as a result of bankruptcies in the recession. This situation is favourable to a rise in prices. This continues during the expansion, as demand pursues its cumulative momentum. The end of the expansion and the crisis see the rise in prices accelerated due to the excessive issue of credit money: credit reaches the maximum growth compatible with the demands of convertibility, while the mass of value tends to stagnate (the insufficient growth of consumption capacity results in enterprises failing to sell and in value losses).

The crisis of overproduction (excess of supply) starts off a cumulative fall in prices and an equally cumulative reduction of the quantities produced (as a result of bankruptcies and of cutbacks in production). The sum total of prices is reduced and the quantity of money in circulation also follows a downward course: at the end of the trade cycle, the excess of money in circulation is completely absorbed.

After the Second World War
Since credit money is not convertible into metal, the magnitude of E is no longer affected by the value of the metal or by the legal definition of the currency:[25] the evolution of E depends solely on the relation between the growth of money in circulation and the growth of the sum total of values. The unit prices of commodities have therefore to be expressed in the following way

$$\text{unit prices} = \text{unit values} \times \frac{\text{money in circulation}}{\text{sum total of values}}$$

How do we explain, from this, the moderate rise in the general level of prices during the period of rapid growth (1945–74) and its accelerated rise during the period of structural crisis (since 1974)? As we saw in the previous chapter, the first period is characterized by marked progress in productivity and consumption, the second by much slower progress both in productivity and in consumption. The problem consists in assessing the effect of this rapid or slow progress on the evolution of unit values on the one hand, and on the evolution of E on the other. As regards E, we will recall the two possible causes of imbalance between the growth of money in circulation and the growth of the sum total of values: on the one hand, the credit-financing of the 'losses of value' inherent in the functioning of the capitalist system (losses due to obsolescence and/or to non-sale), on the other hand, the credit-financing of possible budgetary deficits.[26]

The slow inflation in the period of rapid growth (1945–74). The rapid progress in productivity has the effect of rapidly reducing the unit values of commodities: this in itself tends to *bring down* the general level of prices.

What about the factors causing E to *rise?* The losses of values due to *failure to sell* can be disregarded: the characteristic of this period is precisely the parallelism between the rapid increase both of productive capacity and of markets. Similarly, the credit-financing of possible *budgetary deficits* can be disregarded too: the large increases in productivity make it possible to finance public expenditure by taxation without adversely affecting the scope for wage-earner consumption and for capitalist accumulation. On the contrary, the rapid growth of productivity entails an equally rapid *obsolescence* of plant, resulting inevitably in losses of value and of revenue. Inconvertibility, however, enables the banks to consolidate the debts of enterprises facing losses due to obsolescence: this results in an increasingly serious imbalance between the growth of money in circulation and the growth of the sum total of values and therefore in a continuous rise in E.

In short, the moderate rise in the general level of prices is the result of the contradictory effect of two factors: on the one hand, the fall in unit values, on the other, the credit-financing of losses due to obsolescence.[27]

The rapid inflation in the period of structural crisis (since 1974).   The acceleration of the rise in the general level of prices can be explained by the combined effect of several factors.

First, the slowing-down of the advances of productivity tends to slow down the fall of unit values. The factor making for a fall of prices therefore becomes less powerful than before.

At the same time, the factors making for a rise in E become on the whole stronger than before. The slowing-down of advances in productivity stimulates capitalists into looking for new forms of technical progress (for example robotization): in so far as these forms of technical progress are actually adopted, the phenomenon of *obsolescence* and the losses of value and of revenue associated with it remain significant. On the other hand, the slowing down of advances in consumption increases the losses of value and of revenue due to *failure to sell* and encourages enterprises to minimize these losses through recourse to credit. Similarly, the joint slowing down of productivity and consumption in practice forces the *public authorities* to resort to credit and to the creation of money to finance a proportion of their expenditure: to resort exclusively to taxation would only further reduce the scope for wage-earner consumption and for capitalist accumulation, thus aggravating the structural crisis which the capitalist system is now going through.

This brief analysis calls for the following conclusion. The accelerated inflation which the capitalist system has been experiencing since 1970 is not due to external 'shocks' (the 'shock' of the oil crisis!) or to 'mistakes' of policy (the 'ill-considered' issue of credit money). On the contrary, it is directly linked to the structural crisis of 'contemporary' accumulation: it derives basically from the slowing-down of progress in productivity and in consumption which affects the capitalist system. The capitalist way out of the present inflation will not therefore be through the application of one or other 'technique'; it presupposes a bypassing of the crisis itself and therefore, as we saw at the end of the previous chapter, a joint revival of productivity and of consumption on a world-wide level.

NOTES

1. Originally, the monetary label given to the metal was the same as that used to measure the weight of objects: the metal bar, named 'pound' by the monetary authority, actually weighed one pound.
2. However, the analogy between the measurement of lengths and that of values is an imperfect one. For while the standard of lengths is invariable in time (a metre always measures a metre), the standard of values on the contrary is a *standard* which is *variable in time* (the quantity of metal chosen as a unit of measure has a value which diminishes as productivity in the production of metal increases: the higher this productivity, the less number of hours necessary to produce a given quantity of metal). On the other hand, the 'universal' character of the unit of measure and of its name is extremely relative in so far as money is concerned: a fragmentation of currencies corresponds to the political fragmentation of the Middle Ages and different national currencies to the different national states of the nineteenth century.
3. The monetary authority which defines the metallic content of this monetary unit (in this example, 1 pound = 10 g of gold) can proceed to a devaluation of the currency, that is, a *de jure* reduction of the metallic content defining the monetary unit (for example 1 pound = 5 g of gold). (The converse operation, less frequent in practice, constitutes a revaluation.)
4. Let us be clear that the creation of additional money involves a credit operation but that every credit operation does not necessarily involve the creation of money.
   (1)   The creation of additional money involves credit: as long as the

banks restrict themselves to issuing receipt notes, these are necessarily covered by the metal taken in on deposit.

(2)   Every credit operation does not necessarily involve the creation of money. In fact, the banks can lend out metallic money deposited by individuals: in this case they are merely acting as *financial intermediaries* (who lend out the money they have collected).

5. In so far as the central bank grants credit to credit organizations (to the banks), it acts as 'lender of last resort.'

6. For example, that the relation of notes to metal does not exceed the ratio of 3:1.

7. This new form of money can also be referred to as *checking account money* (American usage) or *demand deposit money*.

8. For example, to ensure that the proportion of checking account money to notes does not exceed the ratio of 10:1.

9. As before (note 4), let us be clear that if the creation of additional money involves a credit operation, every credit operation does not necessarily involve the creation of money: banks can lend notes deposited by individuals, thus merely acting as *financial intermediaries*.

10. As an *international currency*, US dollars held by foreign countries continued to be convertible into gold until 1971. But as the *national* currency of the United States, dollars held by American citizens had ceased, like other national currencies, to be convertible since the Second World War.

11. If the central bank still has the official role of controlling the creation of money, the limits imposed on its creation will depend on internal guidelines or on constraints *other* than the demands of convertibility.

12. In this example, we are not counting the value of the raw materials used and thus the *circulating* constant capital laid out.

13. In this example, we are assuming that simple prices = prices of production = market prices.

14. Although the credit money put into circulation is thus taken out of circulation each time (in the hypothesis of complete valorization), it is however still possible for the total mass of credit money in circulation to increase with time: as we already said, for this to happen it is sufficient that new credits should be granted, before repayment of the previous credits.

15. The unification of the banking system does not in any way rule out bankruptcies (of the banks). Banks which have injudiciously granted too much credit make losses (as they are not repaid) and those losses cannot be compensated for by recourse to credits from the central bank (since the latter is obliged to restrict credit in order to safeguard convertibility). The difference from the case of the non-unified banking system is that the private banks no longer face the additional risk of general demands for conversion due to a loss of public confidence in their own money.

16. To be more precise, the initial imbalance is taken up by a greater reduction of the money in circulation in relation to the quantity of value (which is itself reduced cumulatively in the process of recession involved in the shortfall of sales).

17. We can understand the important effects of the banks' behaviour on the trade cycle. When there is *convertibility*, the crisis of overproduction and the shortfalls in sales which accompany it force the banking system to restrict credit: this accentuates the industrial enterprises' difficulties and the cumulative process of bankruptcies, unemployment and recession. When there is *inconvertibility*, the banking system can on the contrary carry on its credit activities: this helps to mitigate the effects of this cumulative process.

18. A crucial question, which has still to be properly answered, is of knowing the possible limits of this imbalance: can the sector of commodity production increase its debt to the banking system indefinitely?

19. With convertibility, the choice is actually less simple than it appears. For the state can maintain both the amount of its unproductive expenditure *and* the convertibility of credit money, provided it carries out a devaluation of the currency (that is, by reducing *de jure* the metallic content of the monetary unit, for example, of the pound): such a devaluation reduces automatically the quantity of metal required to meet the demands for conversion.

20. As in the case of private credit, we have the question of the possible limits of the imbalance: can the state increase its debt to the banking system indefinitely?

21. As we are dealing with the evolution of the *average* unit price of commodities, we can disregard here the difference between simple prices, prices of production and market prices.

22. Two methods of calculation are theoretically possible: either to relate the sum total of *gross* prices or revenues to the sum total of *present and past* values or to relate the sum total of *net* prices or revenues to the sum total of *present* values. From the practical point of view, the first method of calculation encounters insurmountable problems (calculation of past values) and is abandoned in favour of the second method (cf. chapter 11). From the theoretical point of view, however, it is necessary to argue here in terms of *gross* prices and revenues and of *present and past* values: it is the only way to compare the sum total of prices and the quantity of money required.

23. See chapter 8, p. 185, note 25.

24. In periods during which convertibility has been suspended (for example, in times of war), the imbalance between money creation and value creation did not have to be taken up by restriction of the quantity of money: the maintenance of the imbalance then contributed to the rise in prices (in a way analogous to the situation which was to prevail after the

Second World War, with the permanent adoption of inconvertibility).
25. It is possible that the law may continue to define the currency by reference to a certain quantity of metal (1 pound = x g of metal); but in so far as credit money is no longer convertible, this definition does not have the same significance as before.
26. The principles we have just recalled are sufficient to suggest one important difference between a *Marxist* and a *'monetarist'* approach to inflation. Both theories explain rises in the general level of prices in terms of an 'excess of money'. But monetarists ignore market losses, either through lack of sale or through obsolescence: for them, the state (not private initiative) is thus the only possible source of excess money (the 'ill-considered' issue of credit money to finance budgetary deficits).
27. A more thorough analysis should explain why these two contradictory factors actually result in a *moderate rise* in the general level of prices: the fall in unit values and the rise in E could in theory be such that the general level of prices would tend rather to *fall*.

11

An Empirical Analysis of the Rate of Surplus Labour in Five European Countries (1966–78)

AIM AND SCOPE OF THE EMPIRICAL ANALYSIS

Aim of the Chapter

A basic originality of Marxist political economy consists in emphasizing the reality of the surplus labour provided by the wage-earners, the reality of the exploitation to which they are subject.

Chapters 2 and 3 began by providing a *theoretical* proof in two steps. We first discovered, behind the apparent phenomenon of prices, the hidden reality of value, of labour devoted to producing commodities. We were then able to reveal, behind the visible phenomenon of capitalist profit, the hidden reality of surplus labour provided by the wage-earners in the production of commodities.

Through the analysis of some essential contradictions and tendencies of the capitalist system, chapters 7 to 10 provided a *factual* proof which confirmed indirectly the validity of the earlier theoretical considerations. We saw, for example, how increases in productivity, the breaking-up of non-commodity communities, the growth of female labour, and the worldwide restructuring of industrial production are all clearly in keeping with capitalist logic, as they enable capitalism to expand its sources of surplus value and to increase the rate of surplus value.

The object of this chapter consists in providing a *statistical* proof of the hidden reality of surplus labour. It aims at studying empirically, with concrete and recent statistics, both the rate of surplus labour and the factors affecting its magnitude.

The realities we propose to estimate empirically in this chapter can be specified as follows.

1. The primary reality, of the most general application, is the wage-earners' *rate of surplus labour*. This reality has the most general application, in the sense that it applies to both productive and unproductive wage-earners: blue-collar workers, white-collar workers, officials, all wage-earners (except in exceptional circumstances) provide some surplus labour, for which there is a specific corresponding rate of surplus labour. As one of the essential objects of the capitalist class is to increase the rate of surplus labour – both of productive wage-earners (to increase the mass of surplus revenue created) and of unproductive wage-earners (to reduce the drain of surplus revenue represented by their earnings) – every empirical study of the evolution of the rate of surplus labour assumes a very obvious interest.

2. The magnitude of the rate of surplus labour depends on *labour-time* and on the *value of labour-power*. We emphasized that the evolution of the latter is subject to the opposing factors of the rise in productivity (which causes the value of each of the necessaries of life (the means of subsistence) to fall) and of the rise in the real wage (which corresponds to the increase in the number of necessaries of life consumed). But has the rise in real wages been counteracted by increases in productivity sufficiently great to cause the value of labour-power to fall? Given the well-known trend towards the reduction of labour-time, an empirical answer to this question is of crucial importance for an appraisal of the extent to which the rate of surplus labour is capable of rising.

Scope of the Empirical Analysis

The empirical analysis of this chapter concerns five European countries (Germany, France, the Netherlands, Belgium and the United Kingdom) and covers the period 1966–78 (1973–78 for the United Kingdom).

The choice of five European countries can be explained by the concern to ensure a maximum of statistical homogeneity, relying primarily on the data established by a common organization: the Statistical Office of the European Communities.

Among these data, as we shall see, the results of the triennial surveys of labour costs in industry figure prominently. These surveys were started in 1966 (1973 for the United Kingdom), hence the choice of period for consideration.

GENERAL OBSERVATIONS ON THE EMPIRICAL METHOD

We saw in chapter 4 that the rate of surplus value could be expressed by two different formulae. The first formula related the monetary expression of values (E) to the hourly wage per worker:

$$s' = \frac{E}{w/d} - 1$$

The second formula related the labour-time (*d*) to the value of labour-power per wage-earner (*w*), the latter being the product of the average real wage or of the number of necessaries of life (x) and of the average value per item of the necessaries of life (*px*).

$$s' = \frac{d}{w} - 1$$

or $\quad s' = \dfrac{d}{x.px} - 1$

In these latter formulae, the magnitudes *w* or *px* are obtained by dividing, by E, the wage actually paid (w) or the average price of the necessaries of life (px, as reflected in the index of consumer prices):

$$w = w/E$$

$$px = px/E$$

The method of calculation of the rate of surplus labour suggested by these different formulae assumes that the magnitude of E can be determined; in addition (in the case of the last two equations), it assumes that it is possible, through the mediation of E, to pass from the appearance of prices to the reality of values. The method of calculation of s' therefore raises two problems which assume a wide-ranging significance, for they actually apply to any type of commodity (and not only to labour-power or to the bundle of goods considered by the consumer price index).

(1) First problem: is it possible, and by what means, to determine the magnitude of E?

(2) Second problem (assuming the magnitude of E is known): working from the *actual* (market) *price* of a commodity (the

only phenomenon which can be empirically observed), is it possible, through the mediation of E, to discover the *value* of that commodity?

Let us look at each of these problems, starting with the second.

The Problem of the Transition from Actual Prices to Values

Let us first briefly recall the meaning of E. We saw (in chapter 2) that commodity production must involve the existence of money, and that the value of commodities must be expressed in a certain quantity of money, in a certain price (for example, pounds). The monetary expression of values (E) is merely the relation between values thus expressed in *prices* and the same values expressed in *hours* of labour: it is therefore expressed in a certain number of monetary units (for example, pounds) per hour of labour.

However, if values have to be expressed in prices, actual prices (market prices) normally diverge from simple prices (or theoretical prices corresponding exactly to the monetary expression of the value of commodities). Let us recall the three stages of the transition from values to actual prices: the first is the expression of values in simple prices; the second is the transformation of simple prices into prices of production within the framework of a capitalist society, where the composition of capital varies from one branch of production to another; the third is the transition to actual prices (or market prices), which differ from the prices of production according to the state of the relations between supply and demand and/or according to the degree of protection which the industry in question enjoys. Schematically, in distinguishing the two forms of expression of values (explicit expression in hours of labour and derived expression in prices), as well as three successive levels of abstraction (simple commodity production without monopolies or imbalances between supply and demand – capitalist production without monopolies or imbalances between supply and demand – capitalist production with monopolies and/or imbalances between supply and demand), we can build up Table 11.1 where the three arrows symbolize the three transitions we have mentioned. (The terms in brackets designate concepts not current in Marxist theory.)

The transition from the axis of values to that of prices, or conversely, is carried out through the mediation of the monetary expression of values E. The problem is that, for any commodity, the only magnitude which can be observed is the actual market price:

TABLE 11.1   The transition from values to market prices

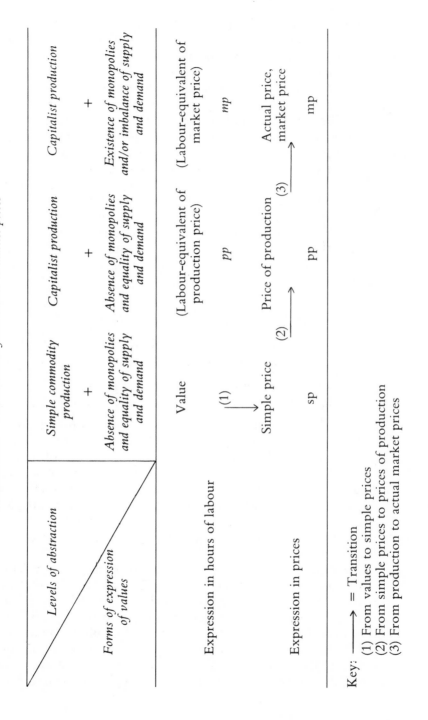

	Simple commodity production + Absence of monopolies and equality of supply and demand	Capitalist production + Absence of monopolies and equality of supply and demand	Capitalist production + Existence of monopolies and/or imbalance of supply and demand
Levels of abstraction / *Forms of expression of values*			
Expression in hours of labour	Value	(Labour-equivalent of production price)	(Labour-equivalent of market price)
	Simple price (1) →	pp	mp
Expression in prices	sp	Price of production (2) →	Actual price, market price (3) →
		pp	mp

Key: ——→ = Transition

(1) From values to simple prices
(2) From simple prices to prices of production
(3) From production to actual market prices

empirical research will therefore only be able to carry out the transition from market prices (mp) to their equivalent in hours of labour (*mp*) but it will never be able to arrive at the actual value of commodities.

This limitation does not invalidate the research we have undertaken, particularly when it is a question of considering the *evolution* of a variable (value of labour-power, rate of surplus labour etc.): in fact, if it is true that there is always a (non-quantifiable) divergence between *mp* and *value*,[1] the essential point for our argument is that the two magnitudes always evolve in the same direction, falling as productivity increases. This same limitation should, however, draw our attention to the imprecision of concepts which will be frequently employed later in this chapter: thus, strictly speaking, w (= w/E) does not represent the *value* of labour-power but the *labour-equivalent* of actual wages; it is only for reasons of simplicity and brevity that we will systematically replace the concept of 'labour-equivalent of actual prices' by the concept of value.

Problems connected with the calculation of E

We know that the magnitude of E is obtained statistically by dividing the sum total of prices or of revenues by the sum total of values:

$$E = \frac{\text{sum total of prices}}{\text{sum total of values}} = \frac{\text{sum total of revenues}}{\text{sum total of values}}$$

The first problem is about whether we should consider prices (or revenues) and values in 'gross' or 'net' terms. In fact, as we have already said,[2] the denominator and the numerator of E can be understood in two different ways: either the sum total of *total* values (including the past values transferred) and the sum total of *gross* prices or revenues (incorporating the cost of the means of production employed); or the sum total of *new* values (excluding the past values) and the sum total of *net* prices or revenues (having deducted the cost of the means of production).

Theoretically, the two methods of calculation are equivalent and arrive at the same result. Let us assume, for example, that in the course of a given year (t_1) the sum total of *present* labour devoted to producing commodities is 3 million hours and the net price of the commodities (or the *net* social revenue) is £30 million. Let us assume in addition that the producers employ in t_1 a set of means of production (tools and materials) made in the course of the previous year (t_0); these means of production cost, in t_0, 7 million hours or £20 million, while in t_1, they are only worth 4 million hours (due to technical progress) but cost £40 million pounds (due to inflation).

The calculation of E in 'net' terms gives us:

$$E \text{ ('net') in } t_1 = \frac{\text{£30 million}}{\text{3 million hours}} = \text{£10 per hour}$$

The calculation of E in 'gross' terms, to be correct, must consider the value and the price of the means of production not in t_0 (the year of their manufacture) but in t_1 (the year of their use, of their incorporation in the production of new commodities);[3] now, from t_0 to t_1, technical progress has brought about a reduction of the value of the means of production, while inflation has brought about an increase in their price (which enterprises must take account of in their amortization policy). Consequently, the calculation of E in 'gross' terms gives us:

$$E \text{ ('gross') in } t_1 \neq \frac{\text{£20 million} + \text{£30 million}}{\text{7 million hours} + \text{3 million hours}} \text{(or £5 per hour)}$$

$$= \frac{\text{£40 million} + \text{£30 million}}{\text{4 million hours} + \text{3 million hours}} = \text{£10 per hour}$$

If the two methods of calculation can be considered as equivalent in theory, it works out differently in practice. For in practice, the calculation of E in 'gross' terms encounters an insurmountable problem, namely the estimation of the value of the means of production: unlike the present value (which can be estimated from the number of labour-hours effectively worked), the past value cannot be the object of any direct observation; this would remain true if we wished merely to quantify the value of the means of production in the year of their manufacture. Consequently, in practice, the only method we can use consists in calculating E in 'net' terms:

$$E = \frac{\text{sum total of net prices}}{\text{sum total of new values}} = \frac{\text{sum total of net revenues}}{\text{sum total of new values}}$$

The denominator of E is provided by the number of hours of *present* labour devoted to *producing commodities*: it is these hours of labour which create new values and new revenues. The denominator is therefore the number of *hours of productive labour, productive in the wider sense*, comprising both waged and non-waged labour (providing these wage-earners or non-wage-earners take part in the production of commodities).

The estimation of the hours of productive labour raises a problem of *statistical availability*: how do we distinguish, in the usual statistics, between productive and unproductive workers? and how do we get to know the average labour-time per productive worker? We shall see, further on, the methods and expedients to which we have resorted in order to resolve these practical questions. But the estimation of the hours of productive labour also raises two more *theoretical* problems which should be mentioned here.

On the one hand, the hours of present labour devoted to producing commodities only constitute productive labour (productive of value and of revenue) in their entirety if all the commodities produced are actually sold. If a proportion of the commodities is not sold, a corresponding proportion of the labour provided does *not* constitute productive labour. As we are unable to measure the degree of non-sale of commodities, we will assume, for simplicity's sake, in what follows that all the commodities produced are actually sold and therefore all the hours of present labour devoted to their production do constitute productive labour.

On the other hand, we cannot ignore the problem of the differences in skill or in the intensity of labour: are all hours of labour equivalent? Is not labour 'worth' more (does it not create more value?) in the case where the labour-power is more skilled (or functions more intensively) than in the opposite case?

We already touched on this problem when we considered the relations between unequally mechanized *enterprises* within the same branch of production.[4] We suggested that (simultaneous) differences in technique, skill and intensity of labour bring about *transfers* of surplus-revenue but do not result in differences in the *creation* of value and of surplus value. The same principles can be extended to relations between *branches* of production. The price of commodities is affected by differences in the 'degree of skill' (or of intensity) of labour among the different branches of industry, just as it is affected by differences in the degree of mechanization and in the degree of protection obtaining in each branch. But in the three cases (difference in the degree of mechanization, in the degree of protection, in the degree of skill or of intensity), it is the price of the commodities which is affected and not the quantity of value itself: in other words, the three cases mentioned only bring about transfers of surplus revenue between branches of production, that is, divergences between the quantity of revenue and of surplus revenue *created* and the quantity of revenue and of surplus revenue *appropriated* by each branch.

Consequently, from the point of view of the creation of value and of revenue, and more generally, of the measurement of labour, we can take it that one hour of labour is always equal to another hour of labour: 1 hour of 'complex' labour (skilled or intensive) equals 1 hour of average labour; 1 hour of specialist labour equals 1 hour of unskilled labour; 1 hour of labour in one enterprise or industry equals 1 hour in another enterprise or industry.[5]

The final problem we must bring up here concerns the numerator of E, that is, the sum total of net revenues (or of net prices). Just as the denominator aims to measure the *value created* in a given economy, the numerator should in theory measure the *revenue created* in the economy (or the sum total of net *simple* prices of commodities). For this aggregate revenue created (or the sum total of net *simple* prices) constitutes the exact translation, in money terms, of the value created. But the statistics available only make it possible to consider the aggregate revenue *obtained* (distributed or spent) in an economy (or the sum total of net *actual* prices of commodities); now the revenue obtained differs from the revenue created (the actual price differs from the simple price) each time there is a transfer of surplus revenue. Making use of the national statistics on aggregate revenue *obtained*, our method of calculation amalgamates the revenue *created* in one country and the revenue *transferred* from one country to another. As a result, there is a risk of 'distortion' in the estimation of E: this distortion may be significant if the international transfers of surplus revenue are themselves significant *and* if they are made systematically in favour or to the detriment of certain countries.

THE ESTIMATION OF THE MONETARY EXPRESSION OF VALUES AND OF THE RATE OF SURPLUS LABOUR

Methods of Calculation

Calculation of E
The existence of relatively homogeneous statistical data published by the Statistical Office of the European Communities (EUROSTAT) has made it possible to estimate the evolution of E in five European countries according to the method described above.

$$E = \frac{\text{sum total of net revenues (or prices)}}{\text{sum total of new values}}$$

$$E = \frac{\text{net national revenue (or product)}}{\text{hours of productive labour (in the wider sense)}}$$

As regards the numerator, the concept adopted is that of the net national product *at market prices.*[6] This is because E is meant to provide the connection between values and their expression in market prices.

As regards the denominator, we first carried out an estimate, year by year, of the number of productive workers, then multiplied this productive labour-power by the average annual labour-time in industry. Let us look at these two stages in more detail.

In order to estimate the number of productive workers, we have used the EUROSTAT statistics relating to the structure of the civilian working population.[7] The published statistics enable us to make the groupings indicated in Table 11.2, and from these groupings we have made a division between workers 'regarded as

TABLE 11.2   *Estimate of productive and unproductive workers based on the EUROSTAT categories*

EUROSTAT categories	Workers regarded as productive or unproductive
1. Agriculture, forestry, fishing (a) non-waged workers★ (b) waged workers	

2. Industry
(a) non-waged workers★
(b) waged workers
  extractive industries
  manufacturing industries
  electricity, gas, water
  building and public works
	Workers regarded as productive

3. Services
(a) non-waged workers★
(b) waged workers
  commerce, restaurants, hotels
  tránsport, communication, storage	

banks and insurance (+ real
  estate and industrial
  services)
communal services (+ social
  services and personal services)
	Workers regarded as unproductive

★Non-waged workers = employers, 'self-employed' and family helpers.

'productive' and others 'regarded as unproductive'. The inverted commas are deliberately used, for such a division does not correspond to a rigorous division between productive and unproductive workers. On the one hand, even within the categories 'regarded as productive' (because the activities carried out in them are primarily directed towards the production of commodities),[8] a certain number of workers (as we saw in chapter 3) inevitably carry out unproductive activities of circulation or of 'internal' non-commodity production.[9] On the other hand, within the categories 'regarded as unproductive' (because they cover primarily activities of circulation or of non-commodity production), we find workers who do in fact carry out activities of commodity production: this is certainly the case of the majority of workers producing 'industrial services' or 'personal services'. In the present state of statistical availability, it is impossible to know whether the number of unproductive workers, wrongly included in the categories 'regarded as productive' is or is not greater than the number of productive workers, wrongly included in the categories 'regarded as unproductive': it is obvious that the two sources of error *tend* to offset each other, but we do not know *to what extent* they do so.

Having estimated the number of productive workers, we have had to estimate the average annual labour-time worked by each of them. For this purpose, we have relied on the results of the 'surveys of labour costs in industry', carried out by EUROSTAT every 3 years since 1966.[10] These surveys provide *inter alia* the *actual* labour-time per manual worker and the *contractual or customary* labour-time per non-manual worker. From here, we have calculated the *average* labour-time per wage-earner (manual or non-manual)[11] in manufacturing industry and we have assumed that this labour-time represented the annual average labour-time worked per productive worker. As the EUROSTAT surveys are only carried out every third year, we have still had to estimate the evolution of the average annual labour-time in the intercalary years: this was done, taking into account the evolution, year by year, of the *weekly* labour-time in manufacturing industry.[12]

Calculation of s'

We recalled at the beginning of the chapter that the rate of surplus labour (s') can be calculated by relating the monetary expression of values (E) to the hourly wage (w/d):

$$s' = \frac{E}{w/d} - 1$$

In addition, we saw in chapter 3 that the most appropriate concept of 'wage' is the concept of 'wage-cost', which takes account *both* of the wage-earners' *individual* consumption *and* of their participation in *collective* consumption.

Having established the evolution of E, we were therefore able to estimate the evolution of the rate of surplus labour from the statistics published by EUROSTAT, on the evolution of the hourly labour cost. More precisely, we estimated the evolution of the *average* rate of surplus labour in the *manufacturing* industry of the five countries in question. We are speaking of an average rate of surplus labour, for this includes all waged workers, with no distinction between manual or non-manual or between productive or unproductive workers.

The EUROSTAT statistics on hourly labour cost (manual and non-manual workers) are of two kinds. We have, on the one hand, direct estimates of this hourly cost resulting from the triennial surveys already mentioned. On the other hand, we have data updating this hourly cost for the intercalary years since 1972 (since 1975 for the United Kingdom).[13] For the intercalary years prior to this date, we have assumed that the hourly labour cost has had a constant rate of increase between survey years.

Results

Table 11.3 shows, for the five countries in question, the calculation of E and of s' in 1966, 1972 and 1978 (1973 and 1978 for the United Kingdom).[14]

Table 11.3 enables us to establish various facts.

(1) The number of productive workers decreases everywhere, both in absolute figures (column L) and in the percentage of the total civilian working population (column L/P). The decline of the ratio L/P tends to confirm the hypothesis of an increase in the proportion of unproductive workers, a hypothesis which is frequently put forward in Marxist writings.

(2) The average annual labour-time (*d*) also decreases (except in the United Kingdom between 1973 and 1978): this reinforces the reduction of the total value created (L.*d* or D).

(3) The decrease of the sum total of values (D) is combined with an even larger increase in the sum total of net prices or of net revenues (R): the result is a rapid rise in the monetary expression of values (E).

TABLE 11.3 Calculation of E and of s'[1] in five European countries: 1966, 1972 and 1978

	L	L/p	d[1]	D (= L.d)	R	E (= R/D)	w/d[1]	S'[1] (= $\frac{E}{w/d}$ − 1)
	(10³)		(hours)	(10⁶ hours) (10⁹)				
Germany					(DM)	(DM/h)	(DM/h)	
1966	21,623	82%	1884	40,738	441	10.81	6.94	56%
1972	20,384	78%	1798	36,650	740	20.18	12.16	66%
1978	18,396	74%	1769	32,543	1145	35.17	21.76	62%
France					(FF)	(FF/h)	(FF/h)	
1966	15,720	80%	2077	32,650	472	14.46	8.24	76%
1972	15,778	77%	1957	30,878	888	28.75	14.96	92%
1978	14,987	71%	1808	27,096	1894	69.88	37.38	87%
Netherlands					(fl.)	(fl/h)	(fl/h)	
1966	3,337	76%	1987	6,631	67	10.14	6.01	69%
1972	3,315	73%	1504	5,970	134	22.42	12.12	85%
1978	3,098	68%	1655	5,127	255	49.82	25.22	98%
Belgium					(FB)	(FB/h)	(FB/h)	
1966	2,855	79%	1958	5,590	806	144	84	71%
1972	2,733	74%	1798	4,914	1397	284	156	82%
1978	2,566	69%	1641	4,211	2706	643	375	71%
United Kingdom					(£)	(£/h)	(£/h)	
1966	18,756	75%	1872	32,494	66	2.02	1.06	91%
1973	17,358	71%	1916	31,721	145	4.57	2.51	82%
1978	16,556	67%						

[1]For the whole work-force (manual and non-manual workers) of the manufacturing industry (enterprises employing at least fifty wage-earners in 1966 and at least ten wage-earners in 1972 and 1978; for the United Kingdom, at least fifty wage-earners in 1973, at least ten wage-earners in 1978).

See key to Table on p. 250.

Key to Table 11.3

L: number of workers 'regarded as productive'.
P: total civilian working population.
d: average annual labour-time per productive worker.
D: (= L.d) total number of hours of 'productive' labour (productive
        of value and of revenue) = sum total of values.
R: net domestic product at market prices = sum total of net prices
        or of net revenues.
w/d: average cost of labour-power (manual and non-manual workers)
        per hour of labour.
h: hours.

---

(4)   While the hourly labour cost (w/d) increases steadily, the rate
      of surplus labour (s') at first increases until 1972, then
      decreases after 1972 (except in the Netherlands where it
      continues to increase).

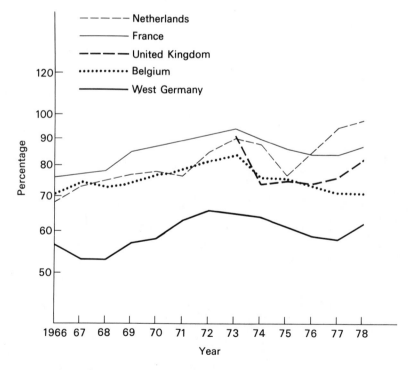

FIGURE 11.1   *Level and evolution of s' in five European countries;*
1966–78

Figure 11.1 shows, year by year, the evolution of the rate of surplus labour. This diagram confirms the general rise in the rate of surplus labour from 1966 to 1972 (or 1973). On the other hand, it leads us to qualify the statements made with regard to the later years: in fact, s' begins by decreasing in every case after 1972 (or 1973) and continues to do so for a number of years, varying from country to country; it tends, however, to recover in the later years, more markedly in some countries than in others (except ĭn Belgium, the only country where s' is even lower in 1978 than in 1975).

TABLE 11.4   *Rate of surplus labour and daily quantity of surplus labour (wage-earners in manufacturing industry, 1978)*

Country	Rate of surplus labour (rounded off) (%)	Relative proportion of		Quantity (per 8 hour day) of	
		Necessary labour (%)	Surplus labour (%)	Necessary labour (hours)	Surplus labour (hours)
Germany	60	62.5	37.5	5	3
Belgium	70	59	41	4.7	3.3
United Kingdom	80	56	44	4.5	3.5
France	90	53	47	4.2	3.8
Netherlands	100	50	50	4	4

Table 11.4 deals with the last year for which we have all the necessary data available (1978). We see in it that the rate of surplus labour in the five countries is (in round figures) between 60 per cent (Germany) and 100 per cent (Netherlands). These same ratios can be expressed in other terms: for a working day of 8 hours, the quantity of free surplus labour is (in round figures) between 3 hours (Germany) and 4 hours (Netherlands).

FACTORS AFFECTING THE EVOLUTION OF THE RATE OF SURPLUS LABOUR

Method of Analysis and Method of Calculation

The analysis which follows has been carried out by taking once again the *average* rate of surplus labour (manual and non-manual workers)

TABLE 11.5 *Analysis of variables affecting the evolution of s'^1 in five European countries, 1966–78 (selected years)*

Base = 1966	d	w/d	w $(= d.w/d)$	px	E	px $(= px/E)$	x $(= w/px)$	w $(= x.px)$	s'^1 $(= \dfrac{d}{x.px} - 1)$
	100	100	100	100	100	100	100	100	100
Germany									
1972	95	175	167	121	187	65	138	90	118
1978	94	314	294	163	325	50	181	90	110
France									
1972	94	182	171	135	199	68	126	86	122
1978	87	454	395	241	483	50	164	82	115
Netherlands									
1972	91	202	183	139	221	63	132	83	124
1978	83	420	350	218	491	44	160	71	142
Belgium									
1972	92	186	171	125	197	64	136	86	115
1978	84	446	374	208	447	47	180	84	100

Base = 1973	100	100	100	100	100	100	100	100	100
Germany 1978	99	159	157	126	156	81	125	101	95
France 1978	94	216	202	166	208	80	122	97	92
Netherlands 1978	93	183	170	146	190	77	116	90	108
Belgium 1978	93	210	195	155	195	79	126	100	85
United Kingdom 1978	102	237	242	211	226	93	115	107	91

[1]For the whole work-force (manual and non-manual workers) of the manufacturing industry (enterprises employing at least fifty wage-earners in 1966 and at least ten wage-earners in 1972 and 1978; for the United Kingdom, at least fifty wage-earnrs in 1973, at least ten wage-earners in 1978).

in the *manufacturing* industry of the five countries in question during the period 1966–1978.

The factors affecting the evolution of the rate of surplus labour can be analysed from the formula

$$s' = \frac{d}{w} - 1$$

or $\quad s' = \dfrac{d}{x.px} - 1$

where d = labour time per wage-earner per annum
$\quad\quad w$ = value of labour-power per wage-earner per annum
$\quad\quad x$ = real wage (number of necessaries of life or means of subsistence) per wage-earner per annum
$\quad\quad px$ = average value per necessary of life

As we saw in the previous section, the EUROSTAT statistics tell us the *annual* labour-time per wage-earner (d) and the *hourly* cost per wage-earner (w/d). The *annual* cost per wage-earner (w) – or average annual wage-cost – is obtained by multiplying these two data:

$$w = d(w/d)$$

The value of labour-power per wage-earner per annum (w) can be calculated directly by dividing this average annual wage-cost (w) by the monetary expression of values (E):

$$w = w/E$$

However, in order to analyse the factors affecting s', it is preferable to calculate w indirectly by estimating its two constituent elements: the real annual wage per worker (x) and the average value per necessary of life (px).

$$w = x.px$$

The annual real wage (x), that is, the number of necessaries of life which a worker can acquire per year, is dependent on the average annual wage (w) and on the average price of the necessaries of life (px):

$$x = w/px$$

On the other hand, the average value of a necessary of life (px) can be calculated, like the value of any commodity, by dividing the price (px) by the monetary expression of values (E).

$$px = px/E$$

The series relating to the average price of the necessaries of life (px) has to be represented in the form of a series of price indices, in practice, the indices of consumer prices.[15] The same applies to the series relating to x and *px* (which are estimated from px). This is why all the data of this section have been expressed in the form of indices. For the purpose of working out these indices, we have chosen, as base, the year 1966 (= 100); however, as the data relating to the United Kingdom are only available from 1973, we have in addition expressed the data from 1973 to 1978, for the five countries in question, taking the year 1973 as base: this improves the comparability of the information for the later years.

The various indices calculated in this way are presented in Table 11.5 for selected years; Figures 11.2 and 11.3 express the evolution of these same indices year by year.[16]

Results

If we consider *the whole of the period 1966–78*, we observe analogous evolutions in the four countries in question. These evolutions can be summed up as follows:

(1) *Labour-time (d)* has decreased in every case (by 6 per cent to 17 per cent according to country) and the *real wage* has increased in every case (by 60 per cent to 81 per cent according to country). These are the most visible and most widely known aspects of what is called 'the improvement of workers' conditions'.

(2) Something less visible and less widely known: in the same period, the growth of productivity has had the effect of considerably reducing the *value per necessary of life (px)* (by 50 per cent to 56 per cent according to country). In reality, the reduction of the *value per necessary of life (px)* is in every case greater than the increase of the *real wage* (x): *px* is in fact reduced by at least half, while x increases but without ever doubling. The result is that the value of labour-power ($w = x.px$) decreases in every case (by 10 per cent to 20 per cent according to country).

(3) The reduction of the *value of labour-power (w)* is greater than the reduction of *labour-time (d)* (except in Belgium, where the two reductions are equal). The result is that the *rate of surplus labour* ($s' = d/w - 1$) is higher in 1978 than in 1966 (except in Belgium, where it remains at the same level).

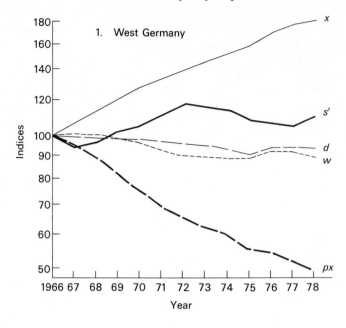

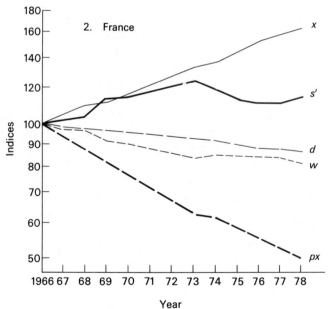

*FIGURE 11.2   Evolution of s' and of variables affecting it; 1966–78
(indices)*

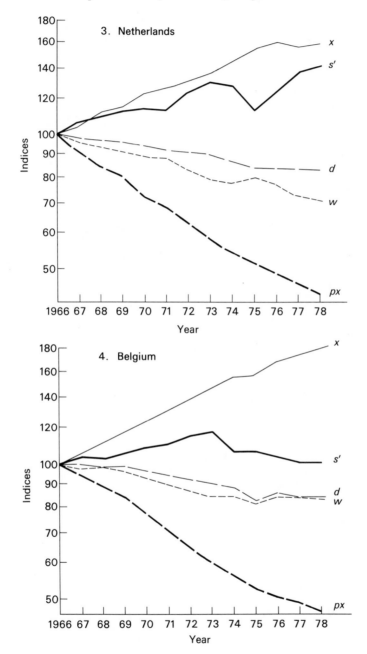

3. Netherlands

4. Belgium

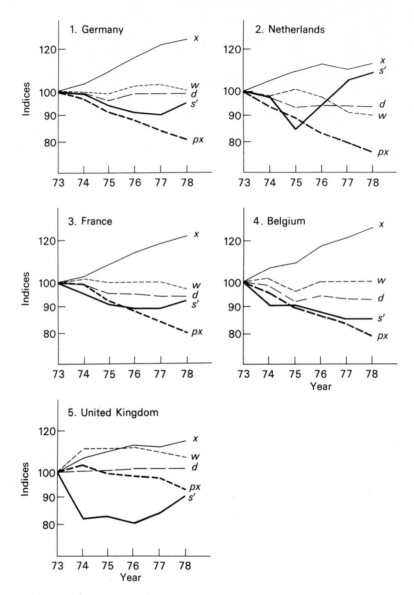

FIGURE 11.3 *Evolution of s' and of variables affecting it; 1973–8 (indices)*

These observations, taken as a whole, confirm an important point of the theoretical analysis carried out in chapters 4 and 8: the rise in real wages is perfectly compatible with stability, or with a rise, in the rate of surplus value. This remains true even when the rise in real wages is accompanied, as in the cases studied here, by a reduction in labour-time. The increase in productivity (and therefore the fall in *px*) has been sufficiently great here to offset both the increase in real wages and the decrease in labour-time.

If we now consider *the later years (1973–78)*, the findings do not necessarily correspond with those made for the whole of the period, and divergences in evolution appear from country to country.

(1) The *real wage* (x) increases in the five countries, but *labour-time* (*d*) evolves in different ways: it still decreases in France, in Belgium and in the Netherlands but it remains constant in Germany and tends to increase in the United Kingdom.

(2) The *value per necessary of life* (*px*) decreases in the five countries but this decrease is generally not greater than the rise in the *real wage* (x): in fact, the *value of labour-power* (*w* = x.*px*) only continues to decrease in one case (the Netherlands) while remaining more or less stable in three countries and even increasing in the United Kingdom.

(3) The effect of these combined evolutions of the *value of labour-power* (*w*) and of *labour-time* (*d*) is that the *rate of surplus labour* (s' = *d*/*w* − 1) is at a lower level in 1978 than in 1973 (except for the Netherlands). Study of the various diagrams suggests, however, that the rate of surplus labour tends to recover in every case (except in Belgium) at the end of the period (from about 1976): we can see here the effect of the initial measures taken to try to move out of the structural crisis of the seventies (measures aiming to raise the rate of surplus value by putting pressure on the workers' living standards).

NOTES

1. The divergence between *mp* and *value* (or between market price and simple price) can be broken down into a first divergence between *pp* and *value* (or between price of production and simple price) and a second divergence between *mp* and *pp* (or between market price and price of production). The magnitude of the first divergence (and its evolution) depends on the composition of capital of the branch in question, considered in relation to the social average (and on the evolution of this relation). The magnitude of the second divergence depends on the degree of protection of the branch in question, considered in relation to the social average (and on the evolution of this relation).

2. See chapter 2, p. 35, note 13 and chapter 10, p. 228, note 22.

3. This remark applies to *all* the means of production used, directly or indirectly, in t_1: not only the means of production manufactured in t_0, but also the means of production used to manufacture *them* and so on. In fact, *all* past labour is thus 'reduced to present labour', that is valued at its value and at its price in the year t_1. This is what explains that, in the example, the relation pounds per hour is, in the end, the same for past labour (40 million/4 million) as for the present labour (30 million/3 million).

4. See chapter 6, pp. 115–16.

5. Note that we approach the problem of more *skilled* labour and the problem of more *intensive* labour in the same way. We do not, therefore, consider that an increase in the *intensity* of labour can be put on the same footing as a prolongation of working-time. Only the prolongation of (productive) working-time brings about a 'production of absolute surplus value'. The increase in intensity constitutes one of the ways of increasing productivity (and so of reducing value) and should be treated in the same way: if it is widespread, it reduces the value of labour-power and brings about a 'production of relative surplus value'; if it is limited to one enterprise or to one branch of industry, it brings about transfers of surplus revenue to the benefit of that enterprise or branch. We see at the same time that the unit of measure (1 hour of average labour) does not constitute a standard which is stable throughout time, since average skill and intensity are not constant.

6. Source: EUROSTAT, *National Accounts ESA-Aggregates 1960–1979*.

7. Source: EUROSTAT, *Employment and Unemployment 1973–1979* (this publication contains retrospective data covering the period 1950–1972).

8. The case of 'commerce' (included in the item 'commerce, restaurants, hotels') is less clear: as we have already pointed out in chapter 2 (p. 23, note 1), merchants carry on production and circulation activities simultaneously.

9. See chapter 3, p. 72.
10. Source: EUROSTAT, 'Surveys of labour costs in industry', in *Social Statistics* no. 4/1969 and 6/1970 (for the 1966 survey), 3/1971 (for the 1969 survey), 4/1974 and 6/1975 (for the 1972 survey), 1978 and 1979 (for the 1975 survey). The results of the 1978 survey have not yet been published but are available on microfiches. The 1966 and 1969 surveys (and also the 1973 survey for the UK) cover all the enterprises or establishments employing at least fifty wage-earners; the later surveys cover all the enterprises or establishments employing at least ten wage-earners.
11. This average has been *weighted* by the respective proportion of manual and non-manual workers in the total waged workforce of manufacturing industry.
12. Source: EUROSTAT, 'Hourly earnings – Hours of work', *Social Statistics*, two numbers per annum since 1965. These statistics provide the *weekly* labour-time worked by *manual* workers in industry. If we compare these statistics with those provided by the triennial surveys, it appears that the evolution of the weekly labour-time (manual workers) follows closely the evolution of the annual labour-time (manual and non-manual workers). Hence the rough procedure adopted for estimating the annual labour-time in the intercalary years.
13. Source: EUROSTAT. 'Hourly earnings – Hours of work', *Social Statistics*, 1980, no. 2, pp. 225 et seq.
14. The complete series, giving the evolution of each of the variables year by year, are given in the Statistical Appendix (1), Tables A1 to A5.
15. Source used: International Monetary Fund, *International Financial Statistics, Supplement on Price Statistics*, IMF, 1981.
16. The complete series used for the drawing up of Table 11.5 and of Figures 11.2 and 11.3 appear in the statistical appendix (2), Tables A6 to A10.

CONCLUSION

The Reproduction of Capitalism

The reality of capitalist exploitation has been emphasized, in the course of the preceding chapters, in three successive and complementary ways. The deductive reasoning of chapters 2 and 3 proved the existence of surplus labour provided 'free' by wage-earners to capitalists. The analysis of chapter 8 showed how numerous basic tendencies of the capitalist system reflect the need to expand the sources and to increase the rate of surplus labour. The empirical data of chapter 11 actually quantified the rate of surplus labour in five European countries in recent years.

It remains to say a few words in conclusion on the reproduction of the capitalist system and of the exploitation which underlies it. This requires us to move out of the somewhat narrow economic framework within which all the previous analysis has been confined.

Various elements combine to make a joint contribution to the reproduction of capitalism: the permanent separation of the workers from the means of production, the repressive or preventive forms of intervention by the capitalist state, the integrative role of liberal ideology.

THE PERMANENT SEPARATION OF THE WORKERS FROM THE MEANS OF PRODUCTION

The reproduction of capitalism is primarily ensured by the fact that *the wage-earners are permanently separated from the means of production.* They can therefore only subsist by continually renewing the sale of their labour-power to the capitalists, who derive from it a continually renewed flow of profit.

However, could not the wage-earners save from their wages, acquire some 'capital' and become 'small-scale capitalists'? On this point, several illusions must be dispelled.

For the vast majority of the working population, savings on wages only pay for the purchase of durable *consumer* goods (a house or a flat in the most favourable cases). To talk about 'property capital' with reference to the house or flats belonging to wage-earners obviously does not put them on the same footing as capitalists.

On the other hand, while some *individual* wage-earners succeed in setting up on their own account, the *general* tendency is towards the progressive elimination of the simple commodity producer, when faced with capitalist competition. And we know that the status of the simple commodity producer is entirely different from that of the capitalist.

Finally, if a number of wage-earners acquire shares in capitalist enterprises, this does not turn them into 'small-scale capitalists'. In fact, 'employee-shareholding' does enable workers to share in the *juridicial* ownership of enterprises and, on this basis, to recover (by way of dividends) some crumbs of the surplus revenue they have created. But these 'employee-shareholders' are still subject to the obligation to sell their labour-power and to create surplus value; moreover they have no share at all in the effective powers of decision-making, or in the real ownership of the enterprises: this ownership remains in the hands of the big shareholders who control a sizeable proportion of the shares and have a voice on the decision-making bodies.

The permanent separation of the workers from the means of production therefore ensures 'spontaneous' reproduction of the wage-earning force and of capitalism; the workers remain sellers of labour-power, the capitalists remain exclusive owners of the means of production and of the product of the wage-earners' labour. Nonetheless, this basic inequality must not be challenged by the workers but must on the contrary be preserved and maintained. It is here that the role of the state and of ideology are to be observed.

REPRESSIVE AND PREVENTIVE FORMS OF INTERVENTION BY THE CAPITALIST STATE

The basic role of the state, in every class-divided society, is to ensure the reproduction of the prevailing social system and to maintain the ruling class in power. The basic role of the state, in a capitalist society, is to ensure the reproduction of capitalism and to maintain the domination of the capitalist class over the workers as a whole.

This role appears clearly in the case of clashes affecting the capitalists' free disposal of the means of production and of labour-power, especially if these clashes are widespread (general strikes, waves of occupation of factories by workers etc.). We then see the *repressive measures of state intervention* set in motion: the police, the army, the courts intervene to break the strikes and the occupations, to restore the 'normal' functioning of enterprises, to deal severely with those workers who are most active in opposition to this 'normal' functioning.

Repression by the state is obviously not limited to cases where the capitalist system as a whole sees itself as immediately threatened. It is also exercised in every localized conflict where the workers challenge the right of capitalist ownership. It is also exercised in response to every action (demonstrations, distribution of leaflets, formation of groups) considered as even a remote threat to the established system.

However, the repressive measures of state intervention (particularly in their most brutal form) do not constitute the most appropriate method of ensuring, in the long-term, the maintenance in power of the bourgeoisie and the perpetuation of the capitalist system. The saying 'prevention is better than cure' applies in this case: better to forestall basic challenges than intervene in order to crush them, better to develop preventive measures of intervention than repressive ones.

The range of *preventive measures of state intervention* is extremely varied. We can point to general legal measures, measures of intervention in the economic and social domain, and on the ideological level.

In the *legal* domain, the legislature and the courts have developed a whole arsenal of legal rules and precedents which *sanction the basic principles underlying commodity exchange and capitalist exploitation*: personal freedom (the workers have to be able to sell their labour-power 'freely'), private ownership of the means of production and labour contracts (the capitalists have to remain in control of the enterprises and to dispose freely of the wage-earners' labour-power), assignment of the products of labour to the owners of the means of production rather than to the producers themselves (the workers have a right to a wage but no say over the product of their labour). These general principles are translated into different legal rules (laws, regulations, decrees, precedents), backed by appropriate sanctions; the whole constitute a fairly ill-defined[1] but powerful means of restriction, intended to dissuade possible opponents of the system and to 'legalize' the repression which can be used against them.

In the *economic and social* domain, the state operates policies intended *to ensure the 'harmonious' functioning of capitalism*. Most of these policies have already been mentioned in earlier chapters: the growing number of *public sector contracts* and their adjustment to the trade cycle provide a guaranteed market for the big monopolistic enterprises and mitigate the cyclical recessions; taking marginal enterprises or branches into *public ownership* allows capitalists to transfer their capital to more profitable sectors, ensures them transfers of surplus revenue by means of favourable public sector prices, makes for a relative stability of employment and so tempers the cumulative process of the recessions; the expansion of *social security* (pensions, unemployment benefit etc.), helps to stabilize the masses' living standards and also to mitigate the effects of the recession.

The objection may be raised that the expansion of social security, like all social legislation favourable to the mass of workers, constitutes measures of state intervention which are in the workers' interests and opposed to the interests of the bourgeoisie. Without denying the importance of social progress which has characterized the post-war years, we must, however, emphasize the origin and the significance of these measures of social progress. In fact, these measures have not in any way been taken on the initiative of the state, but under the pressure (muted or violent) of the struggling workers' movement. On the other hand, the measures of social progress conceded by the state (as well as the rises in wages or the reductions in working hours negotiated without its intervention), never challenge the capitalist system itself but are always confined within the limits of this system: they are only introduced if the 'economic situation' permits and are systematically whittled away when the 'economic situation' (really or allegedly) deteriorates; they constitute a means of stabilizing economic activity in the short term and expanding it in the long term; finally, they are also an important instrument of social peace-keeping, for the improvement of the material conditions of life conceals or makes acceptable the continuous exploitation to which the workers are subject.

To conceal this continuous capitalist exploitation or to make it acceptable is the role of liberal *ideology*, which we shall deal with in a moment. Let us just mention here a third type of preventive state intervention, which as it happens belongs to the ideological field. The state institutions do in fact play an essential role in promoting the propagation of an ideology which suits the interests of the bourgeoisie: they may for instance control the content of educational curricula and the recruitment of teachers; they may control the means of mass communication – radio and television; they may hand out selective subsidies to newspapers in financial difficulties; they may also invoke the maintenance of public order to forbid the distribution of certain leaflets or the organization of certain demonstrations. In short, while proclaiming and formally guaranteeing the freedom of speech and opinion, state institutions intervene massively to organize a certain 'social consensus', necessary to the reproduction of capitalism.

THE INTEGRATIVE ROLE OF LIBERAL IDEOLOGY

If we exclude the systematic recourse to violence to maintain public order, a society can only hold together if there exists a certain 'social consensus', an 'ambient ideology' favourable to the maintenance of the social system in force.

Ideology consists of a whole set of ideas, of mental perceptions, concerning man and society. The *dominant ideology* is the ideology held by the dominant class and propagated through the whole population; its function is to ensure the indispensable 'social consensus' whether by concealing the basic divisions and inequalities of society, or by *making* these divisions and inequalities *acceptable* by *pseudo-justifications* or *evasions*. The pages which follow aim to give some indication of the way in which *liberal ideology* plays this role in the framework of capitalist society.

Liberal ideology, under different complementary facets, *conceals* the reality of capitalist exploitation.

It glosses over the division of society into antagonistic social classes: it presents society as a juxtaposition of free and equal individuals (*liberté, égalité, fraternité,* the slogan proclaims): the owners of means of production and the owners of labour-power are supposed to meet freely and on equal terms.

Liberal ideology glosses over the reality of surplus labour and of surplus value. Supported by the prevailing economic theory, it puts on equal terms all the 'factors of production', that is, 'labour' which 'earns' a wage, 'capital' which 'earns' a profit, 'land' which 'earns' a rent; it lists these different incomes but refuses to see that their sole source lies in the living labour of the producers. Furthermore, it gives countenance to the idea that 'investment is the creator of employment', ignoring the fact that waged labour creates surplus revenue and that it is this surplus revenue which makes new investment possible.[2]

Liberal ideology glosses over the essentially capitalist nature of measures of state intervention. It presents the state as 'the emanation of popular sovereignty' (under bourgeois democracy, cannot all citizens 'freely' choose their elected representatives at regular intervals?) and as the 'guardian of the common weal', the 'arbiter of private interests'. It presents the preventive measures of state intervention as in the 'general interest', the repressive measures as 'necessary for public order'. It puts the emphasis on different *'forms of government'* (democratic republic, parliamentary monarchy, military dictatorship etc.) and conceals the *class nature* common to all capitalist states.

As liberal ideology can never completely conceal all the inequalities and tensions inherent in capitalist society, it must *make them acceptable*, whether by trying to *justify* them or to *make them bearable* for the majority of the population.

A typical example of *'justification'* concerns inequalities of income, for example the differences between the incomes of doctors and of nurses, between those of university professors and of nursery-school teachers, between those of managers and of manual or non-manual workers. While these differences arise basically from the fact that various social groups benefit from an unequal balance of power in society, liberal ideology seeks to justify them by arguments such as 'differences in academic qualifications' or 'differences in responsibilities exercised'.

These arguments obviously provide only unconvincing and superficial answers. The first does not explain why certain social groups and not other have access to advanced studies, the second does not show in what way the responsibilities of some are greater than the responsibilities of others.[3]

As for making the inequalities and tensions of capitalist society *bearable*, we recognize the 'opium of the people' role played by the majority of religious beliefs, where the prospect of a blissful after-life encourages the acceptance of the social *status quo* here below. Other kinds of opium today induce a comparable degree of social apathy, favourable to the reproduction of capitalism.

This applies, in particular, to the improvements in the masses' material living standards and to the liberal ideology of *technical progress* and of the *consumer society*. According to this ideology, capitalism is the most efficient way of introducing technical progress, technical progress is the best guarantee of the masses' material progress and this material progress is itself assimilated to social progress (or even to the disappearance of social classes). As it conceals the basic functions of capitalist technical progress (strengthening of bourgeois domination and increase in the rate of surplus value), such an argument is simply a justification of capitalism; besides which, it encourages an evasion of the realities of exploitation in the pursuit of maximum consumption.

We find another factor of social apathy in the practice and ideology of *participation* and *negotiated agreements*. The practice consists in offering workers some 'crumbs' of participation and in associating their representatives with policies or reforms which still fit into the framework of capitalism. The ideology consists in presenting this participation and this process of negotiated agreements as basic changes, as a sharing of power between employers and workers, the advent of a new society, as it were. The bourgeoisie thus avoids, once again, the head-on challenge to the capitalist system.

It avoids it again thanks to the caricatured correlations, such as '*Marxism* = *USSR* = *poverty and terror*'. This equation is obviously false in all its terms. The USSR, which is in many respects a form of state capitalism, is far from being the embodiment of the Marxist ideal of liberty and democracy; however, without intellectual cheating, it cannot just be reduced to the notorious 'gulags'. But the equation is useful for the bourgeoisie: it makes it possible to discredit at one and the same time, and without the slightest analysis, every experiment of non-capitalist society and also every Marxist critique of capitalist society.

These are some typical elements of liberal ideology: they all help to convince the majority of the population – *workers as well as capitalists* – that capitalism is natural and 'self-evident' or that of the various possible systems, it is the best – or at any rate the least bad. It is in this way that liberal ideology, in so far as it is more or less accepted by the masses, constitutes a powerful element in the reproduction of capitalism. And it is why the workers' struggle against capitalism exploitation *also* demands a struggle against liberal ideology in all its guises.

NOTES

1. The notion of the preservation of 'public order' is as essential as it is ill-defined: this lack of precision makes it possible to interpret arbitrarily the dangers threatening the capitalist system and to deal with them in an equally arbitrary manner.
2. The wage-earners' demand for 'full employment' therefore amounts to a demand for 'full creation of surplus revenue'. It only becomes an anti-capitalist demand if accompanied by a two-fold denunciation of the

outright seizure of surplus revenue by the capitalists and of the incapacity of capitalism to ensure full employment.

3. Since 'everything is settled by the age of six' as regards education, one could retort that the responsibility of the kindergarten teacher is infinitely greater than that of the university professor and that this would justify an exactly reversed scale of income.

APPENDICES

Statistical Appendix

Tables A1 to A5 present the different annual series which have made it possible to calculate the evolution of E and of s' in the five European countries we have chosen. The symbols used in these tables have the following meanings:

L:	number of workers 'regarded as productive'
P:	total civilian working population
d:	average annual labour-time per productive worker
$D (= L.d)$:	total number of hours of 'productive' labour (productive of value and of revenue) = sum total of values
R:	net domestic product at market prices = sum total of net prices or sum total of net revenues
w/d:	average cost of labour-power (manual and non-manual workers) per hour of labour

In columns d and w/d, the parentheses mean that we are using, not data published by EUROSTAT, but data estimated according to the methods indicated in the text.

For sources, reference may be made to the text pp. 245–7, chapter 11, notes 6, 7, 10, 12, 13.

	L	L/P	d^1	D (= $L.d$)	R	E (= R/D)	w/d^1	s'^1 (= $\dfrac{E}{w/d} - 1$)
	(10^3)	(%)	(hours)	$(10^6$ hours)	$(10^9 DM)$	(DM/h)	(DM/h)	(%)
1966	21 623	82	1884	40 738	440.57	10.81	6.94	56
1967	20 720	81	(1855)	38 436	443.94	11.54	(7.56)	53
1968	20 668	81	(1855)	38 339	481.52	12.56	(8.19)	53
1969	20 931	81	1855	38 827	538.83	13.88	8.84	57
1970	21 207	81	(1845)	39 127	610.40	15.60	(9.85)	58
1971	20 930	80	(1810)	37 883	676.43	17.86	(10.97)	63
1972	20 384	78	1798	36 650	739.66	20.18	12.16	66
1973	20 382	78	(1790)	36 484	822.86	22.55	13.70	65
1974	19 852	77	(1770)	35 138	879.87	25.04	15.30	64
1975	18 901	76	1723	32 566	917.00	28.16	17.54	61
1976	18 583	76	(1770)	32 892	997.33	30.32	19.07	59
1977	18 400	75	(1770)	32 568	1066.24	32.74	20.67	58
1978	18 396	74	1769	32 543	1144.51	35.17	21.76	62

[1]For the whole work-force (manual and non-manual workers) in manufacturing industry (enterprises or establishments employing at least fifty wage-earners before 1972, at least ten wage-earners from 1972).

TABLE A.1   Germany – Calculation of E and of s',[1] 1966–78

	L	L/P	d^1	D (= $L.d$)	R	E (= R/D)	w/d^1	s'^1 (= $\dfrac{E}{w/d} - 1$)
	(10^3)	(%)	(hours)	$(10^6$ hours)	$(10^9 FF)$	(FF/h)	(FF/h)	(%)
1966	15 720	80	2077	32 650	472.00	14.46	8.24	76
1967	15 641	79	(2030)	31 751	509.44	16.04	(9.06)	77
1968	15 480	78	(2025)	31 347	555.89	17.73	(9.97)	78
1969	15 667	78	2008	31 459	635.46	20.20	10.90	85
1970	15 732	77	(1990)	31 307	708.08	22.62	(12.11)	87
1971	15 647	77	(1975)	30 903	789.26	25.54	(13.51)	89
1972	15 778	77	1957	30 878	887.82	28.75	14.96	92
1973	15 548	75	(1930)	30 008	1007.71	33.58	17.30	94
1974	15 554	74	(1905)	29 630	1146.10	38.68	20.40	90
1975	15 195	73	1840	27 959	1294.69	46.31	24.95	86
1976	15 119	72	(1835)	27 743	1410.11	53.35	29.00	84
1977	15 104	72	(1820)	27 489	1667.79	60.67	33.03	84
1978	14 987	71	1808	27 096	1893.57	69.88	37.38	87

[1]For the whole work-force (manual and non-manual workers) in manufacturing industry (enterprises or establishments employing at least fifty wage-earners before 1972, at least ten wage-earners from 1972).

TABLE A.2   France – Calculation of E and of s',[1] 1966–78

	L	L/P	d^1	D $(= L.d)$	R	E $(= R/D)$	w/d^1	s'^1 $(= \dfrac{E}{w/d} - 1)$
	(10^3)	(%)	(hours)	$(10^6$ hours)	$(10^9 Fl)$	(Fl/h)	(Fl/h)	(%)
1966	3337	76	1987	6631	67 234	10.14	6.01	69
1967	3289	75	(1950)	6414	73 831	11.51	(6.67)	73
1968	3296	74	(1930)	6361	82 062	12.90	(7.39)	75
1969	3346	74	1917	6414	93 147	14.52	8.19	77
1970	3349	73	(1875)	6279	104 846	16.70	(9.38)	78
1971	3398	74	(1835)	6235	118 310	18.98	(10.70)	77
1972	3315	73	1801	5970	133 820	22.42	12.12	85
1973	3285	72	(1780)	5847	153 550	26.26	13.80	90
1974	3249	71	(1720)	5588	173 200	30.99	16.50	88
1975	3184	70	1663	5295	189 610	35.80	20.24	77
1976	3136	69	(1675)	5253	218 030	41.51	22.49	85
1977	3109	68	(1665)	5177	237 350	45.84	23.56	95
1978	3098	68	1655	5127	255 440	49.82	25.22	98

[1]For the whole work-force (manual and non-manual workers) in manufacturing industry (enterprises or establishments employing at least fifty wage-earners before 1972, at least ten wage-earners from 1972).

TABLE A.3   Netherlands – Calculation of E and of s',[1] 1966–78

	L	L/P	d^1	D $(= L.d)$	R	E $(= R/D)$	w/d^1	s'^1 $(= \dfrac{E}{w/d} - 1)$
	(10^3)	(%)	(hours)	$(10^6$ hours)	$(10^9 FB)$	(FB/h)	(FB/h)	(%)
1966	2855	79	1958	5590	805.98	144	84	71
1967	2812	78	(1940)	5455	862.94	158	(91)	74
1968	2798	77	(1925)	5386	923.38	171	(99)	73
1969	2842	77	1915	5442	1015.30	188	108	74
1970	2809	77	(1875)	5267	1137.54	216	(122)	77
1971	2766	75	(1835)	5076	1248.21	246	(138)	78
1972	2733	74	1798	4914	1397.32	284	156	82
1973	2751	73	(1760)	4842	1593.19	329	179	84
1974	2771	73	(1720)	4766	1865.35	392	219	76
1975	2702	72	1619	4375	2058.64	471	268	76
1976	2651	71	(1660)	4401	2340.00	532	307	73
1977	2614	70	(1640)	4287	2519.70	588	344	71
1978	2566	69	1641	4211	2706.02	643	375	71

[1]For the whole work-force (manual and non-manual workers) in manufacturing industry (enterprises or establishments employing at least fifty wage-earners before 1972, at least ten wage-earners from 1972).

TABLE A.4   Belgium – Calculation of E and of s',[1] 1966–78

	L	L/P	d^1	D (= L.d)	R	E (= R/D)	w/d^1	s'^1 $(= \dfrac{E}{w/d} - 1)$
	(10^3)	(%)	(hours)	$(10^6$ hours)	$(10^9£)$	(£/h)	(£/h)	(%)
1966	18 756	75						
1967	18 261	74						
1968	18 012	74						
1969	17 981	73						
1970	17 791	73						
1971	17 302	72						
1972	17 055	71						
1973	17 358	71	1872	32 494	65 738	2.02	1.06	91
1974	17 309	70	(1890)	32 714	74 078	2.26	(1.30)	74
1975	16 903	69	1898	32 082	93 027	2.90	1.66	75
1976	16 591	68	(1910)	32 376	110 665	3.42	1.97	74
1977	16 619	68	(1910)	31 742	126 862	4.00	2.27	76
1978	16 556	67	1916	31 721	144 999	4.57	2.54	82

[1]For the whole work-force (manual and non-manual workers) in manufacturing industry (enterprises or establishments employing at least fifty wage-earners before 1975, at least ten wage-earners from 1975).

TABLE A.5   United Kingdom – Calculation of E and of s',[1] 1973–78

VARIABLES AFFECTING THE EVOLUTION OF s'

Tables A6 to A10 present the different annual series which have enabled us to analyse the variables affecting the evolution of the average rate of surplus labour (manual and non-manual workers) in the manufacturing industry of the five European countries in question. As we indicated in chapter 11 (p. 255) these series are presented in the form of indices whose base is in principle the year 1966 (= 100); however to ensure comparability with the statistics for the United Kingdom, the data from 1973 to 1978 are also expressed, taking the year 1973 as base.

To recall the meaning of the symbols used in these tables

d: average annual labour-time per wage-earner (manual and non-manual)

w/d: average hourly cost per wage-earner

w: average annual cost per wage-earner

px: average price per necessary of life (means of subsistence)
px: average value per necessary of life
x: real annual wage (number of necessaries of life per annum)
w: average annual value of labour-power per wage-earner

In columns *d* and w/*d*, the brackets mean that we are using, not data published by EUROSTAT, but data estimated according to the methods indicated in the text.

In column s′, the indices have been calculated from absolute figures, obtained from the formula s′ = (E:w/*d*) − 1 (see tables A1 to A5).

For sources, reference may be made to the text, chapter 11, notes 6, 7, 10, 12, 13.

	d	w/*d*	w	px	E	*px*	x	*w*	s′
			(= *d*.w/*d*)			(= px/E)	(= w/px)	(= x.*px*)	$(= \dfrac{d}{\text{x.}px} - 1)$
Base = 1966									
1966	100	100	100	100	100	100	100	100	100
1967	(98)	(109)	107	102	107	95	106	101	94
1968	(98)	(118)	116	103	116	89	112	100	96
1969	98	127	125	105	128	82	119	98	102
1970	(98)	(142)	139	109	144	75	128	96	105
1971	(96)	(158)	152	115	165	69	133	92	113
1972	95	175	167	121	187	65	138	90	118
1973	(95)	197	188	129	209	62	145	90	116
1974	(94)	220	207	138	232	60	150	89	114
1975	91	253	231	147	260	56	158	89	108
1976	(94)	275	258	153	280	55	169	92	106
1977	(94)	298	280	159	303	52	177	92	105
1978	94	314	294	163	325	50	181	90	110
Base = 1973									
1973	(100)	100	100	100	100	100	100	100	100
1974	(99)	112	110	107	111	96	103	99	99
1975	96	128	123	113	125	91	109	99	94
1976	(99)	139	138	118	134	88	116	102	91
1977	(99)	151	149	123	145	84	122	103	90
1978	99	159	157	126	156	81	125	101	95

[1]For the whole work-force (manual and non-manual workers) in manufacturing industry (enterprises or establishments employing at least fifty wage-earners before 1972, at least ten from 1972).

TABLE A.6. Germany – Variables affecting the evolution of s′,[1]
1966–78 (in indices)

	d	w/d	w	px	E	px	x	w	s'
			$(= d.w/d)$			$(= px/E)$	$(= w/px)$	$(= x.px)$	$(= \dfrac{d}{x.px} - 1)$
Base = 1966									
1966	100	100	100	100	100	100	100	100	100
1967	(98)	(110)	108	103	111	93	105	97	102
1968	(98)	(121)	118	107	123	88	110	96	103
1969	97	132	128	114	140	82	112	92	113
1970	(96)	(147)	141	121	156	77	117	90	115
1971	(95)	(164)	156	127	177	72	122	88	118
1972	94	182	171	135	199	68	126	86	122
1973	(93)	210	195	145	232	63	134	84	125
1974	(92)	248	227	165	267	62	138	85	119
1975	89	303	268	185	320	58	145	84	113
1976	(88)	352	311	202	369	55	154	84	111
1977	(88)	401	351	221	420	53	159	84	111
1978	87	454	395	241	483	50	164	82	115
Base = 1973									
1973	(100)	100	100	100	100	100	100	100	100
1974	(99)	118	116	114	115	99	102	101	95
1975	95	144	137	127	138	92	108	100	91
1976	(95)	168	159	139	159	88	114	100	89
1977	(94)	191	180	152	181	84	118	100	89
1978	94	216	202	166	208	80	122	97	92

[1]For the whole work-force (manual and non-manual workers) in manufacturing industry (enterprises or establishments employing at least fifty wage-earners before 1972, at least ten from 1972).

TABLE A.7. France – Variables affecting the evolution of s',[1]
1966–78 (in indices)

	d	w/d	w	px	E	px	x	w	s'
			(= d.w/d)			(= px/E)	(= w/px)	(= x.px)	(= $\dfrac{d}{x.px}$ − 1)
Base = 1966									
1966	100	100	100	100	100	100	100	100	100
1967	(98)	(111)	109	103	114	91	105	96	106
1968	(97)	(123)	119	107	127	84	111	94	109
1969	96	136	131	115	143	80	114	92	113
1970	(94)	(156)	147	120	165	73	123	89	114
1971	(92)	(178)	164	128	187	69	128	88	113
1972	91	202	183	139	221	63	132	83	124
1973	(90)	230	206	150	259	58	137	79	131
1974	(87)	275	238	164	306	54	145	78	128
1975	84	337	282	181	353	51	156	80	112
1976	(84)	374	315	197	409	48	160	77	123
1977	(84)	392	328	210	452	46	157	73	138
1978	83	420	350	218	491	44	160	71	142
Base = 1973									
1973	(100)	100	100	100	100	100	100	100	100
1974	(97)	120	116	110	118	93	105	98	97
1975	93	147	137	121	136	89	113	101	85
1976	(94)	163	153	132	158	83	116	97	94
1977	(94)	171	160	140	175	80	114	91	105
1978	93	183	170	146	190	77	116	90	108

[1]For the whole work-force (manual and non-manual workers) in manufacturing industry (enterprises or establishments employing at least fifty wage-earners before 1972, at least ten from 1972).

TABLE A.8. Netherlands – Variables affecting the evolution of s',[1]
1966–78 (in indices)

	d	w/d	w	px	E	px	x	w	s'
			(= d.w/d)			(= px/E)	(= w/px)	(= x.px)	(= $\dfrac{d}{\text{x}.px} - 1$)
Base = 1966									
1966	100	100	100	100	100	100	100	100	100
1967	(99)	(108)	107	103	110	94	104	98	103
1968	(98)	(118)	116	106	119	89	110	98	102
1969	98	129	126	110	131	84	115	96	104
1970	(96)	(145)	139	114	150	76	122	93	108
1971	(94)	(164)	154	119	171	70	129	90	110
1972	92	186	171	125	197	64	136	86	115
1973	(90)	213	192	134	228	59	143	84	117
1974	(88)	261	229	151	272	56	152	84	106
1975	83	319	264	170	327	52	155	81	106
1976	(85)	365	310	186	369	50	167	84	103
1977	(84)	410	343	199	408	49	172	84	100
1978	84	446	374	208	447	47	180	84	100
Base = 1973									
1973	(100)	100	100	100	100	100	100	100	100
1974	98	122	120	113	119	95	106	101	90
1975	92	150	138	127	143	89	108	96	90
1976	94	172	162	139	162	86	117	100	87
1977	93	192	179	149	179	83	121	100	85
1978	93	210	195	155	195	79	126	100	85

[1]For the whole work-force (manual and non-manual workers) in manufacturing industry (enterprises or establishments employing at least fifty wage-earners before 1972, at least ten from 1972).

TABLE A. 9. Belgium – Variables affecting the evolution of s',[1]
1966–78 (in indices)

	d	w/d	w	px	E	px	x	w	s′
			(= d.w/d)			(= px/E)	(= w/px)	(= x.px)	(= $\dfrac{d}{x.px} - 1$)

Base = 1966

	d	w/d	w	px	E	px	x	w	s′
1966	100	100	100	100	100	100	100	100	100
1967									
1968									
1969									
1970									
1971									
1972									
1973									
1974									
1975									
1976									
1977									
1978									

Base = 1973

	d	w/d	w	px	E	px	x	w	s′
1973	100	100	100	100	100	100	100	100	100
1974	(101)	(123)	124	116	112	104	107	111	82
1975	101	157	159	144	144	100	110	111	83
1976	(102)	186	190	168	169	99	113	112	81
1977	(102)	214	218	195	198	98	112	110	84
1978	102	237	242	211	226	93	115	107	91

[1]For the whole work-force (manual and non-manual workers) in manufacturing industry (enterprises or establishments employing at least fifty wage-earners before 1975, at least ten from 1975).

TABLE A.10   United Kingdom – Variables affecting the evolution of s′,[1] 1973–78 (in indices)

Theoretical Appendix

AN ALTERNATIVE CONTENT FOR THE CONCEPT OF PRO-
DUCTIVE LABOUR

The Approach Adopted in this Book[1]

In chapter 3, productive labour was defined in a broad sense as *labour which creates value (and revenue)* and in a strict sense (specific to capitalism) as *labour which creates surplus value (and surplus revenue)*. Since creating surplus value necessarily implies creating value, the concept of productive labour (in either sense) has been restricted to *labour which creates value*. And as value is created only through the production and sale of *commodities*, the concept of productive labour (in either sense) has been restricted to *labour involved in the production of commodities (which are actually sold)*.

On this basis, various types of labour have been regarded as unproductive, as they are not involved in the production of commodities and of value.

(1) Domestic labour (devoted to the production of *domestic products*).
(2) Directly social labour (devoted to the production of *collective goods and services*).
(3) Labour devoted to the production of goods and services for *internal use* (such as cleaning, book-keeping etc.) *within a commodity-producing enterprise*.
(4) Labour devoted to *circulation* activities (as opposed to production).

An Alternative Approach[2]

While maintaining that the concept of productive labour must be restricted to labour involved in the production of commodities and of value, it is, however, possible to question the previous distinction between productive and unproductive labour on the ground that it is inconsistent with the concept of value adopted in this book.

Value was identified in chapter 2 (pp. 26–8) with *indirectly social labour*, that is labour flowing from a private initiative and recognized as useful to society through the sale of its product on the market. On this basis it can be argued that two of the types of labour regarded as unproductive in the previous concept should rather be regarded as *productive*.

This would apply to labour devoted to the production of goods and services *for internal use within commodity-producing enterprises*. As regards value, the labour performed by cleaners and bookkeepers in an enterprise in the car industry does not differ from that performed by workers directly involved in the technical process of car production: in both cases, it is labour performed on the private initiative of the capitalist who engaged the wage-earners; in both cases, it is the sale of the cars which recognizes this private labour as socially useful. Both types of labour are therefore *indirectly social labour* and count as *value* (and both must be considered as involved in the production of commodities).

The same can be said of labour performed in *circulation* activities. If the circulation labour flows from a private initiative and is recognized as socially useful through the sale of the circulation service (through the payment of a price for the commercial, financial, hiring or letting service rendered), it is just the same *indirectly social labour* and counts as *value* (and the circulation service must also be considered as a commodity).

Following this line of reasoning, only labour devoted to the production of *domestic* products and that devoted to the production of *collective* goods or services would be *unproductive* labour. In these two cases, there is indeed no question of commodity production, or of indirectly social labour, or of value.

This new approach breaks with the traditional Marxist view that circulation services are not commodities and that circulation labour is not productive of value. But it has the twofold advantage, first of ensuring a perfect *coherence* between the three concepts of indirectly social labour, value and commodity and secondly of making these three concepts completely *independent of the specific content* (or use-value) of the activities (the only criterion which remains relevant is whether the activities are indirectly social labour or not).

MARXIST RATIOS WHEN PERIODS AND RATES OF TURNOVER DIFFER FROM UNITY

The Concepts of Period and Rate of Turnover

In chapter 4, Marxist ratios were considered on the assumption that $K = C + V$ represented both the *money-capital advanced* at the beginning of the year (to purchase the means of production and labour-power) and the *production cost* of the annual product.[3] In technical terms, it was assumed that the *period of turnover* of capital was equal to 1 (one year) or that the *rate of turnover* of capital was equal to 1 (one turnover a year). The *period of turnover* can be defined as the interval of time between the moment when the capitalist lays out money-capital (to purchase means of production or labour-power) and the moment when he recovers the money-capital advanced (through the sale of the product); more simply, it is the time necessary to recover the money-capital advanced. The *rate of turnover* is the reciprocal of the period of turnover: it can be defined as the number of times a given amount of money-capital advanced is recovered during a certain period of time.

The following table represents by means of different symbols the sums of *money-capital advanced* (invested at the start) and the *monetary*

	Money-capital advanced (stocks)	Monetary cost of production (flows)	Period of turnover of capital	Rate of turnover of capital
Fixed capital	$\bar{F}$	F	$t_f = \bar{F}/F$	$n_f = F/\bar{F}$
Raw materials	$\bar{M}$	M	$t_m = \bar{M}/M$	$n_m = M/\bar{M}$
Constant capital	$\bar{C} = \bar{F} + \bar{M}$	$C = F + M$	$t_c = \bar{C}/C$	$n_c = C/\bar{C}$
Variable capital	$\bar{V}$	V	$t_v = \bar{V}/V$	$n_v = V/\bar{V}$
Total capital	$\bar{K} = \bar{C} + \bar{V}$	$K = C + V$	$t_k = \bar{K}/K$	$n_k = K/\bar{K}$

TABLE B.1   Money-capital advanced, monetary costs of production, periods and rates of turnover of capital: symbols used cost of production (recovered during the year through the sale of the output produced). The sums of money-capital advanced are *stocks* (amounts of money invested at the start), the monetary costs of production are *periodical flows* (periodically renewed as production and sale are renewed). The ratios between stocks and flows give the *periods of turnover* of the money-capital, the inverse ratios between flows and stocks give the *rates of turnover* of the money-capital.

The following pages start by building up a simplified example in which periods and rates of turnover differ from unity. They then show what the basic Marxist ratios become under these new conditions.

A Simple Quantified Example

The data of the example are as follows.

(1) An enterprise produces four carriages a year (one a quarter). The sale of each carriage immediately follows its production.

(2) The outlay in circulating capital (purchase of materials and of labour-power) is renewed at the beginning of each quarter. This 3-month outlay amounts to 750 000 for materials and 100 000 for labour-power.

(3) The outlay in fixed capital (purchase of machines) amounts to 2 million and is made in full at the beginning of the first quarter. The machines remain in use for 5 years (that is for a production of twenty carriages); one-fifth of their value and price is transferred to the annual output (one-twentieth to each carriage).

(4) The wage-earners' rate of surplus labour is 150 per cent, and profit is assumed to be equal to surplus revenue (P = S).

Using the symbols defined above, the next table shows the stocks of capital invested at the beginning of the first quarter, then the production cost and the selling price of a quarter's and a year's output, finally the period of turnover (in years) and the rate of turnover (per year) of the capital invested.

We see that it takes the capitalist one quarter to recover the stock of circulating capital $\overline{M}$ and $\overline{V}$: so the period of turnover of $\overline{M}$ and $\overline{V}$ is 0.25 (= ¼ year). Reciprocally, the yearly rate of turnover of $\overline{M}$ and $\overline{V}$ is 4: the same amount of money (750 000 for $\overline{M}$, 100 000 for $\overline{V}$) can be used four times a year to purchase materials and labour-power.

Money-capital advanced	Production cost and selling price		Period of turnover (in years)	Rate of turnover (per year)
	One quarter (= 1 carriage)	One year (= 4 carriages)		
$\bar{F}$ = 2 000 000 F =	100 000	400 000	$t_f = 5$	$n_f = 0.2$
$\bar{M}$ = 750 000 M =	750 000	3 000 000	$t_m = 0.25$	$n_m = 4$
$\bar{C}$ = 2 750 000 C =	850 000	3 400 000	$t_c = 0.81$	$n_c = 1.24$
$\bar{V}$ = 100 000 V =	100 000	400 000	$t_v = 0.25$	$n_v = 4$
$\bar{K}$ = 2 850 000 K =	950 000	3 800 000	$t_k = 0.75$	$n_k = 1.33$
—	S = P = 150 000	600 000	—	—
—	Price = 1 100 000	4 400 000	—	—

TABLE B.2   Money-capital advanced, production cost and selling price, periods and rates of turnover of capital: a quantified example

On the other hand, it takes the capitalist 5 years to recover the stock of fixed capital F: so the period of turnover of F is 5 (years), and the yearly rate of turnover of F is one-fifth.

The Basic Marxist Ratios

The rate of surplus value
As before, the rate of surplus value relates the yearly *flow* of surplus revenue created to the yearly *flow* of variable capital laid out. (It is equal, as before, to the rate of surplus labour and expresses the degree of exploitation of the wage-earner).

$$S' = \frac{S}{V}\left(= \frac{600\ 000}{400\ 000} = 150\%\right)$$

Moreover, it is possible to define a '*yearly* rate of surplus value', which relates the yearly *flow* of surplus revenue created to the *stock* of variable capital laid out. This new ratio, symbolized by means of $\bar{S}'$, is equal to the usual rate of surplus value (S') multiplied by the rate of turnover of $\bar{V}$:

$$\bar{S}' = \frac{S}{\bar{V}} = \frac{S}{V/n_v} = S'.n_v \ (= 600\%)$$

The composition of capital
Instead of being defined as the ratio between the yearly *flow* of constant capital and the yearly *flow* of variable capital (C' = C/V), this is now defined

(1) either as the ratio between the *stock* of constant capital and the *stock* of variable capital:

$$\bar{C}' = \frac{\bar{C}}{\bar{V}} \left(= \frac{2\ 750\ 000}{100\ 000} = 27.5 \right)$$

(2) or as the ratio between the *stock* of constant capital and the yearly *flow* of variable capital (which reflects more clearly the degree of mechanization of the production process):

$$\bar{C}' = \frac{\bar{C}}{V} \left(= \frac{2\ 750\ 000}{400\ 000} = 6.875 \right)$$

The rate of profit
This relates the yearly *flow* of profit to the *stock* of capital invested $\bar{K}$ (and not to the yearly flow K representing the production cost):

$$\bar{P}' = \frac{S}{\bar{K}} = \frac{S}{\bar{C} + \bar{V}} \left(= \frac{600\ 000}{2\ 850\ 000} = 21.05\% \right)$$

What becomes of the formula relating the rate of profit to the other two ratios (rate of surplus value and composition of capital?) Each term of the above equation can be divided either (a) by $\bar{V}$, or (b) by V. We thus have:

(a) $$\bar{P}' = \frac{S/\bar{V}}{\bar{C}/\bar{V} + \bar{V}/\bar{V}} = \frac{\bar{S}'}{\bar{C}' + 1} = \frac{S'}{\bar{C}' + 1} .n_v$$

(b) $$\bar{P}' = \frac{S/V}{\bar{C}/V + \bar{V}/V} = \frac{S'}{\bar{C}' + 1/n_v}$$

In both cases, we see, just as before, that the average rate of profit rises as the rate of surplus value rises and the composition of capital falls; in addition, the rate of profit rises as the rate of turnover of variable capital rises.

THE 'TRANSFORMATION PROBLEM'

We set out in chapter 2 (pp. 41–2) and developed in chapter 6 (pp. 116–19) the basic Marxist principle according to which equilibrium prices in a capitalist economy are not simple prices (or the monetary expression of the social value of the commodities) but prices of production (which ensure equal rates of profit between branches).

The transition from simple prices to prices of production presented in Table 6.2 and Figure 6.2 was, however, incomplete. It adjusted the price of the commodities $(c + v + p)$ in order to equalize the rate of profit between branches, but it did not adjust the magnitude of constant capital and variable capital in each branch in order to reflect the changes in the price of the commodities produced (see note 11.2, p. 118).

In this appendix, we first present a more sophisticated transition which takes into consideration both

(1) the need to adjust the price of the commodities $(c + v + p)$ in order to equalize the rate of profit between branches,
(2) the need to adjust C and V in each branch in order to reflect the changes in the price of the commodities produced.

We then proceed to consider some common misunderstandings about the 'transformation problem'.[4]

The Complete Procedure Required to Arrive at the 'Correct' Prices of Production

This complete procedure is summarized in Table B.3, which is based on the following assumptions.

(1) The production sector is divided into three branches or departments. Department I produces the means of production for all departments, department II produces the means of consumption for all the wage-earners and department III produces the means of consumption for all the capitalists.
(2) All the surplus revenue accruing to capitalists is devoted to consumption (hypothesis of simple reproduction, with no accumulation).
(3) The monetary expression of values is £1 per hour.
(4) The period of turnover of both $\overline{C}$ and $\overline{V}$ is 1, so that $K = C + V =$ production cost $=$ capital invested.
(5) The value-composition of capital differs between departments ($450/180$ in I $>$ $200/240$ in II $>$ $100/180$ in III), while the rate of surplus value is identical ($120/180$ in I $=$ $160/240$ in II $=$ $120/180$ in III $=$ 66.6 per cent).

(6)   The commodities produced by each department are reduced
      to only one (composite) commodity: so the total magnitudes
      (C, V, P) may be regarded as also reflecting the unit
      magnitudes (c, v, p) corresponding to each (composite)
      commodity.

The initial situation assumes that simple prices prevail. In such a
case, profits (P) are exactly equal to surplus revenue (S) in each department, but the rates of profit (equal to the rates of valorization) differ
between departments according to the differences in the C/V ratios.

The first round of transformation consists of two steps. Step 1A
leaves C and V unchanged but redistributes the sum of surplus
revenue or profit (400) so as to make the rate of profit in each
department equal to the average rate of profit (29.63 per cent). The
new profit in each department is brought about by a change in price:
C + V + P is raised in department I and lowered in the other two
departments. The 'price multipliers' of the last column express the
exact proportion in which the price of each department has changed.

Step 1B leaves the new prices (C + V + P) reached at step 1A
unchanged but takes them into consideration in adjusting the
production costs: since department I produces the means of production for all departments, C in all departments is raised by applying I's
multiplier (1.0889); similarly, since department II produces the
means of consumption for all wage-earners, V in all departments is
lowered by applying II's multiplier (0.9506) (on the other hand, since
department III produces only commodities for the consumption of
capitalists, its multiplier does not affect either component of the
production costs). These changes in the production costs – with no
corresponding changes in the prices – reduce the total amount of
profit (362.96 < 400) and the average rate of profit (26.17 percent <
29.53 per cent); they still result in differing rates of profit between
departments, though to a lesser degree than in the initial situation.

These differences in the rate of profit between departments make it
necessary to proceed to a second round of transformation, consisting
of two steps as before.

Step 2A leaves the new production costs (C and V) unchanged but
redistributes the new sum of profits (362.96) so as to make the rate of
profit in each department equal to the new average rate of profit
(26.17 per cent). Again, C + V + P is raised in department I and
lowered in departments II and III, though the changes in prices are
proportionally smaller than in step 1A (the price mutipliers are nearer
to unity).

Step 2B leaves the new prices (C + V + P) reached at step 2A unchanged but applies the price multipliers of departments I and II to the various Cs and Vs respectively. Again, the total amount of profit and the average rate of profit are lowered (to 353.25 and 25.29 per cent respectively), though the reduction is less than before; again, the rates of profit differ between departments, though the differences become extremely small.

The transformation procedure may be repeated in successive rounds until the changes from one round to the other are so small as to be negligible. The final situation is one in which the rates of profit are the same in the three departments (25 per cent in the example) and the price multipliers are equal to unity.

Some Common Misunderstandings

Having set out the complete procedure to arrive at the 'correct' prices of production, we need to make some further observations in order to clear up a few common misunderstandings about the 'transformation problem'.

Transforming values into prices of production?

The standard literature about prices of production generally speaks of the 'problem of transformation of values into prices of production'. Marx's imprecise use of the term 'value' (when referring in fact to values expressed in money, that is to what we call simple prices) is partly responsible for this form of expression, which tends to confuse two essentially different problems.

The first problem is of strictly 'qualitative' nature: it is the question of the necessary expression of *values* in a certain *price*, in a certain quantity of pounds (or francs, dollars etc.). This problem of the transition from the sphere of values to the sphere of prices was examined in chapter 2.

The second problem is of both a qualitative and a quantitative nature, but is strictly confined to the area of prices: it is the problem of shifting from one kind of *price* (*simple prices*, which do not ensure an equilibrium in the division of labour in a capitalist economy) to another kind of *price* (*prices of production*, which do ensure this equilibrium). The 'transformation problem' actually considers only this second problem.

(A further 'transformation problem' would relate to the shift from *prices of production* to actual *market prices*. Table 11.1 in chapter 11 clearly distinguishes the three theoretical stages or 'transformations'

TABLE B.3   *The complete transition from simple prices to prices of production*[1]

Dept	C	V	K = C + V	C + V + P	P	P/K (%)	Price multiplier[2]
Initial situation: simple prices							
I	450	180	630	☐750	120	19.05	
II	200	240	440	☐600	160	36.36	
III	100	180	280	☐400	120	42.85	
Total	☐750	☐600	1350	1750	☐400	29.63	

First round of transformation
1A: Prices of production (C + V + P) adjusted to equalize rates of profit

I	450	180	630	816.67	186.67	29.63	1.0889
II	200	240	440	570.37	130.37	29.63	0.9506
III	100	180	280	362.96	82.96	29.63	0.9074
Total	750	600	1350	1750.00	400.00	29.63	

1B: Production costs (C + V) adjusted to reflect prices of production of step 1A

I	490.01	171.11	661.12	816.67	155.56	23.53	
II	217.78	228.14	445.92	570.37	124.44	27.91	
III	108.89	171.11	280.00	362.96	82.96	29.63	
Total	816.68	570.36	1387.04	1750.00	362.96	26.17	

Second round of transformation
2A: Prices of production (C + V + P) adjusted to equalize rates of profit

I	490.01	171.11	661.12	834.12	173.00	26.17	1.0214
II	217.78	228.14	445.92	562.62	116.70	26.17	0.9864
III	108.89	171.11	280.00	353.26	73.26	26.17	0.9733
Total	816.68	570.36	1387.04	1750.00	362.96	26.17	

2B: Production costs (C + V) adjusted to reflect prices of production of step 2A

I	500.49	168.78	669.27	834.12	164.85	24.63	
II	222.44	225.04	447.48	562.62	115.14	25.73	
III	111.22	168.78	280.00	353.26	73.26	26.17	
Total	834.15	562.60	1396.75	1750.00	353.25	25.29	
⋮							

Final situation: 'correct' prices of production

I	504	168	672	☐840	168	25	1.0
II	224	224	448	☐560	112	25	1.0
III	112	168	280	☐350	70	25	1.0
Total	☐840	☐560	1400	1750	☐350	25	

Notes: [1] The actual calculation was made to four significant digits after the decimal point. The numbers shown here are rounded off to two places.

[2]Price multiplier = $\dfrac{(C + V + P) \text{ in current round}}{(C + V + P) \text{ in previous round}}$

which lead from values to market prices: (1) transition from values to simple prices; (2) transition from simple prices to prices of production; (3) transition from prices of production to market prices.)

A sequential process?

Prices of production and equal rates of profit are often presented as the result of a sequential process taking place through time. At an initial stage, simple prices would prevail and rates of profit would differ between branches (for example 10 per cent in branch I and 30 per cent in branch III). The result would be a movement of a part of I's capital to III, bringing about an increase of supply and a fall of prices in III and a fall in supply and a rise in prices in I. The movement would cease, and equilibrium would be attained, at a final stage, when prices of production would prevail and average rates of profit would be the same.

Contrary to this 'sequential' interpretation, it seems preferable to present prices of production and equal rates of profit as logical necessities which impose themselves 'from the start': each competitive branch is supposed to attain a 'normal' profitability (the same average rate of profit), which implies that prices – including production costs – correspond to prices of production (rather than to simple prices). Actual capitalist practice tends to corroborate our 'logical' interpretation: firms tend to fix their supply price by estimating their costs and adding a profit margin sufficient to reach the profit rate aimed at.

A change in the general conditions of accumulation?

Various authors suggest that replacing simple prices by prices of production leads to a change in the general conditions of accumulation, as production costs (C + V) and profit (P) suffer a change of magnitude. This change can be seen in the example of Table B.3: comparing the initial situation (simple prices) and the final situation ('correct' prices of production), it appears that the capitalists will have to spend more on means of production (C is raised from 750 to 840), that the wage-earners will receive less money-wages (V falls from 600 to 560), and that the profit available also diminishes (P falls from 400 to 350 and thus ceases to be equal to the surplus revenue created).

A closer look at the same table shows, however, that these changes in the *monetary* magnitudes have no effect in *real* terms: though capitalists have to spend more on means of production, they cannot acquire more of them as their price is raised in the same proportion (the price in I is raised from 750 to 840); though wage-earners receive less money-wages, their standard of living is maintained at a constant level, as the price of the consumption goods falls in the same proportion (the price of II falls from 600 to 560); though capitalists obtain a smaller profit, they also maintain their consumption level for the same reason (the price in III falls from 400 to 350).

Admittedly, the distribution of the sum total of prices (C + V + P) and of the sum total of profits (P) between the different branches or departments is affected by the fact that prevailing prices are prices of production (equalizing the rates of profit) rather than simple prices. But for the system as a whole, the attainment of prices of production leaves unchanged the total mass of commodities produced and their distribution between investment, workers' consumption and capitalists' consumption.

Constancy of the sum total of prices or of the sum total of profits?
It is worth noting that, throughout the transformation procedure presented in Table B.3, the sum total of prices is kept constant, while the sum total of profits is allowed to change. We have thus:

Σ of prices of production = Σ of simple prices
Σ of profits $\neq \Sigma$ of surplus revenue

Many authors defend the idea that alternative prices of production could be attained through a distinct calculation procedure keeping the sum total of profits constant, while allowing the sum total of prices to change. They thus have:

Σ of prices of production $\neq \Sigma$ of simple prices
Σ of profit = Σ of surplus revenue

It is true that no 'complete' transformation procedure can maintain both equations.[5] But the choice between one calculation procedure or the other is not an arbitrary one. The only correct calculation procedure is the one which maintains *the sum total of prices constant*. The reason for this is that the sum total of prices expresses the sum total of values with a given magnitude of E (Σ of prices = Σ of values × E) and that both factors (Σ of values and E) logically precede any redistribution in the area of prices (any change of particular prices and any redistribution of profits).

Keeping the sum total of prices constant implies that one allows for an inequality between the sum total of profits and the sum total of surplus revenue. But, as we have just seen above, this involves no *real* change for the system as a whole.

NOTES

1. See chapter 3, pp. 70–4.
2. The argument summarized here is based on E. K. Hunt (1979), The Categories of Productive and Unproductive Labour in Marxist Economic Theory, *Science and Society*, and M. De Vroey, On the Obsolescence of the Marxian Theory of Value: a Critical Review, *Capital and Class*, 17, July 1982, pp. 52–6.
3. See chapter 4, p. 91, note 5.
4. The transformation procedure and the subsequent comments presented here are inspired by the following two texts: A. Shaikh (1976), Marx's Theory of Value and the '*Transformation Problem*' in J. Schwartz (ed.), *The Subtle Anatomy of Capitalism*, Goodyear Publishing Co., California, pp. 106–39, and M. De Vroey, op. cit., pp. 44–52.
5. Only such a simplified procedure as that presented in chapter 6 can maintain both equations: however, though defensible as a pedagogical first approach to the problem of surplus revenue transfers, it is clearly neither adequate nor correct.

Further Reading

This short list is intended to provide the reader with a few suggestions concerning (a) alternative textbooks and (b) more specific books on the problems of value, crisis and inflation.

SOME ALTERNATIVE TEXTBOOKS *

Introductory Texts

1. Desai, Meghnad, *Marxian Economics*, Littlefield, Adams & Co., 1979.
2. Fine, Ben and Harris, Laurence, *Rereading Capital*, Macmillan, 1979.
3. Junankar, P.N. *Marx's Economics*, Deddington, Philip Allan, 1982.
4. Sweezy, Paul M. *The Theory of Capitalist Development. Principles of Marxian Political Economy*, New York, Monthly Review Press, 1942.
5. Weeks, John, *Capital and Exploitation*, Princeton, Princeton University Press, 1981.

Advanced Texts

1. Becker, James F. *Marxian Political Economy. An Outline*, Cambridge, Cambridge University Press, 1977.
2. Morishima, Michio, *Marx's Economics*, Cambridge University Press, 1973.
3. Roemer, John, *Analytical Foundations of Marxian Economy Theory*, Cambridge University Press, 1981.

BOOKS ON THE PROBLEMS OF VALUE, CRISIS AND INFLATION

On Value Theory

1. *Review of Radical Economics*, Spring 1982, special issue on Value theory.
2. Rubin, I.I. *Essays on Marx's Theory of Value*, Detroit, Black and Red, 1980.
3. Schwartz, Jesse (ed), *The Subtle Anatomy of Capitalism*, Santa Monica, Goodyear Publishing Co, 1977.
4. Steedman, Ian, *Marx after Sraffa*, London, New Left Books, 1977 (Verso, 1981).
5. Steedman, Ian, et al. *The Value Controversy*, London, New Left Books, 1981.

On Crisis and Inflation

1. Aglietta, Michel, *A Theory of Capitalist Regulation. The US Experience*, London, New Left Books, 1979.
2. Glyn, Andrew and Harrison, John, *The British Economic Disaster*, London, Pluto Press, 1981.
3. Mandel, Ernest, *Late Capitalism*, London, New Left Books, 1975.
4. Mandel, Ernest, *Long Waves of Capitalist Development. The Marxist Interpretation*, Cambridge, Cambridge University Press, 1980.
5. Rowthorn, Bob, *Capitalism, Conflict & Inflation*, London, Lawrence and Wishart, 1980.

Index

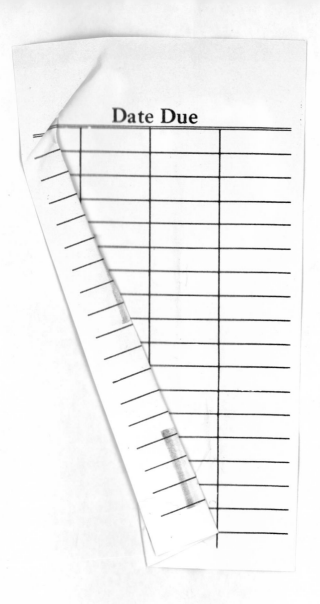

Date Due